Fair Trade Rebels

DIVERSE ECONOMIES AND LIVABLE WORLDS

Series Editors: J. K. Gibson-Graham, Maliha Safri,
Kevin St. Martin, Stephen Healy

*Fair Trade Rebels: Coffee Production and Struggles for
Autonomy in Chiapas*
Lindsay Naylor

*Reimagining Livelihoods: Life beyond Economy, Society,
and Environment*
Ethan Miller

*Carving Out the Commons: Tenant Organizing and
Housing Cooperatives in Washington, D.C.*
Amanda Huron

Building Dignified Worlds: Geographies of Collective Action
Gerda Roelvink

Fair Trade Rebels

Coffee Production and Struggles for Autonomy in Chiapas

LINDSAY NAYLOR

DIVERSE ECONOMIES AND LIVABLE WORLDS

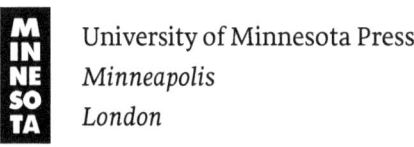

University of Minnesota Press
Minneapolis
London

Portions of chapter 3 were originally published as "Auditing the Subjects of Fair Trade: Coffee, Development, and Surveillance in Highland Chiapas," *Environment and Planning D: Society and Space* 35, no. 5 (2017): 816–35, https://doi.org/10.1177/0263775817694031. Portions of chapter 4 were originally published as "Fair Trade Coffee Exchanges and Community Economies," *Environment and Planning A: Economy and Space* 50, no. 5 (2018): 1027–46, https://doi.org/10.1177/0308518X18768287.

Copyright 2019 by the Regents of the University of Minnesota

All rights reserved. No part of this publication may be reproduced, stored in a retrieval system, or transmitted, in any form or by any means, electronic, mechanical, photocopying, recording, or otherwise, without the prior written permission of the publisher.

Published by the University of Minnesota Press
111 Third Avenue South, Suite 290
Minneapolis, MN 55401-2520
http://www.upress.umn.edu

ISBN 978-1-5179-0577-4 (hc)
ISBN 978-1-5179-0578-1 (pb)

A Cataloging-in-Publication record for this book is available from the Library of Congress.

The University of Minnesota is an equal-opportunity educator and employer.

*To all those who are struggling for a
"world in which many worlds fit"*

Quisieron enterrarnos, pero se les olvidó que somos semillas.

They wanted to bury us, but they forgot that we are seeds.

Contents

Abbreviations and Acronyms	ix
Maps	x
Introduction: A "Window to Better Money"	1
1 Fair Rebels, Fair Coffee? Challenging Capitalist Narratives	23
2 Coffee "Fixes": Decolonizing Development	55
3 Fair Trade Exploitation and Empowerment: Unsettling Narratives	99
4 Fair Trade in Movement: The Possibilities of Being in Common	131
5 Resistance as Agricultural Practice: Rethinking Food Sovereignty	175
Conclusion: Other Worlds Are Possible	209
Acknowledgments	215
Notes	221
Bibliography	231
Index	257

Abbreviations and Acronyms

EZLN Ejército Zapatista de Liberación Nacional (Zapatista Army of National Liberation)

FLO Fairtrade Labeling Organization, now called Fairtrade International

FLO-CERT global certification body for Fairtrade

FTAO Fair Trade Advocacy Office

FTUSA Fair Trade USA, formerly Transfair USA

ICA International Coffee Agreement

INMECAFE Instituto Mexicano del Café (Mexican Coffee Institute)

MAREZ Municipios Autónomos Rebeldes Zapatistas (Rebel Zapatista Autonomous Municipalities)

MAYACERT Organic Certification Organization, Mexico

NAFTA North American Free Trade Agreement

PAN Partido Acción Nacional (National Action Party)

PRD Partido Revolucionario Democrático (Democratic Revolutionary Party)

PRI Partido Revolucionario Institucional (Institutional Revolutionary Party)

PROCAMPO Programa de Apoyos Directos al Campo (Program for Direct Assistance in Agriculture)

PROCEDE Programa de Certificación de Derechos Ejidales y Titulación de Solares (Program for the Certification of Ejido Land Rights and the Titling of Urban House Plots)

Maps

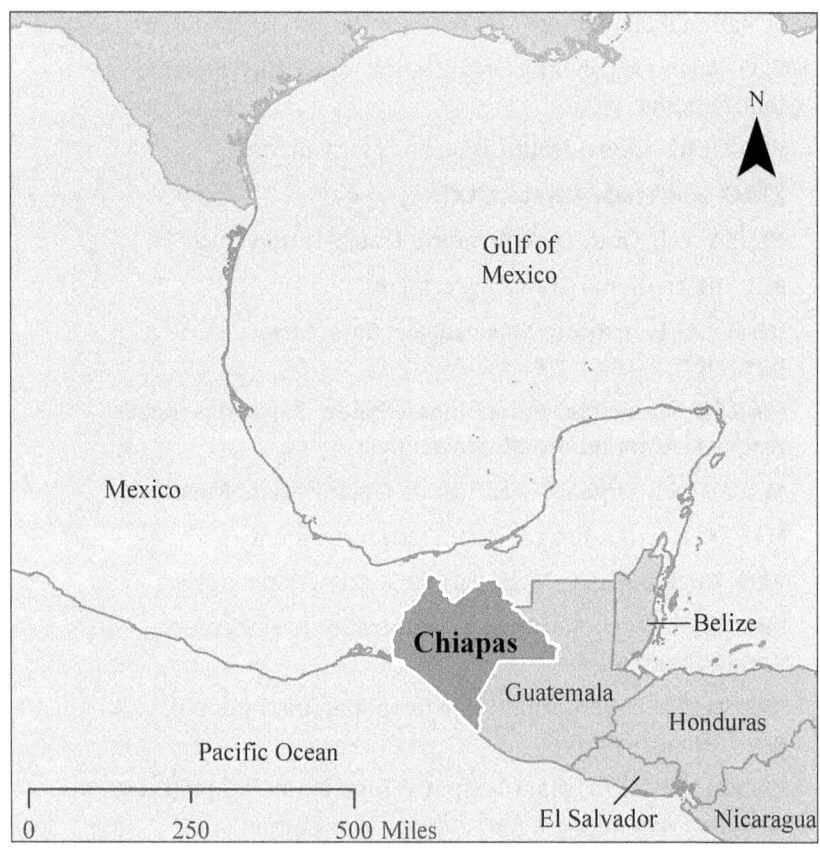

Map 1. Map of Mexico, highlighting Chiapas state. Cartography by Nathan Thayer.

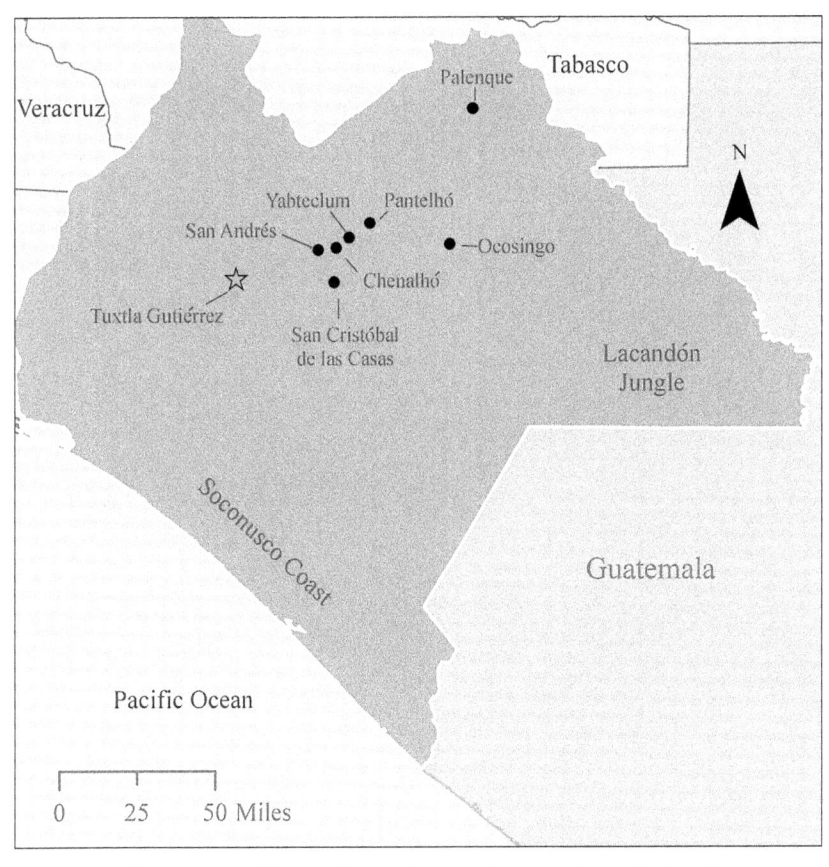

Map 2. Chiapas state, with key cities and towns. Cartography by Nathan Thayer.

Introduction
A "Window to Better Money"

From under the brim of a straw cowboy hat, a rebel *campesino* looked up at the delegation of students and teachers that had come to his community in the highlands of Chiapas, Mexico, to learn about rebel autonomy. "We are in resistance," he declared. "We were obligated to rise up for liberty, democracy, dignity for the world. But the government doesn't want to recognize the indigenous." I sat on a wooden bench at the back, observing and making notes. His words echoing in my ears, I flipped back to my notes from a few days prior. I had spoken with another group of *campesinos/as* about rebel autonomous health promotion. Discussing efforts to maintain healthy communities required a conversation about resistance. The group explained to me that the official government (called the "bad government" by rebel *campesinos/as*) works to destabilize their endeavors. "This is the war of five hundred years, the attack on the indigenous peoples."

Spoken days apart, these statements capture the daily vocabulary of indigenous Maya corn and coffee producers who strive to maintain their ways of life and their livelihoods in a local, regional, and global context that delegitimizes such practices and renders them invisible. In the highlands, daily agricultural acts of cultivating corn and coffee are acts of resistance. These are people who self-identify as peasants *(campesinos/as)* and have been fighting for land and access to resources for centuries.[1] Agricultural production is part of larger autonomy struggles in the highlands. In attempting to maintain their livelihoods as subsistence cultivators, they undertake a number of strategies, and many of these producers cultivate coffee under fair trade certification.

These small producers are not unique, as many peasants worldwide deploy a range of activities beyond those of subsistence. Yet, the livelihood strategies put into practice by rebel *campesinos/as* differ from those of their contemporaries. Peasants around the world are increasingly drawn into state processes and capitalist relations, for example, receiving subsidies or other cash payment programs from the government, selling their labor, or relying on cyclical migration and the substantial remittance economy. Rebel *campesinos/as*, on the other hand, mostly eschew these strategies and have renegotiated economic and state relations through cooperative production, global networking, and struggling for autonomy. While there are many sites of cooperative production, in the highlands, coffee cultivation for the fair trade marketplace represents a key site where local and global forces meet. It was this pivot point that first brought me to Chiapas, where I asked questions about how actors participating in social movements, who had declared autonomy from the state and deployed their production practices as sites of resistance, had harnessed the fair trade marketplace.

Fair Trade Rebels is a book about *campesinos/as* in the highlands of Chiapas, Mexico, attempting to create dignified livelihoods.[2] It is about struggle, and difference, and recognition. At the center of this story are local struggles that are interceded by connections to global networks. A core function of these networks is providing spaces of knowledge exchange and solidarity. While fair trade certification is premised on creating commodity trading relations tied to a price floor, a premium for economic improvement, and standards for sustainable production and community development, its character is changed in this place.

The title *Fair Trade Rebels* speaks to a specific community of people—not bound by borders—and a set of autonomous agricultural practices that facilitate resistance to state processes and capitalist relations. The very existence of this community of people rebels against narratives that seek to explain peasant–state and/or peasant–capitalist relations. Indeed, pro-economic development discourses would describe fair trade certified production as pro-

Figure 1. Patchwork of coffee and corn fields in the highlands of Chiapas. Photograph by the author.

viding better access to commodity markets and fair prices, yet this explanation is limiting when trying to understand the practices of *campesinos/as* in the highlands. Similar to their contemporaries, they do access fair trade as a market and relate to it as a price, yet for some, fair trade provides the possibility of telling a story, not just about capitalist relations, but about community relations and the ongoing struggle of indigenous peoples in their "five-hundred-year struggle." To better understand this struggle and where fair trade fits (or not), I am not asking if fair trade works, but instead I ask how it is understood and practiced in the context of resistance. The findings detailed in this book demonstrate that the production of coffee for the fair trade marketplace both complements and complicates the diverse practices and struggles of indigenous rebel *campesinos/as*. I highlight this crucial point here because this is not a struggle that pits subsistence against neoliberalism, or the so-called binary of traditional versus modern; it is a struggle to live well while making visible indigenous knowledges and practices.

The Five-Hundred-Year Struggle

Although development interventions in the twentieth century highlighted the struggles of marginalized peoples worldwide, the struggles of indigenous peoples stretch across a long history of forced assimilation, otherization, and invisibilization. Indeed, as the end of the Mayan calendar approached in 2012, many popular accounts discussed the Mayan people in past tense, despite their continued existence across the Americas. It is impossible to understand the statement made by the indigenous Mayan *campesino* in resistance at the opening of this book regarding the "war of five hundred years," without establishing its basis in the *encubrimiento* of the Americas and the creation of "Indios."

Prior to the arrival of the conquistadores in the Americas in 1492 and the 1500s, there were no "Indians" in Latin America (Mignolo 2002). Through the conquest, racial constructions were imposed on the indigenous population, simultaneously creating Europe's "other" and distinguishing between the conqueror and the conquered. The creation of narratives of racialized/naturalized difference was utilized as a structure that tied people of diverse origins and belief systems to particular economic statuses that allowed for labor exploitation and dispossession (Quijano 2008). Such narratives of naturalized difference served to maintain the legitimacy of occupation and subjugation of the peoples of what became the Americas (Quijano 2008). The construction of race created new identities for these peoples—as "Indio"—and indigenous identities fell under European cultural, economic, and epistemological hegemony. The conquest also marked, not what has been long hailed as the *descubrimiento* (discovery) of the Americas, but the *encubrimiento* (covering over) or negation of the "dignity and identity of the other cultures" (Dussel 1995, 66). The elevation of the European and invisibilization of the non-European is the foundation of the five-hundred-year war on indigenous practices and ways of knowing and understanding the world.

In October 1992, the quincentennial anniversary of the arrival of Christopher Columbus to the Americas was celebrated. At the same time, an indigenous-led protest against five hundred years of oppression was staged throughout Mexico (Stephen 2002, 136–41).

Both events point to the underlying issue of the fundamental exclusion of indigenous identities, economies, and knowledges in Mexico and made public this long-standing exclusion and desires for recognition. These moments were climactic events that raised questions about the continued celebration of the *encubrimiento* of the Americas and violence against indigenous peoples and set the stage for a long-fomenting rebellion in Mexico.

On January 1, 1994, as the North American Free Trade Agreement (NAFTA) came into force, the social movement and rebel group Ejército Zapatista de Liberación Nacional (Zapatista Army of National Liberation, EZLN) staged a public uprising in the southern Mexican state of Chiapas. Armed and wearing masks, the indigenous Mayan rebels revealed themselves for the first time—on what became a world stage—through the seizure of town centers and the occupation of land in the highlands and the eastern part of the state. Most visible was their seizure of city hall in the former colonial seat of San Cristóbal de las Casas. Their declaration of war, as announced in the "First Declaration of the Lacandón Jungle" (1993), was a proclamation of the continued existence and subjugation of indigenous peoples in the Americas:

> We are a product of 500 years of struggle: first against slavery, then during the War of Independence against Spain led by insurgents, then to avoid being absorbed by North American imperialism, then to promulgate our constitution and expel the French empire from our soil, and later the dictatorship of Porfirio Diaz denied us the just application of the Reform laws and the people rebelled and leaders like Villa and Zapata emerged, poor men just like us. We have been denied the most elemental preparation so they can use us as cannon fodder and pillage the wealth of our country. They don't care that we have nothing, absolutely nothing, not even a roof over our heads, no land, no work, no health care, no food nor education. Nor are we able to freely and democratically elect our political representatives, nor is there independence from foreigners, nor is there peace or justice for ourselves and our children.
> But today, we say ENOUGH IS ENOUGH.

The armed uprising lasted twelve days, but the struggle remains. This struggle is embodied by indigenous Maya, the so-called Indians in Mexico.

On November 7, 2016, the National Indigenous Congress in Mexico together with the EZLN agreed to put forth an indigenous woman candidate for the 2018 presidential race (Zibechi 2016). In a communiqué released by the EZLN, Subcomandante Insurgente Galeano stated that the purpose of running the candidate was not to seek power but to dismantle it from below: "we make a call to construct peace and justice reweaving ourselves from below, from where we are what we are" (Zibechi 2016). Part of the ongoing struggle of indigenous social movements in Chiapas is to retain their visibility not just as rebels seeking autonomy but also as agents of change.

In the two decades that have passed since the uprising of the Zapatistas, Chiapas has changed. It has also in many ways stayed the same. For example, paved roads facilitate the transfer of goods, people, and military supplies, connecting communities in the highlands to municipal seats and the city of San Cristóbal de las Casas. At the same time, the indigenous communities that populate the landscape continue to cultivate corn and coffee and struggle from their long-standing and present position in racialized hierarchies. Although the discourses and practices of resistance take many shapes for rebel *campesinos/as*, they remain sedimented in communities as the struggle continues (Naylor 2017a; see also Nelson 2003). This existence is the struggle of five hundred years, the struggle of indigenous peoples to be visible and to be met where they are.

Campesinos/as in Resistance

Fair Trade Rebels focuses in on the mundane and everyday acts of the people who make up this struggle, the indigenous *campesinos/as* in resistance. It is not focused on the rebellion or the Zapatista movement but on the actors who embody the struggle set forth and who were propelled forward in the watershed moment of 1994 and continue today. The resistance is made up of actors who may support any number of movements, including the Zapatistas, and also solidarity movements within and beyond highland Chiapas; this group includes Zapatistas and their support base members who are adherents to the Sixth Declaration of the Lacandón Jungle as well as members of Sociedad Civil Las Abejas, who are in solidarity with the Zapatistas but are a distinct pacifist group.[3] Because my analysis focuses not on a social movement but instead on a community of people who embody the struggle, I collectively refer to these actors as *"campesinos/as* in resistance." This moniker, along with "fair rebels," allows me to discuss a heterogeneous group of people who have similar strategies but are not all part of the same mobilizations, place-based communities, or coffee cooperatives. I use the term resistance for two reasons: first and foremost because *campesinos/as* refer to themselves as being "in resistance,"[4] and second, because, as *Fair Trade Rebels* will show, there are many ways of knowing and understanding resistance, and indigenous knowledges and practices help to shed light on this. *Campesinos/as* additionally refer to themselves as *socios*, which indicates their membership in coffee cooperatives; I use this term to refer specifically to those participants who are producing coffee. In *Fair Trade Rebels*, the focus is on those *campesinos/as* (peasants, as they self-identify) who are struggling to put autonomous resistance as well as the political and rights discourses made visible by the Zapatista rebellion into practice through maintaining agricultural production for subsistence and also shade-grown coffee for the fair trade marketplace.

Over the past century, the re-formation of peasant identities and diverse livelihoods in Mexico has taken shape alongside demands for recognition, local autonomy, and efforts to build global solidarity networks. In Chiapas State, *campesinos/as* have long observed economic development practices, which are concentrated on "modernizing" rural areas. However, these investments are less concerned with improving resource access for the peasantry and have more to do with capturing rural resources for a wealthy rural minority and a growing urban populace. Hydroelectric projects that disrupted water and foodways were accompanied by electrical lines that ran, not to peasant homes, but over their communities, providing services to a distant urban population. Oil exploration and drilling, deforestation, cattle grazing, oil palm cultivation, and violence (to name a few) displaced peasants from their areas of production. State reorganization around neoliberal principles changed the mechanisms available to peasants for accessing land while also reducing price supports for basic commodities, which fundamentally changed their livelihoods. In these processes and practices, the state forgot who these peasants are.

Access to land and agricultural resources is a long-standing demand of indigenous people in the region and remains a key issue that shapes contemporary political identities in highland Chiapas. Even today, land (and agricultural support) remains unevenly distributed, with the vast majority of lands owned by wealthy individuals and corporations or through the consolidation of newly titled PROCEDE (Programa de Certificación de Derechos Ejidales y Titulación de Solares; Program for the Certification of Ejido Land Rights and the Titling of Urban House Plots) lands, which I will discuss in more depth in chapter 2. Historically, the cry of Emiliano Zapata for "Land and Liberty" in the Mexican Revolution (1910–20) very much represented the landless peasant population (Stephen 2002). In 1930, 4 percent of landowners controlled 67 percent of arable land in Chiapas, and only 3 percent of land was cultivated communally; by 2000, with land reform and land redistribution, 33 percent was held privately and 57 percent was communal land holdings (with 10 percent allocated to national parks and urban areas) (Bobrow-Strain 2007, 136). Thus land reform became an important and hard-won feature of the 1917 Constitution, and although uneven, land redistribution midcentury had the effect of breaking down some large landholdings and redistributing them in Chiapas. Yet there were long delays in gaining access to land that could not be overcome by state–indigenous clientelism (see Bobrow-Strain 2004), and by the time of the Zapatista uprising in 1994, unmet land claims totaled more than one million hectares in Chiapas (Harvey 1998, 216). Indeed, the consolidation of power by the state in the post-Revolutionary period led to an estrangement between indigenous groups and the state (Rus 1994).

Another important event took place in 1992 that demonstrated the long-standing rupture of indigenous relations with the state: the decision of the government to amend Article 27 of the 1917 Constitution, ending land redistribution and calling for the titling/privatization of existing landholdings. An indigenous-led protest against Article 27 reform and the impending approval of NAFTA

Figure 2. Mural painted on the front of a communal meeting space in the Zapatista Caracol of Oventik. Photograph by the author.

was held in Ocosingo, Chiapas, in January 1992. However, by the end of 1992, NAFTA was moving forward, and so was dissent in Chiapas. And here were the murmurings of resistance and rebellion that would later be shouted in January 1994.

The discourses of resistance that are embodied by *campesinos/as* and sedimented in communities in the highlands of Chiapas emerge from social movement foundations that can be traced back to indigenous organizing in the 1970s.[5] Early efforts by indigenous groups were primarily focused on demanding access to government services (e.g., infrastructure, markets, controlled prices, land). The lack of government response to repeated demands led many to begin working with guerilla groups, and in 1980, the EZLN was formed (Stephen 2002, 134; on the origins and split from the FLN [Fuerzas de Liberación Nacional; National Liberation Forces], see Cedillo 2012). The organization of the EZLN and their members' military training were clandestine. EZLN campaigns for membership in the southeast and the highlands took on the more innocuous form of health and literacy programs (Stephen 2002, 134); as a result of this focus, young people, and women in particular, were recruited for armed training outside of the highlands.[6] These campaigns in the 1980s were critical to the early success of the group. However, the collapse of coffee prices in 1989 was perhaps the most important moment of recruitment for the EZLN (Collier and Quaratiello 2005; Martínez-Torres 2006; Stephen 2002); as communities began to feel acutely the loss of income from coffee production, more and more *campesinos/as* started secretly to participate in the EZLN.

In the years of formation, recruitment, and training, the EZLN had as their base the southeastern rainforest. At the same time, other groups took shape elsewhere. In the highlands, indigenous groups continued to experience political and economic injustice, insecure land tenure, and conflicts over land. In 1992, in response to the imbalance of gendered land ownership and a particular incident of violence against women seeking land, representatives from a number of communities in the official highland municipality of Chenalhó formed a coalition to defend women's rights to land (Tavanti 2003, 4) and to protest the violence.[7] The group called themselves Las Abejas, and they quickly merged with Sociedad Civil, a pacifist group established as part of the Catholic dioceses' peace process. Together, they adopted a nonviolent approach to supporting the Zapatista rebellion and took the name Sociedad Civil Las Abejas (Civil Society of the Bees, which I will refer to as Las Abejas) to symbolize their collective work and spiritual identity (Moksnes 2012; see also Nash 2001; Tavanti 2003). Unlike the EZLN, Las Abejas were not clandestine in their struggle. Shortly after their formation in December 1992, the group participated in a nonviolent protest march from the highland town of Yabteclum to the valley city of San Cristóbal de las Casas.

These two groups—the Zapatistas and Las Abejas—are populated by indigenous peoples. In the highlands, these indigenous people are first and foremost corn and coffee producers. These social movement actors take on roles within the resistance alongside their everyday activities as subsistence and fair trade coffee producers. At the same time, these *campesinos/as* are the living, breathing embodiment of the struggle. *Fair Trade Rebels* is about how the struggle and resistance set in motion by social movements are written into the landscape and onto the bodies of the *campesinos/as* who support them. These are the *campesinos/as* in resistance. These are the fair rebels.

"A Window to Better Money"

Why *fair* rebels? *Campesinos/as* in resistance cultivate coffee for the fair trade market, but their identities and politics are not defined by fair trade certification. As noted earlier, *campesinos/as* who participate in social movements in the highlands refer to themselves as "in resistance," and this resistance is a defining characteristic of their everyday lives as *campesinos/as*. As part of their struggle, they demand a fairer price for the goods that they sell in the marketplace. In the case of coffee, this is tied to production for certification. Certified coffee from Zapatista and Las Abejas cooperatives is branded and sold in U.S. markets as "peace" or "rebel" coffee. Yet, when asked about the benefits of fair trade certification, *campesinos/as* in resistance often shrug. Throughout the highlands, fair trade is considered *comercio más justo*, "more-fair trade" (as in more fair than free trade), but as one *campesino* explained, "it's a window to better money." This depiction is not necessarily tied to quantity (as in more money) but is qualitatively different, connected instead to a consistent buyer, their social movement practices, and their stories, which are shared through wide-ranging networks. It is these experiences and perspectives that form the foundation of the analysis in the chapters that follow. In this analysis, I demonstrate that the case of fair rebels provides an opening for thinking about fair trade differently.

Campesinos/as in the highlands have been growing coffee since the 1960s and 1970s, when it was introduced by the National Indigenous Institute as a solution to poverty in rural areas (Martínez-Torres 2006, 53), a history I will discuss in more depth in chapter 2. Prior to the collapse of the International Coffee Agreement (ICA) in 1989 and the dismantling of the state coffee agency, the Mexican Coffee Institute (INMECAFE), producers and cooperatives had a consistent buyer and price expectations. The collapse of the ICA coupled with neoliberal restructuring in Mexico had a significant impact on coffee producers in the highlands, who had to rely on the meager and fluctuating payments offered by intermediaries *(coyotes)* for their coffee beans. Following the 1994 uprising and the declaration that they would not interact with the Mexican state, a number of Zapatista-affiliated coffee producers in the highlands split off from existing cooperatives to form their own. Consistent with the requests of the Zapatista-aligned cooperatives with which I worked, I will not use the names, specific locations, or any other identifying details of these cooperatives. The cooperative of Las Abejas, called Maya Vinic (Mayan Man), was also established through splitting from existing cooperatives and through forming economic relations based on solidarity. Consistent with the demands of Las Abejas for peace and justice, and at the request of the leadership of the cooperative, I use the name of their cooperative and make visible their places of production to create a new space for their stories. The formation of cooperatives and, later, the introduction of fair trade certification created opportunities for producer cooperatives to partner with buyers, lock in a stable price each season, and activate their politics in new ways.

Fair trade, put simply, is simultaneously constituted by movements and a market that are designed to provide secure market access and commodity prices for marginalized producers. It has been hailed by scholars and practitioners as a panacea for impoverished rural populations and damned within the same groups as a neoliberal solution to a neoliberal problem. Fair trade is evaluated as a development fix in impoverished communities and assessed as to whether it is working for producers. The purpose of this book is not to test the successes and failures of the fair trade market but to look at fair trade differently as a site of exchange and to examine how it is practiced by *campesinos/as* in resistance as part of a broader and diverse political-economic approach in their struggle. In the highlands, the harnessing of the fair trade market is just one of many strategies used by *campesinos/as* in resistance in their efforts to maintain their lives and livelihoods while building livable worlds.

If we read fair trade as a "window" for *campesinos/as* in resistance, we can begin to imagine multiple vantage points. Certification is a "window to better money," yet it is also a window on the world, which allows us to ask questions about who opens and/or closes this window and how the view differs looking from the inside out and the outside in. The sale of coffee on the fair trade market is not just about selling coffee; it is about creating connections beyond the highlands and building new nodes in the network of resistance that flows through the highlands. *Fair Trade Rebels* tells the story of a place, but it is not a static, local account of the highlands and *campesinos/as* in resistance. Investigating fair trade certification in the highlands provides an entry point for considering diverse localized political and economic initiatives that are practiced by *campesinos/as* in resistance and how they channel political and economic practices that are global in scale. Indeed, the engagement with the fair trade marketplace by *campesinos/as* in resistance is an example of the local working with and against the global. However, the focus here is not on an isolated local "alternative" that makes a difference only in the lives of the immediate actors. This story is about the transformative possibilities of power "from below." Moreover, this power is not contained within a hierarchy that stretches from local to global but instead trespasses scale, creating, and threading through, communities of people.

Situating Fair Rebels

As Mora (2008, 2017) notes, research in Chiapas is politically charged, a situation that creates particular possibilities and constraints that must be negotiated by researchers and research participants alike:

> During the last fifteen years in Chiapas, scientific research has been forced to reformulate how studies are conducted. Debates on autonomy and self-determination, as part of zapatismo [sic] and prior to the uprising, have generated concrete effects in the ways in which members of indigenous communities accept or do not accept how research is implemented. (Mora 2008, 56)

Chiapas was and remains an area that receives intensive scholarly attention. In an investigation of ethnographies conducted in indigenous communities in Chiapas, Rus (2004) argues that the dominant narrative of Chiapas was driven by a particular group of scholars (the Harvard Chiapas Project begun by Evon Vogt in 1957) and, until the 1970s, was propelled by desire to understand the origins and descent of the contemporary Maya from their ancestors.[8] Moreover, the vast majority of these anthropological studies used one location, Zinacantán, an atypical, closed indigenous community, as the focal point of research; Rus notes that it was the Zapatista rebellion that forced a change in the way people produced knowledge about indigenous peasant populations in Chiapas.

There is a long intellectual history of (mostly white) outsiders debating the extent to which Chiapaneco livelihoods are capitalist—in this case, *Fair Trade Rebels* is an intervention in not conducting a litmus test for capitalist imaginaries but instead examining economic diversity. Much of the analysis presented throughout the book seeks to account for the complex political and economic terrains that *campesinos/as* in the highlands have to navigate on a day-to-day basis to build livable worlds while earning a livelihood in a society structured around neoliberal principles that discourage such practices. Elaborating the philosophical, ethical, and practical dimensions of the methodology employed in this work turns our awareness to these power-laden social terrains and considers the production of knowledge more deeply. Research is performative, and seeing knowledges as multiple and diverse is one possibility for changing our thinking about the world, which in itself can be world changing (see Gibson-Graham 2008). Beyond conducting research and analysis, a diverse economies framing (such as the one used in this book, described more in chapter 1) is invested in constructing (and performing) livable worlds (Gibson-Graham and Roelvink 2009). These knowledges and practices are not uncovered by research but are performed relationally and in place.

It is essential to state going forward in this book that I am not only privileged to be writing it and making attempts to perform livable worlds but to have been able to conduct the research that is at its foundation. As Faria and Mollett (2016) argue, there is a particular mobility of whiteness in the field. They also identify a structural advantage in the production of knowledge, where its workings are normalized and less visible yet continuously privileged (Faria and Mollett 2016, 81; see also Kobayashi and Peake 1994). This privilege, among other important considerations, made it critical for me to evaluate my position in this research. Consistent with the argument of Lugones and

Spelman (1983) that providing an autobiography does not serve to fully acknowledge my position or provide me with a disclaimer, I attempt instead to analyze the system within which I am conducting research (see also Alcoff 1992, 25).[9] Since the late 1980s, feminist and poststructural epistemologies have assisted with decentering the positivist tradition in research and the so-called unbiased researcher through the promotion of reflexive and self-critical examination (cf. England 1994). Feminist geopolitical scholars in particular have attempted to move away from "disembodied" geopolitical analyses by resituating knowledge and a relational ethics in research (Hyndman 2004, 309; see also Routledge 2002; Sparke 2000), and decolonial feminist scholars work to move beyond collaborative and participatory knowledge production to co-production of knowledge, something Hernández Castillo (2016, 38) articulates as epistemic dialogues. As Walsh recognizes, producing knowledge remains a struggle; quoting Anzaldúa (2015), Walsh writes, "How to write (produce) without being inscribed (reproduced) in the dominant white structure and how to write without reinscribing and reproducing what we rebel against" is a dilemma in showing how "decoloniality happens" (Mignolo and Walsh 2018, 20–21).

Research is decidedly not a neutral practice (Alcoff 1992; see also Stephen 2013). As such, I attempt here not only to recognize my positionality but to put into practice self-reflexivity (see Rose 1997; Routledge 2002). However, I am wary of falling into the trap of simply locating myself and exposing my bias so that I can "discover truths" (Pratt 2000). Instead, in positioning and representing myself and others within this research, I recognize that there are many truths and that what is recorded in *Fair Trade Rebels* is not a version of truth but a situated knowledge (see Haraway 1988, 1991), a pluralistic interpretation of something that can be understood in many different ways and that does not fully escape the myriad relations of power at work. It is not only my position as researcher and participant in the research that is at stake, however; there is also the issue of representation, which has been long contested (cf. Ortner 1995; Spivak 1988).[10]

Within and beyond the research period, I attempted to create a measure of accountability to both participants and their ways of knowing and understanding the ideas under discussion (cf. Alcoff 1992; Newdick 2012; Stephen 2013) through a dialogic cycle of sharing ideas, questions, and hopes about the research with participants. As Newdick (2012, 27) pointed out in her work with Zapatista women, working through collective processes creates a space for accountability even as the tensions and contradictions in everyday life and practice are considered. Consistent with the effort toward collective process, a number of my interviews took place with groups of *campesinos/as*, where instead of having a list of questions to be answered, we discussed the broader questions of my research, which participants questioned and dissected and, in many cases, collectively answered. As an example, on one day, I met with four *socios* (members of a fair trade cooperative) to discuss their production for the fair trade marketplace. I started by asking if they had any questions for me or about my research, which led to a lengthy discussion in Tzotzil that was then translated into Spanish by one *socio*. There was a question of what I thought about their coffee production and the price. As a result, we discussed different perceptions of price—for the cooperative, for the *socios*, for the buyer, and especially for the people purchasing coffee in the United States. In this conversation, the participants were less interested in my questions about fair trade (as they noted *comercio más justo*) than in discussing the changes in price and what a good price would be for them. Their desires to talk about price changed the way I asked questions about their participation in fair trade. Having entered the highlands with questions about resistance and market-based production as they related to autonomy and fair trade, the focus on price forced me to start from a place where fair trade exists not just as an intervention but as an income. It was not enough to theorize participation in just one way—as an income-earning strategy, or a form of resistance, or a network of actors, for example; fair trade participation had to be theorized as multiple. The research stage of this project provided opportunities for dialogue and for consistently rethinking and reframing fair trade, the questions I asked, and the considerations I was making.

Dialogue is a task not as easily accomplished at my desk in the United States as I attempt to write "in" (Mansvelt and Berg 2016), in a way that provides some transparency regarding who I am and how I am trying to present the knowledges built in and through this project.[11] Part of this process is reading the geopolitics of knowledge onto my own efforts to produce knowledge in an effort to decolonize it (see Castro-Gómez and Mendieta 1998). Race is a powerful force in the (geo)politics of knowledge production, and it profoundly shapes the lived experience of research.[12] It is not enough to explain racialization; we must also discuss how it is continuously enacted (Faria and Mollett 2016). It is critical to recognize these relations of power and also to adopt perspectives that not only acknowledge power dynamics but, as Hernández Castillo (2016, 39) argues, "demand the rights of indigenous peoples to their own culture and to self-determination." My efforts to develop and enact this research in collaboration with a variety of actors in the highlands of Chiapas do not absolve my ongoing privilege rooted in my ability to move in and out of communities and the region more broadly at will and to take with me the stories and interpretations of autonomy, resistance, fair trade, and so on, of the participants in my research. It does, however, represent an effort to destabilize "normalized" perspectives and knowledge (see Faria and Mollett 2016). In these acknowledgments of my professional and embodied privilege, I seek not simply to reflect on my position but to mobilize it as a way toward a deeper understanding of power imbalances in research and activism and to use this book as a platform to vocalize a deconstruction (and decolonization) of the geopolitics of knowledge and visibilize indigenous knowledges, rights, and futurities.

The analysis presented in this book is drawn from a larger research study centered on fair trade production and autonomous resistance (Naylor 2017a, 2017c). In the process of documenting, observing, and conducting interviews about autonomy and agricultural production, I found that the narratives of fair trade did not map onto self-declared autonomous communities nor *campesinos/as* in resistance very easily. As *campesinos/as* in resistance seek multiple strategies to build livable worlds, I argue that fair trade production both fits into and complicates their efforts. The exchange of coffee in the fair trade marketplace and participating in movements to make trade fairer allow *campesinos/as* in resistance to expand their community to transnational scales, bring in cash income, build solidarity and knowledge-exchange networks, diversify their livelihood strategies, maintain a crop (coffee) in which they have invested for decades, and retain the visibility of their social movement politics and demands for rights and recognition. However, through their participation in the fair trade certification process, *campesinos/as* in resistance are additionally exposed to a project of development that seeks to enfold them into capitalist logics and make them into "rational economic actors"—producers and cooperatives are subject to standards for production and community development that do not fit into their broader struggles and livelihood strategies. The interaction of fair rebels with the transnational fair trade marketplace adds another dimension to these struggles. Here I offer a place-based approach to thinking about fair trade, autonomy, and economic development, asking, what is fair trade, who is it for, and who gets to decide?[13]

Fair Trade Rebels provides an empirically grounded analysis of the diverse economic and agricultural practices of indigenous *campesinos/as* as they play out in self-declared autonomous communities in highland Chiapas; such practices are enacted by *campesinos/as* in resistance who are struggling for dignified livelihoods. This introduction is intended to provide context and a background for understanding fair trade in rebel Chiapas. Although the book draws on stories and experiences coming from the highlands of Chiapas, it is also grounded in a discussion of the nodes of the fair trade network, which necessitates a more zoomed-out approach. In chapter 1, I delve more deeply into the theoretical foundations for the book, drawing out how fair trade is understood in the broader context of economic development and creating a space for a more nuanced analysis of how fair trade is harnessed by fair rebels. Chapter 2 provides the historical backdrop for the cultivation of coffee and is an investigation of the standards for certification and their impact on the lives and livelihoods of *campesinos/as* in resistance. To understand how fair trade certification functions, the dominant narratives of fair trade are discussed in chapter 3. In this discussion, I examine the broader fair trade system, underscoring the divergence of movements for fairer trade and the so-called alternative certified market. This apolitical framing of an alternative economy is taken up and addressed in the context of the struggle of *campesinos/as* in resistance.

Standards for certification and development that are tied to fair trade coffee production are only one side of the coin; on the other side is the social justice activism that is concerned with breaking down the structural conditions that create and maintain unequal trading relations in the world. The activism and solidarity tied to movements for fairer trade are the basis for the analysis in chapter 4, in which I discuss the network that extends from the highlands and into the United States. A specific emphasis on the connections between the producer cooperatives and the roasting cooperatives assists with illuminating different sites of solidarity along the nodes of the fair trade network and possibilities of being in common. While the network in fair trade coffee production extends from the homes of coffee growers in the highlands to the homes of coffee drinkers in the United States, an important part of this discussion is questioning such narrowed economic identities and rethinking, how are we to live well? In chapter 5, I address the practices and processes of making livable worlds through a deeper discussion of economic difference in the highlands. Specifically, I investigate how *campesinos/as* in resistance are cultivating actually existing food sovereignty as part of a diverse livelihood strategy that is at all times based in maintaining autonomy. Here a deeper look at the performance of diverse economies grounds the discussion. Finally, in the conclusion, I come back to the questions around fair trade coffee in the highlands and how it functions as part of diverse and changing economies being enacted by fair rebels, economies that stand apart from the universalizing tendencies of capitalist-style economic development.

I was fortunate to visit the highlands of Chiapas on multiple occasions to be a part of the broader community cultivated by fair rebels. Over many cups of coffee, the multiple and competing experiences of *campesinos/as* in resistance became more visible to me. I offer here a situated knowledge from a snapshot in time and place of the ongoing struggle of fair rebels to create dignified livelihoods and livable worlds.

Figure 3. "Unidos estamos rompiendo el monstruo del capitalismo" (United we are breaking the monster of capitalism). In this mural, the monster's heads are *(left to right)* exploitation, discrimination, dispossession, neoliberalism, repression, patriarchy, and egoism. The protectors at the left foot of the monster are the "federal police," depicted in riot gear. Photograph by the author.

Fair Trade: The "Monster" with a Heart?

I took the photograph in Figure 3 toward the end of July 2010, in the rebel autonomous territory of Oventik, which is administered by the Zapatistas. It was a warm and sunny day in the highlands, and while waiting for a meeting to begin, I sat under the shade of a staircase. Looking up, the staircase revealed to me its message. There are a number of murals in the rebel territories of Chiapas, which are populated by fair rebels. They are evidence of the solidarity relations in which the Zapatistas (in particular) participate, as many murals are painted by outsiders. There are murals about education, about the violence of the state, about resistance, about creating new worlds, and about corn. This one was about capitalism and may have been painted by students, by supporters of the Zapatistas living in Mexico, or even by activists from Europe or the United States.

I was in Oventik to meet with the leadership of a fair trade coffee cooperative. While I sat and thought about the monster of capitalism and its many heads, I tried to understand where fair trade fit. Was it a way to slay the monster? Or was it just a different beast (or a new little head on the existing monster)? What did the farmers think? How did it fit with their self-declared alter-capitalist politics and autonomy?

In our meeting that afternoon, we did talk about capitalism. We also talked about economies, and about the price of coffee. Fair trade is part of a multipronged strategy for cultivating dignified livelihoods in the highlands, but it is not able to be simplified to the growing and sale of coffee for farmers in resistance. Instead, it is a messy and entangled site of negotiation and contestation tied to broader social, political, and economic identities.

I realized much later that capitalism portrayed as a monster means so much more than the violence of profit. Trying to think about where fair trade fit was not really part of the project of "breaking the monster." How then to think about both the monster and fair trade economic interactions?

For in this mural, at the very center of the monster is a heart.

1

Fair Rebels, Fair Coffee?
Challenging Capitalist Narratives

We are living in an era that has produced rapidly increasing global inequality. The multiscalar stratification of people by gender and sexual identity, race and ethnicity, and wealth has created a hierarchy that privileges a very small group of people as global citizens. Through our political, social, and economic practices, many of us are implicated in this stratification. Our actions from the grand to the mundane exist within this hierarchy of people and our earth (nonhuman) others. Indeed, we are so deeply embedded in it that the seemingly simple act of producing or consuming a cup of coffee does not register as a critical political-economic undertaking.

Coffee is a tropical commodity and is a product of colonial and postcolonial relations. On a global scale, economic stratification stemming from colonial and imperial production and consumption practices profoundly divides the world. This division is expressed in discourses of the "Global North/Global South," the "developed and underdeveloped/developing world," and the "First World/Third World," to name a few.[1] The development project of the past several decades is articulated as an attempted transfer of wealth from the global core (dominated by the United States and Canada, Western Europe, and Japan, and by imperial-style accumulation by dispossession) to the global periphery (a vast category that brings together previously colonized states that largely serve as sites of resource extraction) through trade. However, in a global economic system that prioritizes profit over people, this stated project has failed—and not only has it failed but it has failed to such a spectacular degree that in many cases, from the scale of the global to the individual, the economic gap has widened. This failure signals that the system is working in the way it was intended: to concentrate wealth. The redistribution of wealth was a goal in name only.

This chapter provides the framing and foundational context for *Fair Trade Rebels*. To understand why cultivating and/or drinking coffee might register as a critical political-economic act, it is important to consider how theories of economic exchange and development are framed through a capitalist lens. To accomplish this task, I first situate the intervention of fair trade certification in coffee commodity exchanges. Yet, such exchanges are not singular or universal, and as a result, it is crucial to examine economic diversity. Drawing on the body of work produced by diverse economies scholars, I argue that other economies are happening and that in identifying economic difference, multiple economic identities and exchanges are made visible. One of the projects of articulating economic difference is in considering the broader project of economic development that is based in universalizing, capitalist ideas of how to live well rather than in place-based experiences and livelihood strategies. Here I examine fair trade certification as a universalizing project of development and begin the project of deconstructing development, which I will take up again in chapter 2.

A core piece that links the project of deconstructing development and identifying economic difference is decolonizing knowledge. As such, I build on the work of decolonial scholars to demonstrate the pervasive geopolitics of knowledge—which privilege white, hetero-patriarchal, and Western ways of knowing and being in the world—and advocate for a rereading of the struggles to build dignified livelihoods through indigenous ontologies and epistemologies. *Campesinos/as* in resistance seek to build knowledge "from below"; put differently, they are putting power over knowledge production in the hands of people who are otherwise considered marginalized. In the penultimate section of this chapter, I discuss ways of thinking about resistance from theoretical approaches to articulations "from below" to better understand how resistance shapes the ability to build livable worlds. The chapter concludes with a discussion of how we can (re)read fair trade as one strategy and how it can be mapped onto the struggles of fair rebels.

The discourses of fair trade certification, the exchange of coffee through fair trade certification networks, and the production and consumption of coffee provide the foundation for the discussion of multiplying knowledges and experiences of *campesinos/as* in resistance. It is their everyday lived experiences that thread through a deeper discussion of what fair trade is, who is it for, and who gets to decide. A cup of coffee is a starting point; however, coffee is not produced in isolation. While coffee production happens in place, it is also linked through networks that connect localized production and small-scale producers to transnational networks and markets. For many coffee producers, the sale of their beans may be their only cash income for the year. The participation in the cultivation of coffee in a colonial–imperial context places coffee commodity producers in a precarious position on a global scale.

"Lifting Farmers Out of Poverty"

Small-scale producers in the global periphery are among those most impacted by the widening of the global economic chasm. Effectively shut out of international markets, many producers rely on intermediaries to sell their products and in return receive very low prices. In an effort to address the impact of low prices and inaccessible markets, some small-scale producers sought to create direct trading relationships with retailers across the globe. Beginning in the 1960s, these initial efforts, between small producers in partnership with alternative trade organizations centered on political and economic solidarity. These partnerships were the foundation for social justice activism, which was directed at breaking down the barriers to market access, creating direct relations between producers and consumers, establishing more equal terms of trade, and facilitating economic growth and development in producer communities through better prices. The purchase of coffee in solidarity with political movements, such as the Central American Peace and Solidarity Movement (in the 1980s), and handmade crafts by ecumenical organizations, such as Ten-Thousand Villages, in the United States,

Canada, and Western Europe transformed into labeling and certification initiatives designed to codify and regulate these trades and create public awareness (Bacon 2013). In 1988, the first fair trade certification label was created by coffee producers and the Dutch economic development organization Max Havelaar.

Since the late 1980s, economic exchanges under fair trade certifications have increased dramatically. In 2017, the international third-party certifier Fairtrade International reported that 1.6 million producers were certified across seventy-five countries. Fair trade certification is hailed by third-party certifiers as an economic success story and as a strategy for producers to close the ever-widening global wealth gap. This model is called by certifiers trade not aid, signaling that the sale of commodities through global trade rather than injecting funds into communities through development aid is a better way to eradicate poverty. Indeed, U.S.-based third-party certifier Fair Trade USA (2016) proposes certification as a "market-based tool that allows farmers to lift themselves out of poverty." There are some assumptions implicit in this statement. It is part of the project of this book to expose these simplistic assumptions—foremost of which is that producing for profit is the primary way that people participate in economies and build secure livelihoods—and complicate them.

Other Economies Are Happening

Across space, people do not experience fair trade in the same way. If fair trade is considered by *campesinos/as* in Chiapas as *comercio más justo* ("more-fair trade," as *socios* often refer to it, meaning slightly more fair than free trade), why has it been harnessed by *campesinos/as* as an economic practice over other possible livelihood strategies? If selling under fair trade certification is not "lifting them out of poverty," if it is not "working" (Naylor 2014, 282) to reduce the wealth gap and mitigate the problems stemming from political-economic stratification, what purpose does it serve? These are questions about how to live well, based in a narrow reading of how people participate in economies—they are embedded in a "capitalocentric" framing that situates all economic activities as within and/or against capitalism (see Gibson-Graham [1996] 2006a, 6). Considering the economy and capitalism as one and the same has become a totalizing narrative that positions all economic activity on the same (and linear) path, placing some activities as "modern," "formal," and/or "cosmopolitan" and others as "backward," "informal," and/or "provincial." Yet, economic practices the world over are multiple and varied. Over the last few decades, scholars in geography and beyond have cultivated an anti-essentialist frame (Gibson-Graham [1996] 2006a, 11) for viewing economic activity—disrupting the synonymous relationship between capitalism and economy—which has fundamentally changed how we produce knowledge about economic activity. Operating within a theory of economic difference, scholars seek to reframe the way we think about economies (plural) by advancing a diverse economies framework.

The exchange of food and agricultural products through fair trade certification networks is often touted as an alternative to the contemporary neoliberal–capitalist marketplace, which facilitates a more direct connection between economic actors. A diverse economies approach assists with unpacking alternatives to the capitalist marketplace and taking into account multiple and competing economic identities. However, at the outset, we must consider the framing of fair trade as alternative. I argue that this framing is problematic, as it raises the question, alternative to what? Healy (2009) argues that setting up economic exchanges as alternative does a service to capitalism by reinforcing its discursive hegemony. Holding up fair trade commodity exchanges as alternative both supports capitalist ideologies and practices and, as Dolan (2010) argues, makes less visible those services it does in maintaining capitalist relations. Taken as a site of commodity exchange alone, fair trade certified coffee networks appear to be embedded in capitalist-style trade relations.

In calling fair trade alternative, it becomes a referent for capitalist exchanges. It is not viewed as an economic exchange in its own right but as capitalism's other. Fair trade exchanges are just one example of so-called alternatives to capitalism, which sit alongside informal economies, barter exchanges, social reproduction, and otherwise noncounted/incalculable labor and economic practice. In the mid-1990s, writing from a feminist, poststructuralist perspective, Gibson-Graham ([1996] 2006a) put forward an anti-essentialist theory of economies that attempted to recognize this othering through retheorizing economies. This retheorizing rejects a capitalist economy as the main referent for all economic activity. Such "capitalocentrism" (Gibson-Graham [1996] 2006a, 6, 40–43) privileges a particular performance of economy that invisibilizes actually existing economies that are happening within, alongside, and outside capitalism. A critical component of this framework is, drawing on feminist thinking (especially as it relates to undervalued labor), to deconstruct representations of the economy that erase or trivialize difference. The theory of economic difference put forward in 1996 threads through the body of Gibson-Graham's work (cf. Gibson-Graham [1996] 2006a, 2006b, 2007, 2008) and through that of a growing group of scholars focused on making visible economic identities, practices, and exchanges happening worldwide that do not fit into the waged-labor, formal-marketplace, for-profit arena.

In investigating sites of economic difference, economic practices, identities, and exchanges are multiplied. These "diverse economies" (Gibson-Graham 2006b, 60) signal a reclaiming of economic spaces—out of the clutches of capitalism—so they can be examined as economies in their own right. Particular attention is paid to economic activities that are contextualized as "market or capitalist," "nonmarket or noncapitalist," and "alternative market or alternative capitalist" and labor that may be unpaid or receive nonmonetary compensation (Gibson-Graham 2006b, 60–65; see also Gibson-Graham, Cameron, and Healy 2013). I do note, however, that the framing of alternatives within diverse economies is an ongoing project—one that considerations of fair trade exchanges as multiple and diverse assist with building upon. However, crucial to the project of diverse economies and the wider network of scholars contributing to the research network established by the Community Economies Collective is a commitment to not only retheorizing economies (as alternative or otherwise) but also imagining and creating spaces for livable worlds (see Roelvink, St. Martin, and Gibson-Graham 2015).

Diverse economic theory is consistently being advanced through the work of dozens of scholars who have adopted, expanded, and pushed on the reframing presented by Gibson-Graham ([1996] 2006a, 2006b). In this book, I adopt a diverse economies framing and put it in conversation with decolonial theory to break down the geopolitics of knowledge production related to economic development and how to live well. In this way, I expand on diverse economies theory, first through challenging the premise that fair trade is an "alternative" to capitalism, suggesting instead that the fair trade market is an apparatus of capitalism. I note that a closer examination of exchanges in fair trade demonstrates that social justice activism to make trade fairer creates possibilities for being in common and for diverse economic exchanges. Second, through considering the way fair trade is mobilized as part of the political, economic, social, and material practices of *campesinos/as* in resistance, I offer a place-based context that reaches beyond a localized site of community economy and into a transnational space, revealing the messy character of diverse economic exchanges. The new economic ontology offered by Gibson-Graham (2008, 615) provides a mechanism to move away from focusing on or against capitalism to produce work concerned with economic heterogeneity. Reframing economies creates a space for thinking about how, collectively, "humans and nonhuman actants" can live well (Gibson-Graham and Roelvink 2011). It also allows for asking questions that put people and our earth others at the center of exchanges instead of profit, such as, how can we create new forms of economic being? In parallel, scholars are examining forms of social and economic organization that exist or are being developed around community economies. Community economies are spaces of collective action where, in striving to create livable worlds, groups are actively reshaping their economic practices, identities, and exchanges. These economic groupings are not bound by geographical location or particular social groupings (Snyder and St. Martin 2015) but are sites of care, interdependence, and being in common. In this resocializing (e.g., economic exchange as a social relation), Gibson-Graham (2006b, 87–88) envision reintegrating the political and thus making the economy a site of ethical decision-making. The reframing of economies in this way renders visible new and existing social formations around exchange. It is also posited as a way of "reclaiming" the economy as something that is not external to us but transformative and on which we have influence (cf. Gibson-Graham, Cameron, and Healy 2013).

As part of deconstructing and reframing economies, theorists ask questions about the ethical practice of economy and the performance of different economic identities. Scholars use a community economies framing to examine food exchanges and gardening, time banks and community currency, commoning, the Anthropocene, green economies, fisheries, mothering, and care among other topics.[2] There is no clearly defined meaning or single strategy for creating community economies. It is foremost a theory of difference that, through action research and teaching, attempts to make more visible myriad economic activities, identities, and performances at multiple nonhierarchical scales. As part of this project, there is a continuum of reflexivity whereby economic identities are everywhere and always undergoing a process of becoming (both within and independent of the research process). Economic actors may claim any number of economic identities and practices, while also participating in multiple sites of exchange.

One of the core critiques raised in retheorizing economic difference is that it tends toward a Pollyanna-style view of the economy (see Gibson-Graham 2002, 2003), in which scholars are "desperately" searching for spaces not "overwhelmed" by the powers of capitalism (Watts 2003, 28). Moreover, Samers (2005, 883) cautions against a romanticizing of diverse economies, arguing that not all sites of diverse exchange (such as the informal economy) are "progressive" and calling for a more "analytical politics of diverse economies." The idea of an all-powerful global capital and the discursive framing that houses it makes little space for difference, hope, or belonging. A hegemonic capitalism pitted against hope is a vacuum to be filled with criticism. However, even scholars who are actively theorizing economic difference articulate a challenge in locating power in diverse economic exchange. Indeed, it is argued that localized studies of diverse and community economies do not link back up with scalar processes, practices, and politics, thereby neglecting the influence they (may) have (Reynolds and Cohen 2016; see also Glassman 2003; Gritzas and Kavoulakos 2016; Kelly 2005; Laurie 2005; Lawson 2005). Although Gibson-Graham (2006b) argue that relations of power are not deterministic, scholars point out the privilege of researching (cf. Dean 2015) and participating in diverse economies (cf. Miller 2015). Simultaneously, some argue that case studies using diverse and community economic framings often elide possible relations of power (domination and resistance) that emerge alongside diverse economic practice (Miller et al. 2017).[3]

In *Fair Trade Rebels*, I mobilize a diverse and community economies framing not only to elucidate economic difference in fair trade exchanges but also to work toward developing an apparatus for understanding different articulations of power as diverse economic identities, practices, and exchanges occur. Here I extend work that builds an "analytical politics" that is attentive to the more hopeful and positive performance of community economies while also differentiating them from those more mundane livelihood struggles (Samers 2005, 883; see also Naylor 2018). Additionally, here I offer a discussion of a potential community that is networked across space and systems of power that are transnational. To do this, I examine exchanges in fair trade certified coffee chains, which have been identified in the broader diverse economies framework as an "alternative market" (cf. Gibson-Graham, Cameron, and Healy 2013). Returning to Healy's (2009) critique, I want to suggest that fair trade exchanges are in practice not "alternative" at all. I do this for two reasons: first, to reassert the critique that in naming something as alternative, we are essentializing these economic practices by reducing them to a site of "other than capitalism," rather than as economic activities in their own right, which stand outside of a hierarchy that places capitalism at the apex. I make such a suggestion, secondly, to disrupt the idea that coffee consumers (e.g., those individuals who are purchasing and drinking certified coffee) are participating in a nominally different exchange as fair trade certified purchases relate to their daily economic practices. However, dismissing the idea of "alternative" does not thereby reject economic difference. Instead, it multiplies the possibilities for how we produce knowledge about economic exchanges and power relations within them.

To engage a diverse economies framing is not simply to add other economic activities and stir; it is instead an opening up of economic discourse that includes capitalism as one of many types of economic activity that are being performed in multiple places and at multiple scales. An anti-essentialist approach to economic practices is based in recognizing economic difference. In rereading economic practice for diversity, a range of practices are made visible. Worldwide, people interact through different forms of labor activity, value production, and consumption, yet these practices are often viewed through a capitalist lens and theorized in a universal way. If we view fair trade production only as a capitalist endeavor toward economic growth, a host of activities, social and economic relations, and politics are obscured. Economic practices do not all look the same, and the recognition of difference (and the power relations embedded within) can help propel us into less deterministic and unequal futures.

Many studies of fair trade coffee production emphasize its effectiveness as a market-based tool or an alternative to neoliberal trade. Such studies assess the cultivation of producer–consumer relations, barriers to market entry, whether certified production leads to economic and community development, and what labor relations exist in fair trade markets. However, critical readings of fair trade expose it as a tool of neoliberal economic development that masks rather than challenges uneven power relations in trade (cf. Dolan 2010; Lyon 2011). This body of work is important in determining whether fair trade is working the way proponents say it should; nonetheless, it is read through a capitalocentric lens, which significantly limits how we can theorize economic activity.

Fair trade is a market, but it is also tied to social justice movements, and this bifurcation provides an entry point for considering how we might think about it differently and how it features as part of diverse livelihood strategies for small producers. Here I wish to point out something that may seem fairly obvious but is often overlooked: fair trade producers are not solely involved in the production of fair trade certified goods; their identities are not bound to the exploitation of their labor for the creation of surplus value in a world market. Other economies are happening. Hence I paint a different portrait of fair trade. Here I am not asking whether fair trade certification is "working" for *campesinos/as* within and against the global capitalist economy; instead, I ask how *campesinos/as* in resistance are mobilizing fair trade as part of building livable worlds. Pursuing this avenue allows for breaking away from universalizing narratives of what fair trade and development are.

Development and Fair Trade

Since its inception, fair trade *certification* has been tied to economic development targeted at marginalized communities. Chiapas has long been cast as a stagnant and impoverished but resource-rich state in Mexico. The southernmost state and the last incorporated into independent Mexico (annexed from Guatemala in 1824), Chiapas is an ethnically diverse state (with twelve official ethnic groups) and is considered in official records the second most "marginalized" state in Mexico (Consejo Nacional de Población 2011). The vast majority of inhabitants are indigenous subsistence producers who have been petitioning the state for access to resources for decades. Indeed, coffee was introduced into the highlands of Chiapas in the 1960s and 1970s as a way to draw subsistence producers away from household corn production and into the marketplace (Martínez-Torres 2006, 53). As the Mexican state undertook the project of economic "modernization," which followed the Revolution (1910–20) and accelerated through the end of World War II, the promotion of coffee production was viewed as a way to "develop" rural areas in Mexico.

I use the word "develop" in quotes here to signal the competing narratives and practices of development. As Essex (2013, 10) noted, it is apparent that "development is a contested terrain, with no consensus on its meaning, and certainly not on how best to achieve or maintain it." In attempting to explain and understand changes in discourse and practice, genealogies of development tend toward a march through periods of varying (and universalizing) theorization drawing on capitalist narratives. There are two important points here: first, that development theory and practice are bound up in a Western capitalist imaginary, which a diverse economies framing rejects, and second, that development theory and practice produce the periphery (see Escobar 1995 on the "Third World") and subjects of development (Naylor 2014). Development narratives are necessarily focused on the "other" effectively writing impoverishment onto places and bodies. They are bound up in debates about poverty and calculable measurements of progress, they make possible claims to knowledge about lives and livelihoods, and they normalize a capitalist economic imaginary and desires for growth. In many cases, development agendas and discourses are deployed while simultaneously ignoring the intentionally uneven processes of capital accumulation and violent histories and present moments of conquest and imperialism.

Escobar (1995, 3) argues that in his 1949 inaugural address, U.S. president Harry Truman effectively created the so-called developing world, restructuring the discourse with which to manage and "fix" what were viewed as the "miserable" parts of the world. Situating development in the context of post–World War II global relations provides a foundation for telling a particular story about it. As Hart (2001) notes, this more formal period of capital-D development locates development as a product of a new wave of independence and Cold War politics, which is largely institutional. Yet, lowercase-d development describes the ongoing and geographically uneven processes of capitalist growth.

Institutionalized development begins with the apparatus of the state at its center. The establishment of formal economic bodies in the Bretton Woods Agreement normalized a hegemonic core (with the United States at its center) and effectively divided the globe into the "developed" and "underdeveloped." This bifurcation justified state-led intervention following the loss of de jure colonial power. Intervention in the periphery as "development" then becomes, as Rist (2008, 77) notes, "impossible to question. . . . One was quite free to debate its forms, the ways of accelerating growth or distributing its effects more equitably, but the transitive character of 'development'—that is, the intervention it represented into the internal affairs of a nation [state]—was not to be challenged." State-led institutionalization of international development takes many forms, from direct aid to structural adjustment. Many actors participate in doing development; it is not limited to the state or suprastate institutions (such as the World Bank). Concurrently (and increasingly with the neoliberal retreat of the state), nonstate actors take on statelike development roles. Among these actors, capitalist-style development is normalized as a positive and necessary intervention. A core component of universalizing capitalism and growth as the path of development is the "subordination of 'precapitalist' forms" of economic engagement (Gibson-Graham 2006b, 193), which are mapped onto peoples and places that are pejoratively labeled as un- or underdeveloped.

Efforts to decrease poverty in the global periphery tend to be embedded in capitalist imaginaries of economic growth. Infrastructure projects, microfinance, increasing access to global markets, for example—industrialization and urbanization continue to be guiding forces for economic development. Although external aid was and continues to be a key feature of international economic development, a focus on markets and trade (under the mantra of "trade not aid") emerged as part of the development paradigm. This particular narrative is uncritically adopted in emphasizing poverty reduction through economic exchange and is taken up as part of the discourses of fair trade (a point to which I return in chapter 3). In continuing efforts to reduce poverty and increase economic growth, trade is deemed an important feature by suprastate organizations, such as the United Nations, and development agencies, such as the World Bank. However, attempts to more evenly distribute wealth at a global scale operate within systems that require the uneven distribution of wealth and access to resources. Proponents of fair trade rely on the discourse of "trade not aid" as a way to more evenly distribute wealth and resources, arguing that fair trade certification provides a basis to increase access to the marketplace for the most marginalized producers, while making relations of trade fairer.

As Mutersbaugh (2016) notes, geographers are interested in the way that certification (including organic and fair trade, among others) mirrors existing neocolonial relations of trade and development. From a development perspective, the introduction of fair trade certification is a new intervention and fix in marginalized areas (Naylor 2017c). The emphasis of many studies on fair trade coffee production is focused on the benefits accrued by producers and communities through the fair trade price floor and the injection of funds via the fair trade premium that is designated for community development projects and product improvement. The emphasis on whether fair trade certification is "working" for producers stems from scholarly interest in investigating the claims made by fair trade proponents, which point to significantly improving the lives and livelihoods of producer constituents and their communities. However, a rereading of fair trade reveals that situating it as an alternative to free trade and a locus of development in producer communities is rather narrow. We have learned that fair trade producers are better off than their non–fair trade counterparts but that they are not able to improve their economic situations significantly (cf. Bacon et al. 2014; Jaffee 2014; Lyon 2011). Additionally, entry into the fair trade market is restrictive, and the most marginalized small producers are often not reached by certification (Dolan 2010; Lyon 2015a; Smith 2007). Yet these findings are grounded in a perspective that emphasizes outcomes that are considered desirable by outsiders and shaped by neoliberal–capitalist goals (e.g., profit, economic growth).

We desperately need new theoretical approaches to fair trade (and development more broadly). If, as I have argued before, we only ask if fair trade is "working" for producers, our findings can be predicted with some certainty.[4] Yet, if we decide that fair trade does not "work" for producers much better than free trade, why should we continue to investigate and ask questions about it? Investigations of fair trade have allowed scholars and practitioners alike to ask questions about how economic exchange functions in a neoliberal–capitalist system. Nonetheless, this universal perspective has limits, even as fair trade is viewed as an alternative that works "within and against" capitalism. I argue that it is essential to break away from framing fair trade as a project of development. Such a reductionist framing creates producer-subjects whose varied identities and livelihoods become singularly tied to an identity as a fair trade producer and delegitimizes their heterogeneous economic activities and knowledges of how to live well. Producers become a project of economic development that is intended as an intervention to "fix" agricultural systems, individual producers, and whole communities. This "fixing" of producers normalizes them as impoverished producers "needing" to be "lifted out of poverty" and renders their specific and dynamic lives and multiple economic practices invisible. As discussed in the introduction, fair trade both fits into and complicates struggles to build dignified livelihoods. A core piece of this argument is based on considering a geopolitics of knowledge that privileges a singular and particular idea of how certain groups of people should live.

Fair trade is mobilized differently across space (from local to global), and Chiapas is no different. It is not singular or universal. In the highlands of Chiapas, certified coffee is grown in the context of resistance. It is grown by rebels against the state and capitalist marketplace, rebels who participate in self-declared "anticapitalist" social movements. *Campesinos/as* in resistance have been growing coffee for decades: first for the state, then for the neoliberal marketplace (in the wake of the dismantling of INMECAFE in 1989).[5] A major difference has been the creation of coffee cooperatives (which then became fair trade certified) that grew out of social movements in the context of the rebellion of *campesinos/as*. How, then, are we to think about the sale of fair trade coffee in the neoliberal marketplace in the context of resistance? If we consider it only as a (neoliberal) capitalist activity, the actions of fair rebels stand out as contradictory. The challenge is to reread the understandings and practices of fair trade as multiple and varied and to decolonize the way we think about production and certification, as well as who benefits from them.

Decolonizing and Multiplying Knowledge

Decolonizing the ways we think about what fair trade is is essential for seeing and creating other possible worlds. If fair trade is part of the larger project of top-down, capitalist-style economic development, which seeks to intervene and "fix" producer communities, then a decolonial reading creates a different engagement, from below. Decolonizing knowledge is the primary concern of decolonial scholars, who critique contemporary power–knowledge dynamics to confront modernity. For decolonial thinkers, there is no end or after to the colonial period; rather, it is a longer epistemic and ontological project of coloniality–modernity (Quijano 1997) that privileges Western ways of knowing and understanding the world. A decolonized knowledge production—that which attempts to document social injustices and recover subjugated knowledges while challenging paradigmatic racism, sexism, and colonialism—allows for a dismantling of coloniality (Tuhiwai-Smith 1999). It is an attempt to multiply knowledges and move away from universalizing, normalizing, and exclusionary tendencies in knowledge production.

At the core of the decolonial project is the decentering and multiplying of knowledge and power. It is a critique of past and present colonialism and coloniality that attempts to step outside of Eurocentric discourses to untangle colonial modernity. Race, place, and, increasingly, nature, gender, and sexual identity form key sites of examination for decolonial theorists. At the forefront of the decolonial project is the modernity–coloniality research paradigm originating in Latin American thought and driven by the possibility of creating "worlds and knowledges otherwise." The main thread that is pulled through decolonial theory (and that distinguishes it from postcolonial thinking) is that modernity commenced with colonialism. Moreover, there is no end or after to the colonial (Grosfoguel 2011) but a de facto coloniality that continues despite de jure independence. As Alcoff (2007, 83) explains, for decolonial thinkers, such as Mignolo, there is no modernity outside of coloniality:

> Colonialism is constitutive of modernity, of its teleological macronarratives of human progress, and of the material base necessary to provide both the surplus and the self-representation required to imagine Europe as the vanguard of the human race. To put this another way, colonialism is constitutive of both the base and the superstructure of modernity.

What a narrative of coloniality suggests is that a Eurocentric modernity made and continues to make invisible the non-"Western." Knowledge production is generated from particular spaces; for Mignolo (2009b, 160), the imperial and "knowing subject" writes the earth; identifies and classifies people and problems; and makes decisions and designs projects to fix these people and places. Thus universalizing narratives are generated from a particular spatial position, in this case, a Western one, which claims hegemony.

In mobilizing the modernity–coloniality research paradigm, scholars point to a "coloniality of power" and the "colonial difference." The coloniality of power (Quijano 1997) is a global model of power (Escobar 2007) that details the construction of knowledge, identity, and place through hegemonic structures. These structures were emplaced during the period of the conquest of the Americas, and they have been continuously remade alongside the advance of capitalism (Mignolo 2000). Classifying peoples, defining spaces, establishing structures/institutions, and creating (or rendering invisible) knowledge are all ways in which the coloniality of power is reified. For Quijano (2008), the coloniality of power is bound up, first, in the emergence of modernity; second, in the classification of people by race; and finally, in the production of knowledge, which is then imposed via institutional structures. Within this framing, the coloniality of power becomes the organizing principle for ordering the world. Escobar (2007, 185) notes that this model of power, which has been in place since the conquest, "articulates race and labor, space and peoples, according to the needs of capital and to the benefit of white European peoples." Feminist scholars expanded this more narrow reading of hegemony additionally to read gender and sexual identity inequalities as an apparatus of coloniality (cf. Anzaldúa 1987; Gómez-Barris 2017; Lugones 2007, 2010, 2013; Mendoza 2015; Naylor et al. 2018; Schiwy 2007; Zaragocin 2017, 2018).

Parallel to the construction of the coloniality of power is the colonial difference, which Mignolo (2000) argues is what has been erased from social memory through the subjugation of knowledge and displacement of alternate modernities. This subjugation and displacement is inherently geographical, as both Castro-Gómez (2007) and Mignolo (2009b) argue. The colonial difference recognizes the subjugation of knowledge from exteriority and uncovers alterity (Grosfoguel 2008; see also Dussel 1976; Vallega 2014). The modern colonial world system is the legacy of the European encounter with the Americas. The coloniality of power as articulated by Mignolo (2002, 252) "was enacted and continues to rule out everything that did not conform to the principles under which modernity was being conceived," for example, economic exchanges and subsistence practices that are not imagined as aligning with a capitalist model. Yet a reframing through the colonial difference exposes the "forgetting" that happens in and through the project of modernity. In recognizing the artificial differences and othering that were created via the conquest, the structures of power that underlie coloniality can be unearthed. As Walsh notes, "the production of knowledge and theory through embodied practice and from the ground up— that is by subjects, identified or not as women and men, who live the colonial difference—turns the dominant precept of reason and its geography and geopolitics on its head" (Mignolo and Walsh 2018, 28). By locating forms of knowledge via exteriority, or from the "exploited side of the colonial difference" (Grosfoguel 2008, 16), decolonial theorists posit that the modern colonial world system can be resisted. In thinking from the colonial difference, knowledges, practices, identities, spaces, and natures are multiplied.

Out of such deconstruction emerged a number of strategies for constructive dialogue, thinking, seeing, and allying. These approaches include (but are not limited to) relational ontologies, which attempt to erase nature–culture divides (Escobar 2008); transmodernity, which liberates subjugated knowledges (Dussel and Mendieta 1996; Grosfoguel 2011); border thinking, which implores a rethinking from multiple "sides" (Anzaldúa 1987; Mignolo 2000); and those that theorize a geopolitics of knowledge that (re)considers spaces of knowledge production (Mignolo 2002; Naylor 2017a; Tuck and Yang 2012; Tuhiwai-Smith 1999; Walsh 2007). These interdisciplinary perspectives offer opportunities to reframe examinations of multiscalar and multisited processes and interstitial spaces from the global to the body. Decolonial analyses make visible the cracks in universals while simultaneously opening up pluriversal spaces.

Although useful for advancing multiple and diverse knowledges, decolonial theory is rarely deployed to engage gender, sexual identity, nature, or economic difference (Asher 2013; Escobar 2007; Lugones 2007). Such encounters in feminist, postcolonial, and political ecology scholarship are being drawn into these discussions and debates in addressing this glaring omission (Anzaldúa 1987; Gómez-Barris 2017; Escobar 2008; Mendoza 2015; Mignolo and Walsh 2018; Naylor 2017a; Naylor et al. 2018; Schiwy 2007; Zaragocin 2018; Zaragocin, Moreano Venegas, and Álvarez Velasco 2018). In addition to drawing attention to the missing intersectional approaches in decolonial theory, Asher (2013) advances a two-pronged critique, pushing scholars to participate in more critical and nuanced examinations. Asher argues that many decolonial approaches tend to equate the theoretical with the political, rendering it impossible to meet the stated goals of decolonial thinking—in essence bringing tensions to light, but not addressing them. This assessment is expounded by a critique of the silence on representation in decolonial theory. Drawing on postcolonial theory (and arguing that it should be in conversation with the decolonial), Asher deploys Spivak's (1999, 2012) deconstructive work on the messiness of representing the subaltern. Asher (2013, 839) cautions scholars against a romanticization of subaltern knowledges, in which scholarly desires for a "just world for humans and non-humans" are fulfilled. Theorizing knowledges "otherwise," "from below," or at the "underside" risks reproducing oppressive power–knowledge dynamics (or reinstating hierarchies) that decolonial thinking seeks to deconstruct (Naylor et al., 2018).

The decolonial is another way that we can reread economic practice and performance for difference. In work on decolonial feminism, Lugones (2010, 748) articulates this project: "instead of thinking of the global, capitalist, colonial system as in every way successful in its destruction of peoples, knowledges, and economies, I want to think of the process as continually resisted and being resisted today." A core decolonial question Mignolo (2009b, 178) posed is not "how to save capitalism" but "why would you want to save capitalism and not human beings?" What, then, is the practice of decoloniality? How do the struggle and resistance from exteriority push against coloniality? These are questions taken up by Walsh and Mignolo as they examine a decolonial praxis. Walsh (2018, 17) argues,

> With colonialism and coloniality came resistance and refusal. Decoloniality necessarily follows, derives from and responds to coloniality and the ongoing colonial process and condition. It is a form of struggle and survival, and epistemic and existence-based response and practice—most especially by colonized and racialized subjects—*against* the colonial matrix of power in all of its dimensions, and for the possibilities otherwise.

This argument points to a dynamic and place-based decoloniality, which makes visible other ways of knowing and understanding the world that decenter a Western perspective. The project of decolonizing knowledge production must be informed by the geopolitics of knowledge—the why and how of where it is produced. As Gibson-Graham (2006a [1996, 41]) pointed out early on with regard to global economic development, the noncapitalist–capitalist binary forecloses heterogeneity alongside capitalism—instead pitting "islands of localized resistance" within a "capitalist sea." Capitalist-style development and market interaction as a universal pervades knowledge about how to live well. As Escobar (2018, 6) notes, the design of development must be "liberated" from the imagination of the "Global North" and "relocated" within the "multiple onto-epistemic formations of the South, so as to redefine questions, problems, and practices in ways more appropriate to the South's contexts." To decolonize development is to break the hold on a global imagination and create anew in place-based contexts that step outside of universals. Here I assert a decoloniality that is plural and part of the possible.

In identifying fair trade as a tool of economic development that works within and against the market, fair trade scholarship relies on a singular and universalizing narrative of what fair trade is and whom it is for. This book does not. Instead, while I am interested in engaging the questions of what fair trade is and whom it is for, this is tempered too by asking, who gets to decide? Moreover, this question is spatial, considering from where is it decided and how the imaginary of "other" places is projected via that decision-making process. Fair trade is predicated on a development model that universalizes and obscures, and it does this from a particular spatial position—the zero point—erasing other possibilities. The idea of "capitalism's excluded others" (Gibson-Graham 2007, 3) takes on multiple meanings in the context of the practices of *campesinos/as* in resistance. As indigenous peoples, they have struggled against five hundred years of exploitation and marginalization. Their knowledges, practices, and economies were subverted to white, Western, hetero-patriarchal universals. But in considering how to think about economies and economic identities outside of a capitalocentric lens, the pluriversal is opened up and made visible. Fair rebels are engaging in a radical process of place making that comes not from universal imaginaries of development but from a space that puts the politics of place at the center, making visible multiple modernities. Beyond breaking down universals, this approach makes a space for hope.

I aim to retheorize and challenge the way scholars and practitioners think about economic development and resilience by showing that not everyone understands and builds secure livelihoods with profit and growth at the center, and while hopeful, these efforts are part of difficult daily struggles. *Fair Trade Rebels* is an empirically grounded analysis of localized economic practices that mobilize global networks to build wide-ranging networks that are not tied to any one place but to social and economic relations between people. A key contribution is putting decolonial and diverse economies theories into conversation, not only to illuminate the struggles of *campesinos/as* in resistance but also to multiply our understandings of fair trade, development, resistance, and efforts to build dignified livelihoods and livable worlds.

Rebel Coffee

Stepping back from reading fair trade as only a market-based tool for development requires a consideration of movements to make trade fairer and how fair trade is situated in rebel Chiapas (those spaces where *campesinos/as* in resistance have declared autonomy from the state). The production of rebel coffee (coffee produced by *campesinos/as* in resistance for cooperatives that are certified fair trade) forms part of the resistance that is being practiced in the highlands. Yet, fair trade certification is part of the neoliberal apparatus as an ever-expanding, profit-based market, nevertheless the movements to make trade fairer remain. Rather than thinking about fair trade only as "lifting farmers out of poverty," we can also consider fair trade "in movement." Under the larger umbrella of fair trade is a movement and a market—and within each of these may be many different understandings being generated by even more groups about what fair trade is and whom it is for (a discussion to which I return in chapters 3 and 4). The movement and market for fairer trade are entangled and messy spaces that are negotiated by *campesinos/as* in resistance.

In 2011, following the split of the two largest third-party fair trade certifiers, there was an uproar in the larger fair trade community. As part of the response to the split, cartoonist John Klossner produced an image for longtime fair trade organization Equal Exchange (Figure 4).

Considering the question of who owns fair trade is one way we can begin to think about what fair trade is and whom it is for; moreover, the depiction by Klossner (2013) says much about the question

Figure 4. *Who Speaks for Fair Trade?* Copyright 2013 John Klossner, http://www.jklossner.com/.

of who gets to decide. The departure of Fair Trade USA (previously Transfair) from the larger Fairtrade Labeling Organization (now Fairtrade International) is not the site of the rupture between movements and the market for fairer trade; however, it was a turning point for many actors within the broader fair trade apparatus as Fair Trade USA sought to redefine and in essence "own" fair trade. The 2012 "Fair Trade for All" campaign, which was launched by Fair Trade USA following the split, was squarely focused on expanding the fair trade label and market to extend the so-called benefits of economic development to more people (Fair Trade USA 2012). As the fair trade label adorns more products and is extended to more organizations and companies, its meaning changes, creating a distinct path toward answering the question of whom it is for. The discourses of the fair trade movement and social justice activism focused on fairer trade became embedded in the expansion of the market, muddying the different desires, outcomes, and practices of a large group of people.

The expansion of the market at the expense of the movement led Matt Earley (2012), social activist and cofounder of the Just Coffee

Cooperative in the United States, to declare Fair Trade™ dead. This declaration effectively drew a line in the sand between the movement and the market. Movements to make trade fairer are populated by a diverse set of stakeholders worldwide. Taken at its most basic premise, making trade fairer is about valuing people over profit. Making trade fairer crafts coffee production and consumption as political acts. Yet, this simplified understanding masks the different desires and outcomes of mobilizing for better conditions in global trade. Some stakeholders are concerned with making trade "work" for small producers, others with creating more direct trade networks and reducing labor exploitation. Many activists focus on solidarity and awareness raising. Producers also fall in this mix, yet they are also consumers, which adds to the layers of complexity that make up the broader and varied aims of social movements. Movements to make trade fairer are not singular and static but multiple and dynamic. So, we must also consider fair trade in movement. Thinking about fair trade in movement implies a process that has momentum and is moving toward change. Additionally, analyzing the movement versus the market sets up a potentially unhelpful binary. Fair trade reflects not just two realities (market or movement) but many, which are experienced by people in multiple and competing ways. To grasp the nuances of fair trade, we must situate it in place and examine how it is understood and practiced.

For fair rebels, the sale of coffee in the fair trade marketplace is one of many strategies for building dignified livelihoods and livable worlds, even as they resist political and economic violence. In an interview I conducted with the leadership of a coffee-producing cooperative in the highlands early in my research, this point was made very clear: "Our coffee, it sells, and it sends the message that we are still here." For *campesinos/as* in resistance, fair trade is a possibility. It is not *the* possibility but one of many in the pursuit of creating livelihoods with dignity. It is not a means to an end (profit) but something to make them visible, while also gaining cash income for the purchase of items that cannot be produced in their communities. When discussed as a possibility, our thinking on fair trade is opened up and avenues for seeing difference are provided. The cooperatives were begun as a site of resistance, not as a site of capital accumulation. Taking on the fair trade label assists with cultivating a broader community in solidarity with their resistance that is centered, not on coffee and profit, but on people.

Here I discuss local economic practices that harness the global to create a larger network that shapes the pursuit of dignified livelihoods. This discussion is a story about diverse economic practice and resistance. It is about the local and global talking back to each other. Local to global networks and practice are flattened out in this context, disrupting hierarchies that confine local initiatives to their place of origin and put them under the thumb of larger global processes. The localized economies created by fair rebels are more than simply locally shared appropriations of surplus. These community economies are also a form of resistance. Within this resistance lies the possibility of forging relations between local practices and larger outside networks. In many cases, local initiatives are seen as being in response to or undermined by larger-scale practices and processes, yet, in this case, as part of the process of flattening, the local is harnessing (and in some cases manipulating) the global. This flattening is an important theme that threads through the book, and here I seek to understand how fair rebels use local economic practices to extend global solidarity networks and build wide-ranging community economies, which are not tied to any one place but rather are tied to social relations between people.

Here let us briefly consider the questions of what fair trade is and whom it is for in the context of the highlands. Rather than relying on a singular definition, defining it against the capitalist marketplace, or taking up the understandings embedded in movements for fairer trade, I seek here to identify many ways of thinking about fair trade. Multiplying our understandings of fair trade allows for a diversity of perspectives, including those from movements and markets (and beyond). Examining fair trade outside of universal framings opens up opportunities to consider economic practices as a form of resistance. To understand rebel coffee, we must step away from questions rooted in economic development discourses that focus on asking if fair trade is "working" and move toward questions of how it is mobilized and deployed; in the case of fair rebels, we must consider it as part of a broader form of struggle and resistance.

Stzi'kel Vocol: Withstanding Suffering

Resistance is often romanticized, but there is nothing romantic about being hungry. For within each performance of resistance is a membership: people, bodies, practices, and everyday actions that make possible the politics and mobilizations of resistance. In considering the resistance in the highlands, I am not asking about how *campesinos/as* in resistance perform as actors in social movements or originators of subversive acts; rather, I am asking about how they maintain themselves while simultaneously negotiating the politics of their struggle and the creation of dignified livelihoods and livable worlds. Yet, how are we to understand resistance? Resistance is a term that presents many obstacles to scholars and that has been in vogue and fallen from grace in critical geography in the span of a few decades. If we are to examine power–knowledge dynamics and give due attention to the articulations by *campesinos/as* living in rebel Chiapas as a people "in resistance," then revisiting the term is a necessary step in laying the foundation for the book.

As Abu-Lughod (1990, 41) noted, academic interest in resistance was for a very long time tied to emancipation or revolution and an attention to particular global-historical moments. Over the past few decades, geographers have reworked conceptualizations of resistance, moving from a period of examining structural power relationships (Cresswell 1996; Pile and Keith 1997) that tended to mask potential spaces of resistance toward one of analyzing the interactions between intentioned and unintentional acts as well as domination and resistance. These broadened academic conceptualizations of resistance, stemming from work in anthropology by Scott (1985), focused on less visible and more localized resistances. Yet, scholarship on resistance, as Rose (2002) argues, rather than establishing a robust theoretical base, instead created a crisis, which revealed the limits of categorizing resistance and challenged scholars to reconceptualize the relational character of power and space. Critical thinking on resistance opened up the ways that we consider power, yet in many cases, such framings are dichotomous and neglect the interaction between peoples and places.

Although some scholars argue that resistance does not always form in the shadow of hegemonic power (cf. Pile 1997), Sharp et al.

(2000) state that power/domination cannot be separated from resistance, or vice versa, arguing that because domination and resistance cannot be delinked, they necessarily produce "entanglements of power." Drawing extensively from Foucauldian notions of power, Sharp et al. attempt to position resistance in relation to power as it plays out in society and space through the "dyad" of domination–resistance (20). As Rose (2002) points out, both working within the "entanglements" of power as well as attempting to conceptualize resistance outside of domination can have the impact of masking the very power structures, discourses, and actors they seek to make visible. This difficulty brought geographers to an impasse on resistance, to the extent that it became an empty signifier, capturing any and all transgressive acts and characterizing power as necessarily and negatively hegemonic.

Owing to the theoretical stickiness of attempting to capture acts of transgression and resistance (see Naylor 2012b; Spinney 2010), many scholars draw from social movement activism to examine and theorize resistance (cf. Ayres and Bosia 2011; Chatterton and Heynen 2011; Featherstone 2003, 2007, 2008; Routledge 2009). In the more than two decades since the 1994 uprising of the Zapatistas, a range of scholarship has been produced that draws from experiences in Chiapas: some examining the resistances of the Zapatista Movement and others, which use interpretations of Zapatista forms of indigenous, autonomous resistance to understand resistance elsewhere.[6] I draw attention to this use here not to restate or reexamine Zapatista resistances but instead to point to a geopolitics of knowledge production, where resistance and struggle in one place are readily mapped onto other places to explain divergent contexts. In many cases, the performances and practices of Zapatistas are drawn on to explain vastly different forms of struggle, even being levied to explain resistance in core–imperial contexts, which tends to universalize struggle in a particularly Western way.

The very definition of resistance takes on different meanings in the highlands, stemming not from universal notions of freedom, liberty, or counterhegemony but from struggle, suffering, resilience, identity, and material practice. The analytical and methodological starting point for this examination of resistance is a geographically specific place and a set of actors who engage a range of practices but who are not reducible to any one category of resistance. Moreover, the practices examined in this context are not the everyday resistances consisting of "foot dragging" and "sabotage," which lie at the heart of Scott's (1985) theorizations, or linked to particular subversive action or mobilization. Instead, resistance is based in daily struggles, agricultural practices in place, and solidarity network support that is used to materially enact livable worlds. The moniker *"campesinos/as* in resistance" assists with reframing the approach taken and unpacking the power relations and struggles in place. For fair rebels, resistance is not a theory but a reality. Being *campesinos/as* in resistance forms a part of their identities, struggles, and daily lives.

Although coffee makes up an important part of everyday activities and transnational solidarity networking, *campesinos/as* in resistance identify most strongly as *peasants* who cultivate the *milpa* (the three sisters: corn, beans, and squash) for subsistence. As a result, the cultivation, maintenance, and protection of their native corn are paramount; coffee is a solidarity and income relation, but corn is life. The increased threat of transgenic corn spurred some autonomous communities to work with international nongovernmental organizations (NGOs) to create safeguards. One such effort is a seed bank project that I learned about during fieldwork in 2010 from NGO director Peter Brown, who works closely with rebel autonomous Zapatista schools in Chiapas (and who has since published this account; see Brown 2013, 158–60; see also Aguila-Way 2014; Brandt 2014). He described the first meetings of the *campesinos/as* as one where the discussion of safeguarding corn was the focal point of maintaining resistance. In the group conversation about naming the seed bank project, the *campesinos/as* decided on the name Mother Seeds in Resistance, Semillas Madre en Resistencia in Spanish, and Sme' Tzu'nubil Stzi'kel Vocol in Tzotzil (one of the more common Mayan languages spoken in the highlands, along with Tzeltal). He was curious why the word for resistance was two Tzotzil words, *stzi'kel vocol*, and learned through translation and interpretation that it meant "to withstand suffering." Learning this translation was a revelation for Brown (2013, 159). Moksnes (2012, 35–36) also discusses Tzotzil knowledges of suffering, noting that *vocol* (also spelled *vokol*), "suffering," makes up a key part of indigenous identity in the highlands. Indeed, this form and understanding of resistance as a way to withstand the violence of the five-hundred-year war against indigenous peoples stand outside binary understandings of resistance as protest or resistance as a "weapon of the weak," cutting across to reveal everyday, sedimented practices (see Nelson 2003) of resistance tied to agricultural production (Naylor 2017a).

A key way in which *campesinos/as* in resistance are making more visible their subjectivities—not as a project of development and state intervention—is through this narrative of resistance. Not only does this narrative signal a need to expand how, as scholars, we think about resistance; it also provides a signpost for how understanding and theorizing resistance have been monopolized. It is here that we see, not new definitions or understandings of resistance, but a way of knowing and understanding resistance from exteriority. That fair rebels understand and know resistance as withstanding suffering grows out of their experience as exploited indigenous peoples (cf. Escobar 2007; Grosfoguel 2008; Stahler-Sholk 2015).

When *campesinos/as* refer to themselves as "in resistance," it is a way to describe themselves not only as social movement actors but as indigenous peasant producers who are maintaining agricultural practices and cultivating international networks as part of their struggle against the many forces that seek to undermine them. It is a component of building a counterhegemony and an identity, not as powerless, marginalized peasants dominated by state and other neoliberal forces but as powerful *campesinos/as* seeking dignified livelihoods outside the machinations of state-led development. In some ways, this fundamentally disrupts how scholars theorize resistance. Considering highland communities that have declared autonomy from the state as sites of resistance requires expanding geographical epistemologies of resistance.

Ultimately, retheorizing resistance presents a tricky landscape to negotiate. At the same time, however, the moniker "*campesinos/as* in resistance" assists with reframing the approach taken and unpacking the power relations and struggle in place. One *campesino* alluded to the communal ability to withstand the everyday struggle: "we are a people in resistance. There is no other way forward." For it is everyday things and the struggle of daily life that are and become resistance, and fair rebels are resisting cooptation and assimilation through their daily practice(s). Such a practical theory of resistance may not directly address the potentially problematic power/domination dynamic, yet it signals *campesinos/as* as agents of change, which at the very least disrupts it, giving us additional avenues to think through resistance.

A key piece of withstanding suffering is the reframing of identities through striving to create dignified livelihoods as peasants—disrupting the narrative of peasants being subsumed under capitalism. In many ways, fair rebels are redefining and multiplying what it means to be a peasant. One of the key ways that this disrupts the geopolitics of knowledge is through siting the struggle in agricultural production practices. Agricultural production is the leading way that resistance is written into the landscape and onto the bodies of *campesinos/as* in the highlands. It is important to consider how fair rebels make this possible. In many cases, peasant agriculture is viewed as a self-exploiting, noncapitalist practice. Yet, if we are to consider what it means to produce in resistance, viewing these practices as diverse and multiple is necessary. Taken at face value, fair rebels are exercising power over their productive practice and networks. However, these practices are not without their messiness, and they may be in tension as they work within, outside, and alongside capitalist networks. A core component of the diverse livelihood strategies is the building of larger networks within and between rebel territories populated by *campesinos/as* in resistance (and also those who are not aligned with the Zapatistas and Las Abejas), as well as transnational networks to foster solidarity relations. Fair trade certified exchanges in the context of resistance are a "window to better money," as discussed in the previous chapter, yet viewed outside the narrow and universalizing ideas of capitalist development, they open and (fore)close other possibilities.

A Window on the World

Given the framing by *campesinos/as* in resistance of fair trade as a "window to better money," we can ponder the other windows that fair trade opens and closes. This consideration is a piece of the question of "who gets to decide" what fair trade is and whom it is for. There are various decision makers, from coffee producers and their cooperatives to coffee roasters and third-party labeling organizations. As each seeks to "own" fair trade, different viewpoints and openness emerge. As a window to better money within a capitalocentric framing, fair trade certification is reduced to price. As a window on the world, fair trade is part of a larger community. This window is framed by both the market, which is based in profit, successful economic development outcomes, and product improvement, and social justice movements, which are attempting to move toward solidarity, more direct forms of trade, and community building, and also by the networks of resistance, which strike through this binary and demonstrate that the "better" in this phrase might have more to do with building knowledge from below than determining whether fair trade is working for *campesinos/as* in resistance. In the next chapter, I provide a historical context for building livelihoods in the highlands as part of the five-hundred-year struggle of indigenous peoples.

The Shape of Struggle, So It Is . . .

As I had done many times over the past two years, I walked with a member of the coffee cooperative to visit their home and family. Heading out from the bodega of Maya Vinic, we walked down the center of the road, jumping to the right or left every time a pickup truck or taxi raced by. The trucks you could hear from a distance, bumping down the paved but poorly maintained road that connects Yabteclum to Pantelhó. One truck pulled to a stop as we walked, and I watched as a mother and her two young children descended from the back of the truck, laden with packaged goods from town. We talked about the road and the trucks and the community as we walked. "Here our community has changed very much," he remarked as we walked past an old hacienda dwelling that was now in use as a community meeting and Sunday worship space.

It is a community populated by subsistence farmers of varying political affiliations. No matter the affiliation, though, almost everyone works the land in corn or coffee, and as we walk along the road, there is evidence of this. In the foreground is coffee drying on

Figure 5. Husband and wife, members of Las Abejas and the Maya Vinic Coffee Cooperative, stand in front of drying beans and coffee beans at their home within the boundaries of the official municipality of Chenalhó. Photograph by the author.

any (and every) available space. Coffee dries on concrete slabs adjacent to households or on tarps that have been laid on the ground, in the margins of the road, on rooftops and other available flat spaces. In the background, a sweeping vista of cornfields and shade coffee plots extends across the hilly terrain.

Not many in this community are members of Las Abejas or the Zapatistas; they are outnumbered almost three to one by community members who are affiliated with other groups (or unaffiliated). We talk about how this divergence between the numbers of farmers in resistance and those who are not impacts the struggle for autonomy. I ask, "How will you maintain your land and *ejido*?" This question is met with a long sigh. The community has met to discuss PROCEDE. PROCEDE is a government land-titling program that began in the 1990s as land redistribution was halted in the lead-up to the signing of NAFTA. Effectively, it takes communally held land (which before PROCEDE could not be sold) and grants individual titles, allowing for private investment in previously communally held land. For the first time, this land could be titled, bought, sold, rented, or used as collateral. The government has already come and gone, the land has been surveyed, and the community has agreed that their claims to land are not secure without title.

The community has decided that they will accept PROCEDE and receive titles to their land. "We all agreed that we are going to get title and that we would not sell our plots. So it is." Another long sigh. *Así es,* or "so it is," is an oft-heard refrain in Chiapas. It reminded me of Vonnegut's "so it goes." And it still rings in my ears as acceptance of struggle. Being outnumbered in their community adds another dynamic to their resistance and to how they interact with the state, or not. It forms another key part of daily struggle as they negotiate how their struggle should be shaped.

2

Coffee "Fixes"

Decolonizing Development

In late December 2012, I traveled outside the highlands to visit communities in Northern Chiapas near the archeological site of Palenque. I was assisting with translation and interpretation for a group that had come to learn about rebel autonomous education. They were visiting a new school that was being built with the support of a U.S.-based NGO. I was not aware at the time of our visit that the Zapatistas would shortly be closing their government offices and staging a mass mobilization in cities and towns across Chiapas. This mobilization was timed with the coming of the Sixth Sun, a new *b'akt'un* or historical cycle in Mayan chronology. Prior to their march, I was chatting with an education promoter about the agroecological training that was planned for the new school and about the division of labor between the student attendees. Following this discussion, I remarked that I had seen many foreigners arriving near Palenque to "witness" the end of the world that misinterpretations of the meaning of the Sixth Sun had falsely prophesized. I asked what he thought about the apocalyptic visions coming from outside Mexico, which were spurred by the supposed end of the ancient Mayan calendar. "We think it is funny," he remarked. "People think that the Maya are a people of the past." However, what the calendar meant for *campesinos/as* in resistance was not an end but a new beginning.

On December 21, 2012, the world did not end. Instead, at dawn, thousands of indigenous Maya Tzotziles, Tzeltales, Tojolobales, Ch'oles, and Mames emerged from Zapatista centers and quietly marched on the cities of eastern Chiapas. Masked in balaclavas or handkerchiefs, they silently filed through the cities. They built stages but made no speeches. Each Zapatista ascended the stage, fist in the air, and continued their silent march. That afternoon, the Zapatistas issued a communiqué:

> Did you listen?
> It is the sound of your world crumbling.
> It is the sound of our world resurging.
> The day that was day, was night.
> And night shall be the day that will be day.
> Democracy!
> Liberty!
> Justice! (Ejército Zapatista de Liberación Nacional 2012)

In the fervor leading up to the Sixth Sun, the indigenous Maya were cast as a magnificent ancient civilization to be celebrated and remembered as part of a golden age prior to the conquest of the Americas. Such narratives are tied to what Mora (2017, 16) identifies as a trope that uses representations of an "extinct" and glorious civilization to contrast current Mayan peoples as degenerate and in need of assistance. As part of the erasing of colonial–imperial geo- and body politics, the indigenous Maya of Chiapas (and they are not a unique case) are recast as inherently unable to participate in modernity. Such an imaginary is a core piece of the colonization of knowledge that renders non-Western ways of knowing and being invisible. The reassertion of indigenous existence is one way that we might consider a decolonizing of knowledge.

What *campesinos/as* in resistance are making visible through their knowledge building and material practices toward dignified livelihoods are the ways in which their struggle is sedimented in place and the present. Their rebel autonomy and resistance emerge from geohistorical violence, structural oppression, and the denial of indigenous ontologies and epistemologies. Knowledge is produced in place and is not divorced from historical context or imperial imaginaries. Mignolo (2009b, 160) argues that the "geopolitics of knowledge goes hand in hand with geo-politics of knowing" and questions "who and when, why and where is knowledge generated?" Mignolo draws from this larger query about situated knowledges to further understand why Western ways of knowing became universal, concealing and delegitimizing the multiple and varied knowledges that existed and continue to shape non-Western worldviews and struggles. This understanding of knowledge production as "sitting in places" (see Escobar 2001) contrasts with colonial–imperial imaginaries of modernity, which elide the geopolitical and geohistorical contexts of cultivating ways of knowing and being in the world. This imaginary provides the foundation for an apolitical, aspatial, and universalizing idea of what is modern and how people should live. Visions for economic development and economic exchanges begin from these universalizing narratives, and the struggle of *campesinos/as* in resistance provides concrete examples for how we might consider the decolonization of knowledge from struggles in place, which are not confined to the local but reverberate throughout broader networks and sites of solidarity. Simultaneously, these examples demonstrate that the experience of the "struggling peasant" is not a quixotic universal.

Many events tied to land and the cultivation of corn and coffee assist with understanding how development is perceived and "done" in Chiapas. This chapter is a deeper investigation of the development narratives and programs in Chiapas and their impact on the lives and livelihoods of *campesinos/as* in resistance. It should be noted at the outset of this historical chapter, though, that there is a politics of narrating history and the danger of single story. There are multiple historical narratives at work, and one component of being in resistance is crafting that narrative. Here it is in the context of the five-hundred-year struggle; however, it also serves as a counternarrative to official state accounts and as a site of looking backward to move forward.

After the Zapatista uprising in 1994, demands made by *campesinos/as* in resistance for access to land and resources were permeated by desires for "modernity," including technical agricultural packages and market access. Spurred by the attention that the uprising focused on Chiapas, *campesinos/as* drew on official narratives of the "backwardness" of Chiapas to agitate for the state to develop rural areas. Discourses of the invisibility of indigenous peoples by the state formed the basis of these demands. Following the uprising, where indigenous peoples "covered their faces to be seen," they finally had the attention of the state and hoped that the promises of "development" would follow.[1]

However, what followed in the wake of the uprising was economic and political violence. NAFTA arrived, bringing competition from the United States and Canada, and in its defense, soldiers.[2] New roads were rapidly built, connecting some areas in the highlands to the valley for the first time. These new roads were constructed with the pretense, not of assisting small-scale producers with getting their products to market, but of eliminating *campesinos/as* in resistance. When discussing the change from demands on the state to declaring autonomy from the state and what that meant for agricultural production, one *campesino* explained how indigenous groups (both those intertwined with the resistance and those who were not) responded to state assistance during this period:

> Before the [Zapatista] insurgency, with the price of coffee, people had to leave their land. Those who stayed farmed the *milpa* but NAFTA brought more chemicals to the highlands. *Campesinos* who worked as laborers on the *fincas* saw the immediate successes and tried to bring them to their own small plots, so it is. People were using two or three times more the amount of fertilizer and after a few years the land was dead.

Desires for modernity, bound to universalized knowledge about how to develop, form a key piece of why *campesinos/as* sought to replicate industrial agricultural practices—something that most *campesinos/as* in resistance later deemed a continuation of the war of five hundred years, where state intervention in land and agricultural resources was based in the elimination of the indigenous peasant in Chiapas. Following the collapse of the 1996 San Andrés Accords and the declaration of autonomy by *campesinos/as* in resistance, a slow violence of government interference and market fluctuations settled in the highlands. The infiltration of government programs into the highlands in 1994, as a way to destabilize the resistance, assists with understanding the deployment of universal forms of development; programs such as PROCAMPO, PROCEDE, and Oportunidades (formerly Progresa, 1994–2001), and lately Prospera (since 2012) (see Mora 2017, 161), are used by the state to incentivize *campesinos/as* away from the resistance and enfold them into state biopolitical (power over bodies and body politics) and economic control. Indeed, Stahler-Sholk (2005) notes that the neoliberal agenda in Mexico is intimately tied to efforts to create neo-patron–client relations and foster divisions among dissenting parties.

When talking about agroecological practices currently being used in *milpa* production, a group of *campesinos* with whom I spoke talked about the government program Programa de Apoyos Directos al Campo (Program for Direct Assistance in Agriculture, PROCAMPO), which was introduced in 1994 (following the uprising), and the rampant use of chemicals, and one of them remarked on how his organic practices and efforts to learn about agroecology differed from the industrial–technical methods encouraged by the state: "the credit to *campesinos* for pesticides and herbicides, because it was government support people believed that it was the best way to farm, but the effects, they were never explained. The effects on the health of the people or the land." Another *campesino* supplied, "And after, we reaped the reward of a bad system."[3] The changing relations with the state and agricultural production currently and historically are important touchstones for the resistance that is practiced in the highlands today, and they shape the knowledge building and responses of *campesinos/as* as they seek to resist development programs that label their practices (subsistence and small-scale agriculture) as an unproductive use of land that inhibits development in the region.

The delivery of technical–industrial agricultural packages through PROCAMPO and the forcing of small-scale producers onto an open coffee market are part and parcel of a development paradigm that obviates the peasantry. Attempts to "modernize" Chiapas are focused not on people but on capitalist enterprise as historical and contemporary efforts emphasize cattle ranching, petroleum extraction, and large-scale farming of commodity crops such as African oil palm. Programs centered on indigenous *campesinos/as* tended to be distributed unevenly (often peaking during election campaigns) and lack staff and/or resources. Following the 1994 uprising, such programs and projects increasingly became a way to undercut indigenous resistance politics and "improve" indigenous people's health and agricultural practices under the umbrella of government programming, while simultaneously keeping them at the margins. Indeed, Mora (2008, 184–85) argues that these programs, Oportunidades (now Prospera) in particular, became new spaces to govern indigenous activities and, especially as they related to indigenous women, had the impact of recasting them as "pillars of the neoliberal state." Fair rebels, in their resistance and since their declaration of autonomy, have eschewed such programs and assistance of the state and instead have focused on those activities that the state continues to attempt to distance them from: small-scale, subsistence, and commodity agriculture. It is in this way that *campesinos/as* in resistance enact the processes of building livable worlds.

Government programming and narratives focused on development are more than attempts to assert political and economic knowledges and forms of control in the highlands (and elsewhere). Drawing on the work of Cumes (2014), a Kakchiquel scholar, Mora (2017, 10) argues that past and present biopolitical, economic programs became ways to control life, putting indigenous peoples in spaces of servitude and nonindigenous peoples in places of "racialized economic privilege." These forms of colonial–imperial domination are correspondingly tied to the geopolitics of knowledge. Such universalizing forms of knowledge about how to live are inextricably part of colonial–imperial projects of development, which shape understandings of what it means to be "developed" and "modern."

The aftermath of World War II brought new attention to the geographies of inequality, and critical development scholars argue that the so-called developing world was invented through discourses that located poverty as an object of analysis and facilitated economic interventions that were shaped by Cold War geopolitics (cf. Escobar 1995; Rist 2008). Critiques of the project of development point to a rationalizing tendency that reproduces uneven power relations, delegitimizes non-Western knowledges, and otherwise subjugates and erases the particulars of place. This practice is concurrent with the normalization of poverty and the depoliticizing of economic relations (see Escobar 1995; Ferguson 1994;

Mosse 2005)—a point that is salient if we consider that the projects of development and fair trade are largely bound up in concerns that emanate from postindustrial and high-consumption contexts (Hart 2001; Rist 2008). Ferguson (1994) observed that the development problematic occludes forces for change that are not based in the project of the state. More than two decades on, with a significantly reduced role of the state, we can amend this observation—many forces for change are now excluded that are not based in the market. The power of development and neoliberal discourses has to some extent foreclosed questioning whether economic development as deployed is even "desirable or necessary" (Rist 2008, 3). Indeed, the postwar project of development ignores legacies of conquest, colonization, and enslavement, all the while making the global periphery into a site of intervention for governance, improvement, and market integration.

Since the 1970s, global-economic restructuring has had a significant impact on the peasant way of life—signaling to some the death of the peasantry (cf. Collier 2008; Hobsbawm 1994).[4] More than a century ago, Karl Kautsky ([1899] 1988) asked if capital was infiltrating agricultural production, destroying old forms of peasant production and creating new ones. In a macro-scale analysis surveying the agrarian question, Akram-Lodhi and Kay (2010a, 2010b) suggest that neoliberal agricultural production on a global scale reframed peasant production strategies in the capitalist marketplace, rather than eliminating them. They argue that "agriculture continues to be relevant for capital and capitalism in an era of neoliberal globalisation" and that "small-scale petty commodity producing peasant farming still has a role" (Akram-Lodhi and Kay 2010a, 180). They further note that it is "necessary to understand the diverse and uneven ways in which rural production processes and agrarian accumulation are or are not being transformed by the capitalist mode of production" (Akram-Lodhi and Kay 2010b, 266). However, such an argument neglects alternate conceptualizations that move away from the binary of capitalist–noncapitalist; furthermore, it positions capital as the locus, closing out alternate explanations for diverse peasant livelihood strategies, such as those under way in Chiapas. Not only does this framing miss the varied and multiple ways that people form their lives and livelihoods but it assumes that they do so only in response to the pressures of capitalist systems and not as agents who may be pursuing capitalist (cf. Li 2014) and other economic activities.

To put efforts for modernization and development in context, I begin this chapter by discussing the "state" of Chiapas, detailing the resource-rich, poverty-stricken narrative that pervades political and scholarly discourse about southern Mexico. With this foundation set, I proceed to a discussion of the development of the coffee economy in Chiapas, focusing in on changing patron–client/peasant–state relations and access to land and resources. Critical to understanding how fair trade functions in Chiapas is an understanding of the formation of the coffee cooperatives that are the basis of this research—in the third section of this chapter, I discuss how each was formed, illuminating the violence and crises present in the highlands that led to their creation. Once this history and trajectory have been established, I then turn to the introduction of fair trade standards into the highlands and the complicated and contradictory effects of participating in a certification program that applies universal development paradigms. In wrapping up this chapter, I seek to decolonize the way we think about development as it relates to building dignified livelihoods and participating in the fair trade marketplace.

The State of Chiapas

Chiapas is the southernmost state in Mexico, sharing an international border with Guatemala. Chiapas is the eighth largest state in Mexico and the sixth most populous (out of thirty-two) (Instituto Nacional de Estadística y Geografía [INEGI] 2015). The 2015 census completed by the Instituto Nacional de Estadística y Geografía (National Institute of Statistics and Geography, INEGI) in Chiapas recorded 5.2 million inhabitants, almost 36 percent of whom self-identified as indigenous.[5] This figure represents twelve ethnic groups, but the majority population is Tzeltal and Tzotzil speaking (INEGI 2015). These ethnic groups primarily populate the central highlands and eastern lowlands of Chiapas. In addition to demographic data, the government records data on marginalization, stating that Chiapas is the second most "marginalized" state in Mexico, and within Chiapas, the highlands have the highest degree of marginalization (Consejo Nacional de Población 2011).

In arriving at the measure of "marginalization," the government takes into account formal income and economic activities, housing and access to basic infrastructure (e.g., running water), education, health services, and migration. Many in Chiapas live and work in rural areas with scant access to such services; for example, in the official highland municipality of Chenalhó, where the coffee cooperatives I worked with are based, the vast majority of inhabitants are subsistence corn producers who have been petitioning the state for access to resources for more than five decades and endured a long history of indentured servitude and resistance prior to land reform efforts (see also Mora 2017). By other official measures, Chiapas is rich. Resource extraction in the form of minerals, petroleum, timber, oil palm, coffee, and hydroelectric energy makes a significant contribution to the national economy. Moreover, Chiapas is home to the second most biodiverse rainforest on the planet, the Lacandón. Twenty percent of Chiapas's territory is under official protection as federal natural areas, and the state is increasingly a target for ecotourism projects (Flores 2014). Such ecological richness is measured against extreme poverty in Chiapas, creating a stark contrast on the landscape.

Not unlike other sites targeted for "development," Chiapas is frequently treated by the state and by many scholars as a problem. This framing is based in the "impoverished population"–"rich land" contrast described here. Statistics on marginalization and resources are based in official narratives of economic development and "acculturation" of the indigenous *campesino/a*. The state's statistical representation of Chiapas is used to cast Chiapas and its population as a site for social, economic, and environmental "improvement." In the 2013 Gubernatorial State Plan for Chiapas, Governor Manuel Velasco Coello wrote that his government would help to "put Chiapas in the place that it deserves, away from backwardness and closer to prosperity. The road to a successful Chiapas implies that development, economic betterment and welfare are present in each of the homes of each Chiapaneco family" (Gobierno del Estado de Chiapas 2013, 7). Such official narratives provide a static snapshot of marginalization and strategic resource availability. This snapshot masks the complex spatial–historical processes that produce and maintain marginalization as well as the long-standing resistance to these relations of power and exclusion on the part of the so-called marginalized. It is also a universalizing narrative that claims ownership over what development is and who it is targeted at.

This singular vision of development that simultaneously tokenizes and ignores geohistorical contexts and cultural difference was at all times present in the highlands while I was conducting my fieldwork. The Chiapas state government, in its ongoing campaign against *campesinos/as* in resistance, makes visible and scattered changes to the landscape. To arrive in self-declared autonomous communities in the highlands, I would travel along a postinsurgency road, now designated part of La Ruta Maya (Mayan Route), a road that promises tourists a journey into the past. Stretching from southern Guatemala to the northeastern edge of the Yucatan Peninsula in Mexico, the Route emphasizes the culture and history of the ancient Maya, placing indigenous peoples as part of the region's past. This rendering makes invisible indigenous peoples in the region, relegating them to an ancient past and a contemporary status as vendors of cultural artifacts outside the ruins of Palenque or in government-sponsored shops, which essentialize and exploit indigenous people living along the Route. This example is one of the ways that the state promotes a particular geopolitics of knowledge regarding development. It is an aggressive ownership over what development is, who can participate, and in what capacity. The already existing systems of indigenous peoples in the region and their rebel autonomous activities are delegitimized.

The semiotics of the government efforts to maintain the Maya as a group in and from the past range from the pervasive signage related to the Route itself to the development efforts in the highlands. One of the most overt state campaigns against the rebel autonomy movement is evidenced in the slogan of the Chiapas state government's development efforts: "son hechos, no palabras" (deeds, not words). The phrase emphasized with a red slash underscoring the "deeds" adorned most posters promising improvement in communities. This slogan is meant to undercut the resistance by suggesting that indigenous social movements are incapable of bringing about concrete changes and instead are simply spouting empty or nonsense words. *Campesinos/as* in resistance refer to the slogan as the "big lie of the state." One *campesino* remarked to me that "they put up signs with their slogan, that's all they do. It's just lies." Every year on my way to the coffee bodegas, I saw the same weathered sign promising concrete floors in every house for a particular community, still yet to appear.

Such signs are apparently made up only of state promises, but other changes are more visible on the landscape. As political campaigns intensify during election periods, tangible efforts to gain the votes of the indigenous population appear in the form of investments made that are visible from the main road: basketball courts, latrines, fresh coats of paint on houses, and, less often, health clinics and schools. These are the signs and symbols of the state fighting an ideological war, attempting to regain the former patron–client relations enjoyed prior to the organizing of peasant groups (which began in the 1970s). State development efforts are clearly tied to a particular vision of the future, where indigenous peasants shed their indigeneity and become wage laborers and live in ordered communities, where they can be counted, purchase municipal services, and pay taxes. Universalizing visions such as these can also be seen in the direct aid programs deployed in 1994 and introduced at the beginning of this chapter. The efforts to establish neoclientelistic roles through direct payments are one way that the state attempts to intervene and change the culturally and place-specific knowledges and practices of *campesinos/as*. As Stahler-Sholk (2005, 36) observes, "PROCEDE undermines the management of communal landholdings by offering individual titles to those who opt out of the collective agrarian *ejidos* . . . and PROCAMPO gave direct per-hectare compensation payments to producers as price supports for peasant agriculture were being dismantled." This programming contrasts strongly with the demands of indigenous groups to have rights to self-determination and autonomy instead of new forms of control through patron–client relations (Stahler-Sholk 2005). Mora (2017, 173), who focuses explicitly on Oportunidades (Prospera)—which is a direct payment program for women, who receive a bimonthly payment in return for sending their children to state schools, participating in health workshops, maintaining a "hygienic home," and receiving annual gynecological exams—argues that the program creates a site of co-responsibility between women and the state.[6] Indeed, the program reinforces particular gender roles in indigenous households (who is responsible for social reproduction), while also reinforcing the primacy of state knowledge of how to live.

Development in the contemporary period for the highlands (and elsewhere) mediated by neoliberal designs is predicated on the state providing opportunities for the "marginalized" to improve themselves through learning about the "right ways" to be educated, healthy, and financially solvent. *Campesinos/as* in resistance see these programs as just another part of the war on indigenous peoples spearheaded by the government (Mora 2017; Naylor 2017a). Yet, state-led development programming in the highlands directed at exploiting peasant labor and decreasing subsistence lifestyles is not a product of the insurgency, however the form has changed over time. Leading up to the 1994 uprising and subsequent declaration(s) of autonomy, state–peasant relations in the highlands are best understood through struggles over land rights and the production of coffee. Coffee is historically a colonial–imperial commodity, one that tied peasants to large coffee plantations (50–150 hectares), or *fincas* (Martínez-Torres 2006; Rus 1994) and that is now being used as part of the resistance through reappropriating and decolonizing it.

Coffee as Development

Despite the early annexation of Chiapas into Mexico (1824) following independence from Spain, Collier and Quaratiello (2005, 23) argue that it took the better part of a century for independent Mexico to politically and economically integrate Chiapas. Racial hierarchies and inequalities cemented during the colonial period in Mexico persist in Chiapas, where indigenous peoples continue to struggle against their anchoring at the bottom of an increasingly deep socioracial system. Struggles for self-determination and land acquisition ebb and flow through long periods of subjugation by elites and the state. Simultaneously, this history is deeply connected to relations of clientelism, where indigenous demands for improvement were tied to loyalty. These relationships enjoyed by both elites and the state are part of a larger and well-established politics of the *indio permitido* (permitted Indian), where the patron acquiesces to small demands, while the larger demands for rights to self-determination, land, liberty, and justice are ignored (Hale, cited in Moksnes 2012, 13).

In the 1800s, indigenous occupied lands were viewed as *terrenos baldíos* (vacant lands) and were sold to nonindigenous elites (Stephen 2002, 92), displacing indigenous peoples and effectively forcing the sale of their labor on plantations (including coffee *fincas*). This loss of land, along with labor regimes that created systems of debt peonage, had a dramatic impact on indigenous livelihoods (Mora 2017). Servitude on haciendas and in logging camps was common; moreover, in 1846, the first coffee *fincas* (plantations) were established on the Soconusco Coast (bordering the Pacific Ocean), and through a system of *enganchar* (recruited labor contracts), many indigenous peoples from all over Chiapas provided labor in the coffee fields (Martínez-Torres 2006, 50–51).

Following the Mexican Revolution (1910–17), patron–client relations between *ladinos* (mixed race) and indigenous laborers took on a new character. Such relations, while still remarkably unequal, were based in reciprocity and in some cases allowed for *campesinos/as* to receive aid or other "favors" from landlords. These relations articulated with national efforts to accelerate land reform and "develop" rural areas during the presidency of Lázaro Cárdenas (1934–40). Government programs sought to incorporate the indigenous population into the economic plan of Mexico. Attempts to depoliticize race and the peasantry were ongoing in Mexico and Latin America more broadly (Martínez-Echazábal 1998; Reyes Ramos 1992) as a single and authentic Mexican identity was embraced in the discursive framing of *mestizaje*. *Mestizaje* was mobilized as a unifying nationalist ideology that was promoted as the mixing of race toward the "one-race nation" (Stephen 2002, 85). New forms of state–peasant relations became bound up in racialized state structures that sought incorporation and assimilation. Although *mestizaje* emerged as an ideology during the Porfiriato Period (1876–1910), it only became a state project in the post-Revolutionary context (Lewis 1997). Plan de Ayala (the 1911 proclamation of agrarian reform by revolutionaries; see Womack 2011) as it was incorporated into the Mexican Constitution of 1917 was used by the Partido Revolucionario Institucional

(Institutional Revolutionary Party, PRI), to integrate indigenous peoples into the nation-state through an assimilationist model.

Indigenista policies, which were focused on the whitening and "Westernization" of the indigenous population, were developed alongside land reform in the 1940s and 1950s (Bobrow-Strain 2007, 91). Although the promise of land reform reverberated across the country, it was not immediately enacted (Collier and Quaratiello 2005, 31). By the 1940s, the state turned its attention to industry and economic development, which had the impact of turning the "Indian problem" into a technical one to be fixed, not through addressing unequal societal and economic relations but through assimilation and economic development (Lewis 2005; Rus 2004). Land reform finally reached Chiapas through government development planning in the 1930s and 1940s. As a result, the presence and power of the local and federal government grew; Rus (2004, 247) notes that the "hope of eventually receiving an agrarian reform grant served as a profound form of social control," effectively tying indigenous peoples to their petitions for land. The promise of land reform gave the state a tremendous amount of support from peasants for government programming and politics (Hernández Castillo 1994; Moksnes 2012; Rus 1994). As Bobrow-Strain (2007, 91–92) notes, these policies attempted to reshape indigenous identity in a manner that suggested a greater relationship between *campesinos/as* and the state; thus the Mexican government replaced the *hacendado* (estate landowner) in the patron–client relationship in Chiapas, offering resources and other forms of aid to *campesinos/as*. This transition in clientelism is evident in indigenous *campesino/a* livelihood strategies and demands for recognition from the mid-1900s until the beginning of the neoliberal era, although it was not without some recognition that in their efforts to effectively petition the state for land, indigenous links to the state grew tighter. Rus (1994, 267) describes this process as one in which indigenous communities became "institutionalized revolutionary communities" that were "harnessed to the state." This harnessing went beyond pushing for land reform and is also tied to participation in state programs that enabled greater access to goods, services, and the market, as well as loyalty to the ruling political party (Reyes Ramos 1992).

The experience of cultivating coffee for income serves as an important example of economic regimes in post-Revolutionary Chiapas. *Campesinos/as* initially relied on corporatist state formation—where they were grouped together as coffee producers who sold to the state. The state acted as a market intermediary, and coffee producers were subject to significant change in their relations with the state following neoliberal restructuring, which forced a retreat of the state from managing the coffee sector. Changes in the coffee sector and in land tenure help to set the stage for indigenous organizing in the 1970s, when peasant groups began to unite and pull away from the state. The next two sections detail the changing coffee regimes in Mexico following the redistribution of land and state promotion of small-scale coffee production.

Coffee and the Corporatist State

In a region that relied on patron–client relations and, for the indigenous population, subsistence production to maintain livelihoods, the introduction of small-scale coffee to the highlands (1960–1970s) assisted with bringing new forms of political–economic organizing and income to communities, as well as a shift away from peasant reliance on a landowner patron to a relation with the state (Martínez-Torres 2006, 53). As a project of economic "modernization" was undertaken by the Mexican state following the Revolution and accelerated by the end of World War II, the promotion of coffee production was viewed as a way to develop rural areas in Mexico. During this period, coffee production in the highlands became a state-sponsored activity that facilitated the organizing of indigenous peasant groups into coffee producer cooperatives, a lasting legacy that bolstered efforts of the Catholic Church to organize peasants.[7]

In a study of organic coffee growing in Chiapas, anthropologist Maria Elena Martínez-Torres (2006) explains that coffee growers are among the most organized indigenous peasant groups in Mexico to date. Martínez-Torres's findings, which demonstrate that organic farming is a productive means of cultivating coffee, also reveal that in combination with subsistence production of crops, coffee producers are able to survive in places that are considered by official accounts to be marginalized. While coffee had traditionally been grown on plantations in Chiapas, the Revolution and the agrarian reforms that followed enticed highland peasants away from the Soconusco Coast, and many returned to the highlands with coffee seedlings (beginning as early as 1914) (Martínez-Torres 2006, 52). However, despite the increasing number of coffee plants entering the highlands (between 1914 and 1960), Martínez-Torres argues that peasants were wary of adopting coffee production; as there was little market for the sale of green coffee beans, the vast majority of coffee was produced for household consumption. The production of coffee was also hindered by lack of access to land. Indeed, many in the highlands recounted selling their labor to large landowners who were early adopters of coffee production.

Following the Revolution, the number of peasants growing food and coffee on small plots increased slowly, whether through land invasion or constitutionally mandated redistribution (the results of which were mixed in Chiapas; see Bobrow-Strain 2005, 2007; Reyes Ramos 1992).[8] An increase in coffee production in the 1960s was facilitated through promotion by the National Indigenous Institute as a solution to impoverishment among peasants in the highlands (Martínez-Torres 2006, 53). However, coffee production only became viable for small producers in the highlands with increased access to land, which Martínez-Torres attributes to the large-scale invasions of coffee lands in 1974 (such acquisitions led to a 900 percent increase in total area planted by 1990) (54).[9] The ability to sell the coffee to an intermediary, called a *coyote*, was also a significant contributor to the widespread adoption (or maintenance) of coffee on newly acquired lands.

As indigenous peasants gained access to land, state programs to promote and facilitate small-scale coffee production were critical. Consistent with other economic development strategies being deployed in the region, the government, in the period of import substitution (1940–80), created a state-run institution for the regulation of coffee production and marketing. In 1959, the INMECAFE was established by the Mexican state to provide technical assistance, conduct research, administer ICA quotas, and issue export permits (Renard 2010, 22). By 1973, INMECAFE had expanded its patron role through the purchasing and processing of coffee, which displaced the *coyote* as the middle person and created somewhat of a reliance on the state for coffee producers (Renard 2010, 22). However, as early as 1979, groups of small producers began to collectively organize in favor of reducing the cost of transporting coffee and protesting the delay in compensation after the sale of coffee to the institute (Stephen 2002, 121). In the period leading up to the debt crisis, these groups grew stronger. Yet, at the same time, oil development boomed in Chiapas during the 1970s, and many who had been producing coffee sought better opportunities for cash income, abandoning their coffee plots in search of wages (Martínez-Torres 2006). Indeed, on a larger scale, oil production in Mexico became an economic boon that the state used to fuel efforts toward economic development and global-economic competitiveness.

Neoliberal Restructuring and Colonial–Imperial Relations

U.S.-based banks provided substantial loans to finance development efforts in the 1970s in Mexico. The "petro-dollars" generated by the oil price hike in 1973 manifested in significant debt in Mexico (and Latin America more broadly). The debt was taken on as part of the development plan of the state—designed to "modernize" and "stabilize" the economy as well as promote state-led industry and social support (the increased state intervention was premised on import substitution industrialization models and was also a response to the 1968 student riots; see Lustig 2000, 14–18). The default of Mexico on its loans in 1982 set into motion events that reified global colonial–imperial relations and fundamentally changed socioeconomic interactions throughout the country and is critical to understanding how state–peasant relations in the coffee sector (and for peasants in general) shifted in ways that fed growing indigenous dissent in the country. Structural adjustment following the 1982 debt crisis sought to reduce the role of the state in the market (through deregulation and fiscal austerity measures) while also integrating Mexico into the global market under "free trade" principles (Cook, Middlebrook, and Molinar Horcasitas 1994). Mandated by the International Monetary Fund (and supported by a pro-reform and PRI-led government), this market-led economic agenda in Mexico was focused on generating development (and earning foreign exchange necessary to make payments on debt) through promoting the freedom of domestic economic elites and foreign capital. State-owned industries, the cornerstone of the previous model of import substitution and industrialization, were systematically privatized throughout the 1980s and beyond. To combat inflation, wages were frozen, and price protections that had assisted with accessing food for economically marginalized groups were eliminated. The culmination of this agenda came in the form of NAFTA, negotiated in 1992.

Neoliberal restructuring in the 1980s in particular generated a severe economic crisis for the majority of Mexicans as the dismantling of trade barriers reduced jobs in large and small businesses, decreased the competitiveness of the agricultural sector, and caused the decline of the real value of wages. This in turn generated political crisis, as the tools of political control within a corporatist state (where a large part of the economy is controlled by the state) were dismantled as part of the neoliberal agenda (Harvey 1993). Two moments of severe political discontent stand out. The first was the disorganized response of the Mexican government in the aftermath of the devastating earthquake in Mexico City (1985), which emboldened a popular urban movement and also critics of the PRI regime (Saiz 1990). A second flashpoint of contestation was located in the constitutional reforms undertaken in the early 1990s to make Mexico's legal system "work" with the expectation of enacting NAFTA. Consistent with other colonial–imperial relations, the systems of Mexico had to be aligned with those of the United States and Canada to participate. On a global scale, the geopolitics of knowledge played out between states, as the economic and legal systems of Mexico were viewed as incompatible with economic growth and development. That knowledge built about financial and legal systems in the United States and Canada could or should be mapped seamlessly onto Mexico represents a privileging of whose knowledge counts. The practices implemented concurrent with the negotiation and commencement of NAFTA solidified global neoliberal hegemonies initiated during the debt crisis.

Although it was an uneven process over time and space, the debt crisis and neoliberal restructuring severely impacted the lives of peasants throughout Mexico. The 1982 debt crisis foreclosed many opportunities for peasants to earn wages in the oil and other industries respectively, and many from Chiapas returned to their subsistence and communal *(ejido)* plots by the mid-1980s (Harvey

1998). Yet, the inability to access credit significantly limited capital improvements that small producers could make, which meant that many continued their small-plot subsistence and coffee production. Neoliberal-style reforms and the 1989 ICA collapse (and crash in the global coffee price) precipitated the dismantling of INMECAFE from 1989 to 1993 (Jaffee 2014; Martínez-Torres 2006). As the Mexican state sought to recover from the debt crisis and introduce neoliberal policies leading up to the signing of NAFTA, *campesinos/as* were increasingly closed out of the economic development plan of state.

The restructuring that followed the 1982 debt crisis impacted economic segments in Mexico in different ways: in the coffee sector, it took little more than a decade for the state to abandon coffee producers (Martínez-Torres 2006). The withdrawal of the state from the coffee-producing areas of Chiapas was a critical component of the end of the former patron–client relations enjoyed by the state. Indeed, scholars point to the collapse of coffee prices as a key moment in the formation of contemporary indigenous rebellion and resistance movements (Jaffee 2014; Martínez-Torres 2006).[10] The removal of state support for coffee production combined with increased emphasis on large-scale farming over small-plot production placed *campesinos/as* as an obstruction to neoliberal development (Bobrow-Strain 2007). A number of small producers abandoned their coffee plots following the price collapse, either seeking new opportunities for paid labor or planting corn in its place (Jaffee 2014). Although some *campesinos/as* began to rely on selling their labor, Bobrow-Strain (2007) argues that attempts by the state to incorporate *campesinos/as* in the newly organized economy of the state (as contract producers or wage laborers) were largely met with failure as they continued to cultivate small plots of corn and petition for land. Indeed, many *campesinos/as* mobilized under their coffee-producing cooperatives to demand agricultural support as well as continued land distribution (Martínez-Torres 2006). However, the end of INMECAFE signaled the end of patron–client relations with the state for many indigenous producers, and their allegiances waned as they began to see the state as the source of their marginalization (Rus, Hernández Castillo, and Mattiace 2003).

State support for small-scale coffee production diminished at the same time as protections for basic foodstuffs (corn and beans) declined. NAFTA for the Mexican government and economic elites was a signal of economic progress—price supports and land redistribution (as well as the communal landholdings of peasants) were viewed as a hindrance to economic efficiency and development. The 1992 amendment to Article 27 of the Constitution, which canceled land reform and facilitated the privatization of communally held land (largely concentrated in indigenous communities), was a difficult prospect for many *campesinos/as* to face. Despite efforts at distributing land to indigenous peasants in the 1940s and 1950s, in 1992, there were more petitions outstanding and conflicts over land tenure yet unresolved in Chiapas than anywhere else in Mexico (Bobrow-Strain 2005, 2007; Harvey 1998).[11] In place of state land reform efforts, the government promoted the privatization of communal land through a new program called the Programa de Certificación de Derechos Ejidales y Titulación de Solares (Program for the Certification of Ejido Land Rights and the Titling of Urban House Plots, PROCEDE).

This neoliberal intervention in Chiapas and the highlands more specifically strikes a contrast from the previous decades of patron–client relations experienced by *campesinos/as* in the region. The privatization of land and the withdrawal of the state, however, did not signal the end of intervention in rural areas but a new way to intervene and "fix" what were viewed as places of economic stagnation. PROCEDE is a program designed to incorporate rural peoples into the neoliberal fold. Obtaining a title to land was marketed as a way to guarantee the "freedom" of the individual (Stahler-Sholk 2007). As discussed earlier in this chapter, PROCEDE is one of many programs initiated by the neoliberal government to "modernize" rural areas and peoples (e.g., pursuing large-scale industrial agriculture rather than subsistence production). Mora (2008, 120) argues that PROCEDE "represents new development interests directed at the rural sector, including the production of new peasant-subjects which more effectively respond to emerging market options." By privatizing communally held lands, individual plots could be held as collateral or purchased and consolidated into larger landholdings by private entities. Something that is important to note here is that neoliberal restructuring and global imperial relations are filtered through the state into indigenous communities perpetuating universal imaginaries of development as well as property and economic exchange. It also suggests that at a global scale, a corporatist state and import substitution are considered responsible for economic stagnation and, scaled down, that communal forms of living and producing food and agricultural products are responsible for marginalization and poverty in indigenous communities, erasing the colonial–imperial contexts of uneven development.

As a result of these socioeconomic changes, peasant groups in Chiapas mobilized to protect their land and livelihoods.[12] Following the 1994 uprising, peace talks between the government and the Zapatistas began in the highland town of San Andrés Larráinzar; these talks were moderated by Bishop Samuel Ruiz García and attended by government and Zapatista representatives as well as scholars and peacekeepers from around the globe. Las Abejas and other indigenous groups participated in conversations about the demands that would be leveled at the government, and many members were present outside the talks as part of a larger group of people who formed a "peace belt" that surrounded the building where the talks took place (Moksnes 2012, 207–8). The peace talks were held intermittently from 1994 to 1996 even while the federal government launched new military campaigns against Zapatista support bases (Harvey 1998; Stephen 2002). In 1996, the Accords of San Andrés on Indigenous Rights and Culture were signed between government and Zapatista representatives, and the Zapatistas withdrew from the public eye while they waited for the Accords to be written into federal law and implemented.

This period of time was something that very few *campesinos/as* in resistance wanted to discuss during the course of my fieldwork. When welcoming guests visiting the Zapatista autonomous health clinics and schools, the history of the rebellion and the violence of the 1990s is recounted to contextualize their work and their continued struggle. One member of a group retelling this history remarked that their struggle continues because "many people died in 1994 and we will not betray their blood, we will always be in resistance." But beyond such statements, many outside of such gatherings preferred instead to discuss their ways of moving past the violence. They do not see it as contained to one story or one period but as part of the five-hundred-year war still raging against the indigenous peoples of Mexico. This larger context gives weight to the importance of reflecting on the spatial and geohistorical contexts of their resistance to the erasing of indigenous ways of knowing, being, and understanding the world. The resistance that is being practiced in place today is part of a larger process of struggle to maintain and practice dignified livelihoods as indigenous peoples from and where they are and in ways that are bound to difference and their own imaginaries of social, political, and economic life.

The signed 1996 Accords were never codified or implemented by the Mexican state. As a result of the continuous violence against their groups and the government's unwillingness to recognize their right to self-determination, both groups reinforced their original declaration of autonomy from the state.[13] To date, neither Zapatista nor Las Abejas supporters participate in state-sponsored politics, and they do not receive any funds, subsidies, health care or educational services, or any other support from the state.[14] Autonomous zones are not contiguous and are made up of community-level Zapatista support bases, larger-scale municipalities (Rebel Zapatista Autonomous Municipalities, MAREZ), and regional government zones (called *caracoles*). They are spaces of multiple and competing politics and power (see Stahler-Sholk 2010), not confined to official government borders and boundaries, and may overlie one or many official government cartographies of the highlands (and eastern Chiapas more broadly).[15]

These autonomous zones are populated not with homogenous communities of *campesinos/as* in resistance but with diverse political, social, and economic groups (Naylor 2017a). It is especially important to note that the cartographies of these places are neither fixed nor singular but are in a continuous process of becoming and struggle over different knowledges of how to live well. At first glance, communities may look fairly similar, with familiar groupings of housing, *milpa* agriculture, and coffee plots, with chickens traversing the terrain, but a deeper look shows that even though the vast majority of the population of the rural highlands comprises peasants working the land in corn and coffee (and other subsistence and commodity goods), wildly divergent politics and economic practices underscore their labor and livelihoods. Many of these families are members of coffee-producing cooperatives, some predating the uprising and others having been established as a part of rebel autonomy and as a way to build dignified livelihoods.

Cooperatives out of Crisis

Coffee production is not new to Chiapas. What has changed in the intervening periods of production are the social relations of production. International connections made through solidarity with *campesinos/as* in resistance combined with hostile relations in heterogeneous communities were important to the creation of new cooperatives. Although the existence of rebel coffee cooperatives was not an immediate effect of broader political maneuvering in the highlands, their establishment forms an important component of knowledge building and solidarity relations that extend within and beyond the highlands. The 1996 Accords, as written, supported the demand for autonomy and stipulated linguistic, territorial, and political rights for indigenous peoples in Mexico (Eber and Kovic 2003). However, the government held back the implementation of the San Andrés Accords and began issuing warrants for the arrest of key leaders of the Ejército Zapatista de Liberación Nacional. A low-intensity conflict had begun in Zapatista support base communities. As noted earlier, critical to the state's strategy is creating divisions in communities through the distribution of aid programs, as well as goods and services to those community members who offer their support to the government; in some cases, arms and training are given in encouragement of community-based paramilitary activity (Solomon et al. 1997; see also Naylor 2017a).

Through government supply and support, armed conflict in the region and the number of paramilitary groups grew.[16] To legitimize this violence, political and economic elites actively constructed the *campesinos/as* in resistance as a threat to the economic development of Chiapas and Mexico. The most well-known example of this narrative is the January 1995 Chase Manhattan Bank memo, authored by political scientist and advisor to the bank Riordan Roett, that suggested that the Mexican government would need to "eliminate the Zapatistas" to establish their territorial hegemony and demonstrate effective security. This warfare is not only in response to the existence of so-called rebel indigenous groups but is part of the attempted assimilation and integration of indigenous peoples into a neoliberal economy. The low-intensity warfare practiced against indigenous communities in Chiapas goes beyond armed conflict and is a militarization and racialization of the political, economic, and social that is written into the landscape and onto the bodies of indigenous people in Chiapas.

As Mora (2017, 182), who discusses the possibilities of a "life politics" in Zapatista communities, articulates, the low-intensity war and counterinsurgency tactics of the Mexican state were multiple, including burning harvests, destroying crops still in the ground, stealing livestock, and using checkpoints to restrict the movement of people, especially those people making the journey to their *milpas* or *cafetales* (which can sometimes be hours away from their homes). Members of Las Abejas recalled the impromptu checkpoints that would come and go in the highlands, disrupting their harvest schedule and instilling a fear that violence may erupt at any moment. These practices remain visible on the landscape; however, the stress brought on by constant struggle and fear of violence also manifests in health issues such as gastritis and depression (Antillón Najlis, cited in Mora 2017, 183).[17] This militarization of everyday life for *campesinas* in particular speaks to a long history of attempted domination and control through sexual violence and other tortures directed at female bodies.

And so they resist and build their own livelihoods. Along with other cooperative production (e.g., bread, weaving, metal working), coffee-producing cooperatives are a critical locus for solidarity interactions globally and locally. The Zapatista-affiliated coffee cooperatives are supported by a membership of more than one thousand producers, and they primarily sell their coffee to solidarity markets, where it is branded "Zapatista Coffee" or with the name of the cooperative (at the time of writing, Café Zapatista is being sold by Higher Grounds Trading Company).[18] These cooperatives operate in a liminal space as they negotiate market access and government demands. The first cooperative established by the Zapatistas had their coffee-processing equipment confiscated by the state government.[19] In an interview, the former treasurer for the cooperative explained, "The cooperative was closed because of the bad government [Zapatista reference to official Mexican governing bodies], they said we were not paying our taxes, that we owed millions in back taxes." However, it was not worth the time or effort to remove their coffee plants, which are a perennial crop and represent a long-term investment (decades of production), and so *campesinos/as* in resistance continued to harvest coffee and looked for ways to maintain their political identities—as in resistance—and form export cooperatives.

Since the disbanding of the first cooperative, two new cooperatives have been established. One cooperative member explained the start of their cooperative in the context of resistance in this way: "We became organized so we could work on our own, but better and so we could continue to feed our families." These cooperatives maintain organic certification and rely on certification *por palabra*—or by word of mouth—and their coffee is purchased and sold at fair trade prices by coffee importers in the United States and Europe. Despite the problematic character of trying to maintain autonomy and ignore state processes, Zapatista-affiliated producers continue to work within new cooperatives that have been established. On my last trip to the highlands in 2013, one of the newest cooperatives was in the process of constructing a bodega for processing and storing cooperative members' coffee.

The Maya Vinic coffee cooperative took a different approach to interacting with me as a researcher, and in one of my first conversations with the leadership of the cooperative, we talked about the efforts of Las Abejas to remain visible to the international community. We discussed anonymity in research and what the result of participation might look like and that I should use the name of the cooperative. This strategy is consistent with Maya Vinic's efforts to preserve the memory of the violence against indigenous peoples, and particularly those in resistance. The *Pillar of Shame*, one of a series of installations sculpted by Danish artist Jens Galschiøt, which I passed on every trip into Acteal, serves as a harrowing reminder of the violence inflicted upon *campesinos/as* in resistance following the 1994 uprising.

In the years leading up to and especially following the 1994 uprising of the Zapatistas in Chiapas, highland communities experienced fragmentation and conflict over land rights and access to resources (Delfin-Fuentes et al. 2011). As discussed in earlier chapters, the Sociedad Civil Las Abejas (Bees Civil Society) was organized out of two groups, the Sociedad Civil and Las Abejas, in response to land conflict and injustice against women (Tavanti 2003) and a desire to promote a space of pacifist support for Zapatista demands (Moksnes 2012). The combined group was formed out of a need and desire to work collectively in spaces that were increasingly being torn apart through outmigration, land conflict, state-sponsored violence, and divergent community politics. A key piece of the low-intensity conflict in communities that had been declared autonomous was the increased militarization of the highlands both through arms trafficking and the establishment of military outposts. Following the failure of the San Andrés Accords, tensions in the official highland municipality of Chenalhó were heightened (Nash 2001). During 1996–97, there was a series of murders and attacks—more than fifty—perpetrated by and against *partidistas* (supporters of the major Mexican political parties, e.g., PRD, PRI, PAN), Zapatistas, and Las Abejas members alike (Tavanti 2003, 9). The violence in the municipality caused the expulsion of families from their home communities and significant displacement as Abejas and Zapatistas sought refuge in the newly declared autonomous communities in the highlands.

By December 22, 1997, almost 250 Abejas had sought refuge in the highland community of Acteal (Tavanti 2003), which is located within the official municipality of Chenalhó. On that day, members of a paramilitary group called Máscara Roja (Red Mask) opened fire and visited considerable violence on the refugees in Acteal, killing forty-five men, women, and children and wounding twenty-five others (Stahler-Sholk 1998, 63; see also Moksnes 2004, 2012; Stephen 2002; Tavanti 2003). This gruesome attack is further evidence of the violence on the landscape and on bodies that is deployed to weaken the resistance and prevent particular groups (e.g., women) from participating in political processes (Hernández Castillo 1998; Mora 2017) and furthermore are acts of dehumanization that reinforce racialized hierarchies and colonial–imperial imaginaries of domination and control.

It is important to note that members of paramilitary groups are not generally from outside of the communities that they are threatening with violence. Owing to the violence across the highlands and the horrific events of Acteal, which took place at what would have been the start of the coffee harvest, many Las Abejas members had to flee their homes and abandon their *milpas* and *cafetales*. Following the massacre, international attention and pressure led to investigation and some arrests. Moreover, some members of the Maya Vinic cooperative recall international solidarity groups arriving in Chiapas to support their families and accompanying members of Las Abejas, escorting producers into their *cafetales* so that they could harvest their coffee.

Many who participated in the massacre were either never arrested or have been released from prison on appeal and live side by side with families who lost members in the massacre (SIPAZ 2012). They are additionally surrounded by military encampments and subject to daily patrolling by the Mexican state. It is a particularly painful piece of the history of the Abejas and of Maya Vinic and also their present because there has been no peace, no justice. In 2010, in the city of San Cristóbal de las Casas, members of Las Abejas gathered to recognize the anniversary of the release of the perpetrators of the massacre from prison.[20] In a peaceful demonstration outside the cathedral, members gathered to construct a memorial and to display photos of the children, women, and men who were brutally murdered in 1997. Crosses and pine needles were placed on the cobblestones, and songs of protest sung in Tzotzil filled the square. A banner censuring the government was pinned up in the square outside the cathedral: "Mexico está cubierto de impunidad y sangre de los martires de Acteal" (Mexico is covered with impunity and blood of the martyrs of Acteal). The massacre is ever present as members of Las Abejas seek justice while living under the threat of violence and state intimidation.

At the same time, through events such as the one pictured here, Las Abejas are countering the dominant narrative of the massacre that is perpetuated by the government—the state denied any influence or participation of state actors in the massacre. Indeed, the government perpetuated the idea of the "indigenous problem" by indicating that the massacre was the result of intercommunity resource conflicts that had been ongoing in the highlands (Moksnes 2012). However, through the public censure of the government and continued interaction with solidarity networks, Las Abejas produce and disseminate their knowledge of the event, which challenges official accounts of the massacre.

Figure 6. Las Abejas members gather in San Cristóbal de las Casas to memorialize the Massacre at Acteal and censure the government. Photograph by the author.

Figure 7. Crosses and pine needles in the square. Photograph by the author.

Figure 8. Singing revolutionary songs in Tzotzil outside the cathedral in San Cristóbal de las Casas. Photograph by the author.

As I noted earlier, my conversations with Abejas were less focused on the painful reconstruction of the past and instead reflected hope for the future. When discussing the beginning of the Maya Vinic coffee cooperative with *socios* (cooperative members) who have been with the cooperative since the beginning, the massacre is an agonizing part of their story:

> Maya Vinic was not founded for earning money, but because of the conflict in the communities. Many of us had been in the cooperative of [name removed] but after 1997 there were divisions in the communities and within the cooperative and there were some who had participated in the massacre, which caused many problems. So we talked as Abejas and decided to start our own cooperative.

This approach is consistent with the pacifist character of the Abejas movement and is their constructive response to the horrific events that happened and continue to take place in their communities. As part of our conversation about the founding of the coffee cooperative, one *campesino* described this moment to me:

> When the massacre happened it was very bad. My family, with my little boys, we had to leave the municipality. When it happened there was more violence done to us even afterward. They were robbing us too. We had to leave the municipality for more than five months and when we returned they had taken everything, the wood, and the lamina from our houses, the stored coffee and corn. They had taken the fruit from the trees and had hurt the coffee plants. There was no food. There was nothing. Nothing.

This violence is interwoven with the importance of the cooperative not as a space for development or participating in the market but as a space of memory, solidarity, and resistance. A member of the leadership made this clear: "We need people to remember Acteal, to remember us.... We want people to see us, here in our communities." Others shared similar thoughts and stories of displacement. Some had been forced out of their homes and communities for months, others for years, but they returned. "We came back to our place." Out of the trauma and violence of displacement, *campesinos/as* in resistance seek to rebuild their lives and livelihoods in a dignified way. This form of memory and place making provides spaces for reframing what fair trade, cooperative production, and development are in the highlands and for fair rebels. Coffee cooperatives are just one piece of this puzzle, which is now more complex due to the addition of fair trade and organic certification.

Out of the violence, *campesinos/as* in resistance came together and created their own rebel coffee cooperative to support their community of producers. Maya Vinic was established in 1999 and received fair trade certification from FLO (now Fairtrade International) in 2001; it has since expanded production beyond coffee to honey and, in 2013, claimed a membership of 640 *socios* representing fifty-two communities in the highlands and eastern Chiapas. The establishment of the cooperative provided three key benefits to members of Las Abejas; first, it provided a shield against the threat of declining coffee prices; second, it extended and solidified solidarity network assistance established in the aftermath of the Acteal Massacre; and finally, it created an internal network for knowledge gathering (about coffee production and political organizing, for example) and material assistance for coffee growers who were part of the autonomy movement and were no longer willing to claim any form of government aid as part of their rebel autonomy and resistance.

Cooperatives established by *campesinos/as* in resistance have created connections outside of Chiapas and Mexico to assist with the purchase of their coffee. These connections create an important basis for international support and recognition as well as for cash income in self-declared autonomous communities. In this way, demands for recognition and economic development by indigenous communities in resistance have changed from making demands on the government to generating their own systems of governance as well as economic and social ties that seek to bypass the state and conventional market relations. *Campesinos/as* in resistance have stepped away from the racialized problematization of their livelihoods as indigenous peoples and begun to build a "world in which many worlds fit" (Ejército Zapatista de Liberación Nacional 1996). The importance of the cooperatives notwithstanding, the introduction of fair trade (and organic) standards into self-declared autonomous communities populated by fair rebels deserves a closer look as the income gained from production for the fair trade market is contingent upon compliance with standards for production and community development that do not map onto the livelihood strategies of *campesinos/as* in resistance.

The Fair Trade Standard: Developing Producer-Subjects

In one of the first conversations I had with a fair rebel about *comercio justo* (fair trade), I learned that many people bristled at the phrase. "We here do not believe it is fair trade. It cannot be fair trade unless all community members have the same opportunities and access. For example, we should all have the same type of houses and be able to send our children to the same school." This signals a disconnect between how fairness is understood, and knowledge about what is fair is constructed across different groups. Fair trade certification is often positioned by third-party certifiers as a tool of empowerment for farmers, yet uneven relations of power and the structural conditions of economic inequality persist, raising questions about the "fairness" of fair trade (cf. Bacon 2010; Dolan 2010; Jaffee 2014; Lyon 2007, 2011; Naylor 2014; Renard 2005; Renard and Loconto 2013). Indeed, many *campesinos/as* in resistance refer to it as *comercio más justo* or "more-fair trade," signaling that they consider working with a cooperative and having a consistent buyer and annual price better than selling to an intermediary, but that it does not live up to their expectations of fairness. Returning to what fair trade is, who it is for, and who gets to decide, in this section, drawing from the discussion of development from chapter 1, I consider fair trade as a tool of economic development. While fair trade certification was begun as a solidarity based, direct trade relation to facilitate market access and awareness (movement + market), it has transformed into a development apparatus that third-party certifiers claim allows for economic development and improvement in producer communities.

Certification provides a price floor and credit, but participation in fair trade also requires adherence to standards for production and community development that are created by third-party certifiers. These standards themselves are an important locus for development in fair trade producer communities, as they provide funds to be used for the "improvement of producer communities." However, the fair trade premium that is given every year is to be used toward the Fairtrade Development Plan, which extends the reach of fair trade third-party certifiers from the coffee plots (where standards for production are applied) into producers' homes, communities, and cooperatives. A universal idea of what development is or should look like is pervasively normalized through fair trade narratives. One of the main goals of Fairtrade International is to promote business and economic development. The standards have guidelines describing the "requirements that are unique to Fairtrade":

> Fairtrade should lead to the demonstrable empowerment and environmentally sustainable social and economic development of producer organizations and their members, and through them, of the workers employed by the organizations or by the members, and the surrounding community. (Fairtrade International 2011, 28)

Fair trade certification operates as a development corrective through providing market access. As market-oriented institutions, certification organizations take on what is described as a "trustee role," which Li (2007, 4) argues is "defined by the claim to know how others should live, to know what is best for them, to know what they need." In the case of fair trade, I argue that this is articulated as a "Northern" trustee enabling a "Southern" producer (Naylor 2014). Yet, third-party certifiers "render technical" (see Ferguson 1994) the relations of coffee production for small producers, reducing their livelihoods to their role as "marginalized" coffee producers in need of economic development. To render something technical, a problem and solution are identified by "experts," who establish an us–them dichotomy that is anti-political (Li 2007, 7; see also Ferguson 1994), thereby dismissing the political economy of development, unequal trade relations, and politics in place in fair trade producer communities (Naylor 2017c). The trusteeship of third-party certifiers extends to the fair trade audit—as the audit is premised on translating the standards for certification and development into measurable results, which have a universal character (Dolan 2010, 40–41; see also Mutersbaugh 2002, 2005a, 2005b). This "audit culture" takes on greater scope as it not only measures accountability to certification standards but also seeks to improve their implementation and outcomes. So while the third-party certifier sets the standards and claims to have an increasingly hands-off approach to implementing development programs (something that has changed over the past twenty years), the independent audit that is conducted annually with certified producer cooperatives serves as a mechanism to reassert control over bringing development to others.

Fairtrade International (2017) claims that fair trade standards are "designed to support the sustainable development of small producer organizations and agricultural workers in the poorest countries in the world." The objectives of these standards are to guarantee a price, distribute a cash premium for development projects, facilitate financing, create long-term partnerships, and establish criteria that assure consumers that the conditions of production were responsible. As they relate to development, Fairtrade International standards require that producers work continuously [to] improve and to invest in the development of their organizations and their workers. This concept is developed for the target group of Fairtrade: *disadvantaged producers and workers*. It encourages sustainable, social, economic and environmental development of producers and their organization. (Fairtrade International 2015, 2, emphasis added)

Fairtrade International is the largest third-party certifier for fair trade and claims that its standards impact the 1.6 million farmers and laborers it represents. Across the many certification labels, fair trade sales in 2016 reached almost US$10 billion (Fairtrade International 2016a). When certification standards were expanded and developed beyond their origins (direct trade between solidarity groups and farmers), they were done so with a different imaginary. Standards largely began to be implemented with the imaginary of creating better lives and livelihoods for "disadvantaged producers and workers." And so the relation of market exchange changed from one based on breaking down structural inequities in global trade and facilitating solidarity exchange to a "helper" form of exchange based in poverty reduction and universal economic development ideals. The standard-setting agencies and executive leadership have long been populated with industry insiders and individuals who are not representative of the group that they are charging with meeting certification standards (something I discuss in greater depth in chapter 3).

While many third-party certifiers and other proponents claim that fair trade gives power to producers, Fairtrade International makes assertions of empowerment by arguing that certification is "giving farmers more control over their own lives" (FLO 2008, cited in Wilson 2010, 85). However, certification standards fail to give producers control and instead attempt to structure producers' lives around certified coffee production, and noncompliance with standards results in exclusion from the market (Renard and Loconto 2013). Contemporary fair trade certification agencies are gatekeepers and standard setters. They control the certification of producer products and of importing agencies. Third-party certifiers set standards for production and development and work with independent verification bodies for external reviews and certification audits. Third-party certifiers also set a minimum product price and a premium for community development. The price is set with consideration of labor hours, inputs, and costs and is designed as a safety net. The premium is set in relation to the price; its use is "restricted to investment in the producers' business, livelihood and community" (FLO-CERT 2011) and, consistent with the broader stated goals of certification, it is meant to assist smallholders with organizing and building "thriving businesses" (FLO-CERT 2013, 5).

Examples of those development projects that are supported by third-party certifiers include projects to increase the productivity of individual producers, which may include interventions in the *cafetal*, such as developing organic fertilizers; education initiatives, which range from production techniques to financial management; and/or the purchase of production-related equipment, in the case of coffee production, household-scale depulping tools or concrete patios for coffee drying. It is these investments that are seen by third-party certifiers as an appropriate use of funds and which cooperatives are effectively coerced into participating in to maintain their certification.

The cooperatives established by fair rebels came from the need to form new economic and sociopolitical relations outside both the

Figure 9. A *socio* of Maya Vinic stands next to his household's coffee depulper. Photograph by the author.

state and the neoliberal marketplace. However, their interaction with the fair trade marketplace has introduced new forms of development and surveillance in their communities. As I argue elsewhere (Naylor 2017c), there is a dangerous assumption made by third-party certifiers that market integration is desirable and that small-scale coffee producers only cultivate coffee. I reported on this exchange, which took place during the audit of Maya Vinic:

> AUDITOR: Who has the smallest plot here?
>
> SOCIO: I have one-quarter hectare and get about two hundred kilos from the harvest.
>
> AUDITOR: How do you survive with two hundred kilos?
>
> SOCIO: It is difficult.

Here the auditor operated under the assumption that coffee is the main economic strategy of the *socio*. However, in many cases, for highland producers, coffee is one component of a diverse livelihood strategy that may include seasonal labor migration, subsistence food production, weaving or other handicraft, and other income- or non-income-generating subsistence, labor, or exchange activities. However, in the dialogue between the *socio* and the auditor, the meager amount of coffee is not presumed to be able to support the producer or their family. There is a concern that the *socio* is not growing their "business" or trying to "improve their product." There is a knowledge that is advanced by third-party certifiers and their ancillary organizations about who producers are and what they and their communities need that is part of the broader geopolitics of knowledge about how people should live. The fair trade premium for development and annual certification audit are an attempt to create and maintain producers as fixed subjects. This is important, because third-party certification organizations' foci on community-wide development and the desire to improve economic behaviors of cooperatives and their members fail to take into account the particulars of farmers' daily lives and politics in place. The universal character of the standards for development are strongly shaped by a capitalocentric worldview that maintains that generating profit in the marketplace is the right way to build livelihoods. Herein rests an important component of what fair trade is, whom it is for, and who gets to decide. The certified market and fair trade brands are becoming dangerously close to speaking for fair trade, something that I will address in the next chapter in unsettling the dominant narratives of fair trade.

Decolonizing Development

The idea of development as part of fair trade discourses is a piece of a universalizing paradigm that places everyone on the same trajectory toward so-called modernization. Fair trade certification is grounded in the idea of perceived differences; it is mired in binaries: north–south, consumer–producer, wealthy–poor, and so on. Fair trade certifiers advertise commodities and producers in the same breath, selling not only a product but the knowledge of production and producers' impoverished livelihoods. For fair trade to exist, it requires a producer in need of "improvement." These discourses of improvement are part of broader paradigms that bifurcate the world into haves and have-nots and seek to move people along a universal(izing) path of "modernization."

When interviewing ranchers about the land occupations and redistribution following the Zapatista uprising, Bobrow-Strain (2007, 21) learned their perspectives on peasant agricultural systems; ranchers whose land had been occupied and had watched their pastures converted to *milpa* decried the "waste" and the "laziness" of subsistence producers. A landscape once occupied by concentrated landholdings populated by cattle shifted to subsistence, and human labor–powered production. What the ranchers saw was "nothing" (159). When pressed to explain why *milpa* production was characterized in such a way, one rancher told Bobrow-Strain that it was "not that the land is producing nothing, but that 'it's not producing what it should. . . . They grow their crops for household consumption, not, productivity'" (161–62). A peasant way of life is delegitimized and ridiculed. Corn is considered the "crop of failure" (Snyder 2001, 209, cited in Bobrow-Strain 2007, 179). Small-scale, indigenous production is considered unproductive and as an impediment to the development plan of the state. The way farming in the region is discussed by *campesinos/as* exposes this fractured landscape of production; one *campesino* explained to me,

> There are many problems with farming here in Chiapas, there are problems with the transgenic seeds and the crops grown for fuel. The government wants to turn Chiapas into an export producer. Calderón [Felipe Calderón, president of Mexico from 2006 to 2012] says we should stop growing corn, that we can just buy it from the United States.

However, in highland Chiapas (and elsewhere throughout the state), the production of corn and other agricultural goods on small plots is a critical component of community economies and everyday life of *campesinos/as*. It is especially important as a part of their resistance. Communities that are populated by *campesinos/as* in resistance share similar issues as other subsistence and coffee-producing communities in the highlands, yet simultaneously, they stand out. One key similarity has been the experience of the "lean months," which is described by Bacon et al. (2014, 140) in the context of fair trade coffee producer communities as the summer months of seasonal hunger. The lean months fall when household food storage has been depleted (or rationed), there is little or no income for the purchase of food, and/or when families have to rely on credit to purchase basic food items (Bacon et al. 2014; see also Fernandez et al. 2013). Such season-to-season realities demonstrate the multipronged strategies of *campesinos/as* in resistance and also the imbalances in how these strategies work out; despite their desire to limit their interaction with the market and the state, many households must purchase corn at some point in the year. For fair rebels, coffee production in the fair trade market is not a panacea, nor is it the personification and portraiture of community sustainable development that is considered desirable by U.S. and European imaginaries.

The trade of certified products is described by third-party certifiers as taking place in a "fairer market where small-producers can build sustainable livelihoods" (FLO-CERT 2013, 5). However, how this is put into practice cannot be universal in character. Despite dominant narratives that construct neoliberal development as inevitable and without alternatives (see Ferguson 2010), *campesinos/as* in resistance continue to maintain subsistence livelihoods that are bolstered by interactions with coffee cooperatives connected to the fair trade marketplace. To have cash income for the purchase of food in lean times and for items that they cannot produce at home, fair rebels, in this case, encounter trade-offs between their politics and practice. They struggle for autonomy and continue to engage in diverse livelihoods, some of which are linked to global exchanges, which subjects them to standards that are incongruent with community practices and politics (something I discuss in more depth in chapters 3 and 4).

A diverse economy approach is useful to decentering capitalism and conventional economic development as the prevailing lens with which peasant economic activities are viewed. Within dominant discourses of economic development, peasant producers are viewed as noncapitalist (the myth of subsistence) and needing to be integrated into the capitalist marketplace. By pushing against capital as the organizing principle, a whole range of activities are made visible. The agricultural and economic practices in the highlands (sale to fair trade markets, subsistence production, cooperative production of goods, and so on) force a rethinking of economic imaginaries and a "dislocation" of capitalocentrism (Gibson-Graham 2006b, 59). This dislocation is due to the diversity of practices and economic relationships that take place in self-declared autonomous communities, which cannot be fully captured by locating activities as only "capitalist" or "peasant."

Breaking down a geopolitics of knowledge of what development means and how it is/was constructed, and who benefits, is a key piece of decolonizing development. Put differently, seeing where knowledge is built and deployed as part of white, Western, patriarchal imperialism is an essential component of rereading and reframing development from different spaces. As part of these considerations, I discussed economic realities with *campesinos/as* in resistance. These discussions were an important piece of examining how I understood economic exchange and the different forms that economies might take. These economic performances—economies, economic practices, and economic exchanges—are situated in multiplicity. I detail in the following paragraphs three key ways that economic performances help to reread "economy" and decolonize development: first, the economy as violence; second, economy as family; and third, economy as community.

My introduction to the use of economy in self-declared autonomous communities was framed by discussions of the war of five hundred years and the resistance struggle. *Campesinos/as* in resistance related stories about the bad government (official Mexican governance bodies) seeking to divide communities through economic means; one *campesino* declared that the government would "bomb us economically" to describe a lack of market for cooperatively produced goods. Government economic interventions were also tied to past patron–client relations, about which one *campesina* remarked that "the government buys people with bad houses and food, they look to buy off people's consciences." Another explained that paramilitaries operate their own economy, trying to "buy us . . . but you can't buy peace and justice with money." Such narratives appear to be tied to the violence of state clientelism. Yet, simultaneously, *campesinos/as* in resistance discuss their own economic activities and economies. The same word is used to describe different approaches to exchange and well-being.

When discussing the importance of everyday activities in food and agriculture consumption and production for *campesinos/as* in resistance, one *campesino* offered that "the base of the capitalist economy is to get people to buy food." However, fair rebels disrupt this particular vision. As part of building dignified livelihoods, *campesinos/as* attempt to resist this base, reducing potential dependencies on the market, and instead build anew. It is not an anticapitalist approach, as the sale of coffee and the purchase of corn in the "lean months" underscore a capitalist relation, but rather a diverse approach, where the "economic base" is about more than market-based, for-profit, wage-labor exchanges. I asked about the role of fair trade in their households, and a consistent response was that it was "a little money"; nonetheless, *campesinos/as* narrated a range of household economic activities. "The family is the economic base of the household," one *campesino* articulated. "There are the chickens and the coffee, and the honey; but there is also the drying of the beans and the harvesting of *elote* [fresh corn]." Other discussions about the economic base of the household centered on exchange:

"families do exchange, maybe you see families exchanging the little animals, or some corn. There is a lot of exchange within and between the communities this way. They can also exchange clothing and other things." Such exchanges may take any number of forms, from barter and trade to support during a time of *cargo* (translated as "burden" and functions as democratically elected, community-based volunteer work) or maybe filial care.

Other types of exchange are based in maintaining subsistence livelihoods as economic practice. Part of their resistance to state forms of development is bound up in fair rebels' desire to maintain the *ejido* and communal forms of food and agricultural production. Subsistence cultivation is one type of economic practice, and maintaining communally held lands is another. One memorable occasion of walking through the community with a family on the way to their *cafetal* navigated us through the communal corn plot, where they weeded and even harvested a few ears of corn as they walked through. Corn forms the foundation of indigenous economies and livelihoods, and as there are incursions by nonnative seeds, communities of *campesinos/as* across the state of Chiapas are working together to maintain their communal production. This extends the community beyond ideas of bounded space and into communities of people, who may not live and work the same land or land race but who are exchanging knowledge of seeds and agricultural practices (something I discuss in greater detail in chapter 5). These communities of people are working together to maintain and build their own vision of living well—to live as communities of indigenous peasants in a world where indigenous people are continuously dispossessed.

To decolonize means also to consider indigenous futurity (Naylor et al. 2018). Decolonizing development is not only about recognizing different forms of building livelihoods and living well but also about recognizing the structural oppression and struggles that shape these differences. Different understandings of economic performance are one potential avenue. Crucial to this project is seeing multiple performances that are stimulated by any number of resistances but also as embodied difference. Put differently, economic and development imaginaries need to be expanded on as sites of difference that are attentive to the geohistorical context of indigenous struggles in place. If the "colonial modern world" began with the *encubrimiento* (enclosure/concealment) of the Americas, as Mignolo (2002) suggests it does, a hegemony over knowledge production and the othering of indigenous lives and livelihoods is intertwined with the centering of capitalism as *the* basis of economic exchange and improvement.

Other modernities are invisible or rendered invalid in the primacy of Western (and Anglo) imaginaries (Zaragocin 2018). What development programming and narratives fail to take into account is multiple and competing worldviews and the importance of promoting and maintaining pluriversal approaches to living well. We need multiple worldviews as a human community. Although universalizing development narratives and standards for development through programming remain an important part of fair trade market relations, fair rebels are not passive recipients of fair trade–led development. In the next chapter, I discuss the multiple meanings of fair trade and how negotiating social justice movements and the market for fair trade coffee became a key piece of the resistance and the messy reality of building livable worlds for fair rebels.

"Son Hechos, No Palabras"

I am sitting with several *socios* and members of the cooperative leadership for Maya Vinic in the community kitchen adjacent to the bodega waiting for a meeting to start. We are sharing kilos of tortillas and avocados with salt that I brought from the city that morning. The avocados are exquisite. Everyone has gathered for a meeting to discuss the honey harvest and to set up contracts with a buyer from Europe. While we are waiting for the representative of the buyer to arrive, we chat about honey. I ask for the Tzotzil word for "honey" to add to my growing (but meager) vocabulary: *pom* (Tzotzil) is *miel* (Spanish) is honey (English). There is a smattering of discussion in a mix of Spanish and Tzotzil, and I catch bits and pieces about the performance of honey and desires of increasing production to meet the demands of buyers. To my surprise, Maya Vinic has a few buyers for their honey, and one of them is a family-owned entity in Eugene, Oregon, where I live in the United States—another node in the network, another connection.

Figure 10. Sketch of the Chiapas state slogan from my fieldwork notebook: "Son Hechos, no palabras" (Deeds, not words). Photograph by the author.

The representative from Europe arrives with one of the cooperative staff from the city, and formal discussions begin. It is a lot of discussion about contracts (which are in Spanish) and increasing production. At one point, the buyer raises a concern about *socios* possibly selling their honey to the *coyote* to get fast cash instead of selling to the cooperative. This raises some pretty baffled looks on the faces of the representatives from Maya Vinic, until someone finally explains that there is not really such a thing as a honey *coyote*.

I am not a participant in these exchanges as much as a fly on the wall, but I do get to share in the samples of honey and enjoy hot coffee as I observe the proceedings. Out of the five hundred plus members of the cooperative, about 25 percent have beehives in their *cafetales*. The honey we are enjoying is coffee honey, produced from the flowers of the coffee plants. Many *socios* want to diversify their products, but not everyone wants to deal with bees. I make a remark about this to the *socio* sitting next to me, and he laughs, telling me that he gets stung all the time during honey harvesting; he laughs again, saying, "My blood is now used to it."

After the buyer's representative departs, many of us remain at the table chatting and drinking the remaining coffee; I put a little of the honey in mine. The treasurer for the cooperative is sitting with us, which has kept him from being available to make payments to *socios* who are delivering their coffee today. One of the *socios* locates the treasurer in the kitchen so he can be paid. After the administrative work of recording the payment is done and the *socio* has the cash in his hand, he says to the table at large, "Son hechos, no palabras!" This exclamation, which is a slogan of the state of Chiapas, is met with great amusement. We all agree it is funny, because they do not accept any state programs or presence, and it is a part of the propaganda machine of the state anyway.

It is a joke.

3

Fair Trade Exploitation and Empowerment
Unsettling Narratives

When I started my preliminary examination of fair trade coffee in Chiapas and was puzzling through some of the contradictions that I saw at work in the highlands, I would describe the use of fair trade as a market that had been harnessed in the service of resistance by social movements. In a conversation about my nascent work, a colleague asked, "Do you really think you are going to go to Mexico and find that people aren't being exploited [by fair trade]?" And in this question, all agency was removed from the people with whom I was working; my colleague already imagined them as exploited and participating in a neoliberal market context. It also pitted their resistance as one of struggle against neoliberal capitalism, which simplified the historical (e.g., the five-hundred-year struggle), place-based, and racialized contexts of their attempts to build livable worlds. This question further troubled me because I saw *campesinos/as* in resistance as being agents of change rather than neoliberal subjects continuing to facilitate their own dispossession. Reflecting on this conversation in the context of reading, writing, and coming to know the geopolitics of knowledge, I continue to align myself with scholars who advocate for multiple epistemologies, such as decolonial, feminist, and queer theorists. As a group actively working to produce knowledge, scholars are uniquely positioned to shape ontologies and epistemologies (and how we educate others). Even as *campesinos/as* in resistance had been categorized and known as "marginalized," as "impoverished," as "disadvantaged coffee producers," there is no reason to suggest that this framing is the one way to consider their identities or how they know, understand, and perceive themselves and their world. Reframing and dismantling such colonial–imperial subjectivities is crucial if we are to be held accountable for decolonizing knowledge (Naylor et al. 2018). This accountability is part of conducting research with groups who may be normatively categorized at the "margins" and is a component of the performance of research discussed in the introductory chapter to this volume.

In considering fair trade exchanges through the lens of diverse and community economies, inevitably, the ubiquitous binaries that populate fair trade discourses must be addressed. "Trade not aid," "a movement and a market," "producer and consumer," are all important phrases adopted across fair trade literature and form a key part of the capitalist (and especially neoliberal) imaginary of fair trade. Drawing from the work of Sedgwick (2003) on paranoid theory, Roelvink (2016, 30) suggests that scholars contribute to capitalist hegemony because they "know about neoliberal capitalist globalization, they feel morally and ethically compelled to document, analyze, and theorize this systemic force of oppression to be able to oppose it." Because we are aware of the structural oppressions of capitalism, many tend to fall into the trap of maintaining its primacy, while trying to make visible how it works for a particular group of people through the exploitation of other groups, rather than seeing such "exploited" groups as having identities outside of these framings, which may be tied to capitalism or not. It is this particular framing that must be interrogated in thinking through what fair trade is, whom it is for, and who gets to decide. Ultimately, these questions have no one right answer, and my goal in this chapter is not to make claims as an arbiter but to open up possibilities for rethinking economic exchange by disrupting capitalocentric binaries. In the performative act of research and writing, I use this platform as a way to consider economies in a manner that moves away from the singular imaginary of a capitalist economy and toward diverse and multiple economies (Gibson-Graham 2006b). In this examination, I intend to dislocate long-standing binaries enmeshed in fair trade networks and open up the possibilities for thinking about an ethic of care in economic exchange that is not based in otherizing dichotomies and knowledge production. A main point I draw through this chapter is that we cannot begin from a space where people producing for the fair trade market are singular ("marginalized" commodity producers) and on a universalizing path (toward capitalist markets and development).

My goal in this chapter is, drawing from the foundational discussion of development in chapter 1, to unsettle the major narratives produced by scholars and practitioners of fair trade and make the case that the universalizing and capitalocentric paradigm that shapes certified exchanges (driven by attempts to "develop" producers into rational economic actors) reifies subjectivities of "there is no alternative." Even as fair trade proponents claim certified exchange to be a different approach (e.g., binaries of trade, not aid), a closer examination shows that fair trade does not produce difference in and of itself. In this chapter, I draw from literature written by scholars and practitioners of fair trade, with specific attention to the discourses used to perpetuate the dominant narratives of fair trade and historical changes in representation of voices within fair trade markets and movements. I ground this textual analysis with empirical data from interviews with *campesinos/as* and extensive observation and participation in everyday activities in the highlands of Chiapas over the period of fieldwork. These data sets were transcribed and coded thematically with a focus on binaries of movement/market, producer/consumer, for example.

In the three sections that follow, I examine in more detail how dominant narratives about fair trade are put into practice. In the section "Trade Not Aid," I draw on the discussion of fair trade as development from chapter 2 to consider how fair trade certification maintains long-standing economic development paradigms. With an understanding of the blurry line between trade and aid, and how universalizing desires to improve the "other" are at work as part of third-party certification systems, I then discuss the idea that fair trade is both a movement and a market. Many authors argue that the fair trade movement allows for the success of the market, and I build on this critique and argue that the fair trade movement is not separate from the market and that distinct movements to make trade fairer have emerged. Finally, I examine the producer–consumer binary and attempt to disrupt the singular producer-subject through thinking from the colonial difference and making visible and multiple their economic identities. Ultimately, I discuss the need to unsettle the narratives of fair trade as a way to decolonize the geopolitics of knowledge production and consider the possibility of fair trade in movement, which is the subject of chapter 4. Thinking through these fair trade debates is a theoretical activity; however, it has a practical application—how we think about and theorize fair trade shapes the way it is developed and deployed. Currently, as I argue in chapter 1, it is something that is "done" by and for "producer-subjects." If we begin to open up universalizing narratives and normalizing binaries, we might find that it can be more for *campesinos/as* in resistance.

"Trade Not Aid"

Current fair trade certification strategies are based on recognition on the part of third-party certifiers that the promises of globalization and development have failed particular groups. Yet as a global system of accumulation by dispossession and resource concentration that has restored power to the wealthiest people on the planet (Harvey 2001), it is a system functioning exactly as intended (Smith 1984). As I noted in chapter 1, the larger-scale adoption of development aid in the post–World War II period was based in creating a spatial fix, by facilitating a transfer of capital to former (*de jure*) colonial states. However, while global development aid continued, in the context of a TINA ("there is no alternative")-shaped neoliberal globalization, there were stronger calls for free trade and decreasing development aid.[1]

Proponents of fair trade extol certification as a way to address poverty through "trade not aid" (cf. Sarcauga 2004). A key component of this advocacy is to distance fair trade certification from discourses of charity and giving to the "poor," instead imbuing "marginalized" populations with business skills and market access. Moreover, many claim that private entrepreneurship is the primary mechanism that should be used to address poverty (cf. Knapp 2009; Nicholls and Opal 2005; Nicholls 2010). Knapp (2009, 53), executive director of Fair Trade Australia and New Zealand, in examining the challenges of promoting development through a market-based system, wrote,

> It is within the context of this extensive challenge that it is possible to best understand the central logic of the Fairtrade Labelling system's strategic approach: the advancement of a joined-up approach to development and trade justice which attempts to embed goals of poverty reduction, social development and democratic governance at the centre of the international trading system, and thereby to help realize the full potential of the international trading system to promote agendas of both economic development and social justice. The Fairtrade Labelling system's new business model is designed with this ambition: to take Fairtrade firmly into the mainstream with the scale and integrity to redefine global business objectives in order to achieve broad-reaching development and empowerment through trade.

Through such an approach, we are meant to understand that fair trade can achieve what free trade cannot and thus create global entrepreneurs and more even distribution of wealth within a capitalist system. Remarkably, Nicholls (2010, 245) refers to this approach as one that has the possibility to create an "economics of virtue," which challenges the neoliberal market model, also noting that the narratives that shape fair trade have "diversified" from emphasizing social justice and resisting conventional trade to engaging "conventional market models and market practices." The trade of certified goods is viewed as a better way toward development, one that maintains the steady march onward to "modernization" and high-mass consumption. These approaches are clearly shaped by a neoliberal paradigm as fair trade organizations seek to mold small-scale producers into capitalists who can increase their scale of production through successful integration into global markets and realize the virtue of a free (but regulated) market. This effort is particularly evident in the annual fair trade audit. For example, when the auditor from Fairtrade International arrived to conduct the annual audit of Maya Vinic in 2013, they frequently spoke with the leadership about organizing their office and documentation in specific ways, as well as having written contracts for their employees. The auditor also voiced concerns about a more senior certified cooperative needing to run their organization in a more business-like manner to compete better.

Fair trade as development is an important component of the mantra of trade not aid. Trade is held up as the single best way to achieve "development" for "marginalized" groups. Yet, the broader market and mainstreaming of fair trade in the past decade represent a certain economic myopia, which results in universalizing and Western-centric framings and means of addressing "under-" and "undeveloped" economies.[2] The narratives of development and "trade not aid" represent a landscape of marginalization of peoples and places. As Fisher (2018) notes, the logic of producing capital under certification in many cases is not congruent with producers' ideas of practicing "dignified work." Examining a fair trade sewing cooperative in Nicaragua, Fisher further notes that similar to development, "fair trade is at once a global project, made coherent by its own rules and norms" (75–76), which neglects producer understandings of what dignified work (lives) look like. Fair trade as defined by a handful of scholars and proponents answers the questions of what fair trade is and whom it is for: development for impoverished producers (who will then become rational economic actors). It is a singular (and neoliberal) vision of living well.

The Fairtrade International *2016 Global Strategy Report* describes this ongoing mission for fair trade:

> Our mission is to connect disadvantaged producers and consumers, promote fairer trading conditions and empower producers to combat poverty, strengthen their position and take more control over their lives. (3)[3]

This set of goals from the largest fair trade, third-party certifier in the world speaks volumes about how fair trade has changed over time to align with the paradigm of international aid, which seeks a "responsibilization of the poor" (Lyon 2015b, 163) in "lifting themselves out of poverty." These goals are backed by standards for certification, which are largely developed and controlled by organizations in the United States and Western Europe, placing people who are producing commodities for the fair trade marketplace in the position of subjects or recipients of fair trade. The broader definitions for social and environmental standards of production of fair trade products remain strained by colonial–imperial relations of power (Bacon 2010; Renard 2003) that operate very similarly to aid programs. Moreover, many producers were already participating in market-based trade of commodities prior to the introduction of certified trade. The introduction of a label based on standards for production and development simply changed its character. As Renard and Loconto (2013, 53) argue, fair trade certification standards are not without bias and instead are "the outcome of the interests of those who participate in their creation." As fair trade certification systems grew and became more market oriented, the inclusion and representation of producer voice(s) was minimized:

> Many of the decisions that were made by the administration of FLO [now Fairtrade International] were completed "behind the backs," or contrary to the opinion, of the producer organizations; the latter, in turn, were marginalized in the processes of registration for members and users of the label, the standards development process, and the commercial decisions taken by NIs [Northern Labeling Initiatives] and integrated committees of Northern representatives. Thus while claiming representation, inclusiveness was not the result. (53)

Indeed, it was not until after significant pressure from producer organizations that any representatives from these organizations were given a seat at the fair trade decision-making table.

The voluntary (and, since 2003, fee-based) certification for fair trade coffee began as a smallholder initiative for empowering producers in the marketplace and can currently be better described as a volume-, sales-, and revenue-driven endeavor (Renard 2015); this is part of the broader neoliberal paradigm that emphasizes the primacy of productive output and profit over other forms of value, such a social reproduction, mutual aid, and other methods of exchange. Standards for social, environmental, and governance practices have changed in the intervening thirty years since the first label of Max Havelaar; as Renard (2015, 481) synthesizes, the "professionalization of certification processes and the creation of professional agencies result in the disempowerment of those who initially created the regulatory systems" (see also Jaffee 2012; Renard 2010; Renard and Loconto 2013). A principal reason for drawing attention to this change is that, similar to aid organizations, the leadership and decision-making power of third-party certifiers lacked representation from small producers. As longtime fair trade scholar Renard has chronicled, the Board of Directors for Fairtrade International (which, until 2011, was the umbrella organization for all regional third-party certifiers) gradually acquiesced to the demands of small producers (particularly those from Latin America) to expand representation to them. There are two main governance bodies of Fairtrade International—the Board of Directors and the General Assembly. It was not until 1999 that producers had representation at Fairtrade International, when two producer representatives—one for Latin America and one for Africa—were added to the board (Renard 2015, 481; see also Bennett 2016).[4] These changes were hard won, and Figure 11 details voting representation change from the first label, governed by the organization Max Havelaar, to present representation for Fairtrade International.

Renard (2015, 481–82) articulates these changes as producers "winning votes, but not power," as their votes remain isolated and otherwise marginal to the issues that are brought to a vote, such as the inclusion of mining operations (certified gold was proposed in 2009 and was opposed by the producer networks yet came into force in 2011) and the certification of coffee plantations. Furthermore, Fair Trade USA remains devoid of diverse representation (at the time of writing), having no governance seats occupied by producers. It is not entirely clear why Fair Trade USA remains obstinate about producer representation. Bennett (2016, 340) observes that "Fair Trade USA's Achilles heel may be legitimacy. It lacks transparent governance; [and] is not endorsed by key movement actors." Moreover, the move by Fair Trade USA to certify coffee plantations remains a point of contention among small-scale coffee producer cooperatives, which may offer an explanation for why they are not offered a seat at the table.

The story of representation illuminates the disconnect between the goals of third-party organizations and organized producer

Figure 11. Historical Governance Changes and Producer Representation

Change	Year	Governing Body	Role of Producers
First Label	1988	Max Havelaar Board; Producer Assemblies	3 of 13 votes (Board); Producers retain all votes, decisions ratified by the board (assemblies)
New Labels	1992-1997	National Fairtrade Organizations (NFOs)	1 vote in Transfair Germany and 3 votes in Max Havelaar (Boards; only 2 of 16 NFO Boards have producer representation); Producers retain all votes, decisions ratified by the boards (assemblies)
Establishment of Umbrella Organization (Fairtrade Labeling Organization)	1997	FLO General Assembly; FLO Board of Directors	No Producer votes (Board); No producer votes (Assembly)
Producer Inclusion	1999-2005	FLO General Assembly; FLO Board of Directors	2 votes (1999); 4 votes (2001) (Board); Producers have 3 of 23 votes (2005) (Assembly)
Establishment of Fairtrade International	2011	Fairtrade International General Assembly; Fairtrade International Board of Directors	4 of 11 votes (Board); 50% producers; 50% NFOs (Assembly)

Adapted from Bennett (2016); Renard (2015)

groups and also sheds light on the complications of enforcing auditing standards that were, for the most part, created by people residing in core countries on behalf of those in the global periphery. This problematic extends from issues such as the static price floor for coffee (the price has only been raised twice in thirty years, once in 2007 and again in 2011, something that has not escaped the notice of fair rebels and that was frequently commented on) (see Bacon 2010; Jaffee and Howard 2016) to the restrictive aspects of inclusion, noting that the smallholders who might benefit the most from fair trade are often not able to meet the requirements for initial certification or are otherwise systematically excluded (Dolan 2008). The Latin American and Caribbean Network of Fair Trade Small Producers and Workers (CLAC) found that many small producers continue to be excluded from fair trade certification (CLAC 2004, cited in Renard 2015). These realities suggest that the goal of bringing trade rather than aid to groups lacking secure trading markets is complicated by the very certification processes that are being promoted. Furthermore, the lack of representation by producers resulted in the creation of standards that do not separate trade and aid but fuse them together. Moreover, it presents a tension in the neoliberal paradigm of fair trade, in discursively constructing certification initiatives as promoting producer responsibility and agency, yet simultaneously reducing their role to value creation, but not the governance of the distribution of that value or broader policies that shape its distribution.

As part of their efforts toward transparency, fair trade third-party certifiers, which are umbrella organizations and gatekeepers, conduct annual reports, commission research studies, and make these available to the public on their websites. In 2017, as part of a response to claims that coffee producers were not being "lifted out of poverty" by selling under the fair trade label, Fairtrade International released a report (Fobelets, Rusman, and de Groot Ruiz 2017) on income earnings in one season of coffee production for seven countries: Rwanda, Tanzania, Uganda, Kenya, India, Indonesia, and Vietnam (representing roughly 20 percent of coffee producers certified under their label, and notably lacking key production areas in Latin America, where about 75 percent of certified producers are located; Fairtrade International 2018, 53). The 2017 report, which was commissioned by Fairtrade International and compiled by TruePrice from data collected by fair trade field staff, found that on average, coffee sales amounted to about 50 percent of producers' total household income for that year (4), and producers in Kenya experienced income losses through the cultivation of coffee (21). Critically, this report signaled somewhat of a recognition that third-party certifiers artificially homogenize coffee producers. Field staff found that in most cases, producers had multiple income earning strategies (consistent with long-standing findings by scholars on peasant production; cf. Akram-Lodhi and Kay 2010a, 2010b; Ploeg 2010, 2014). Yet, simultaneously and consistent with many long-term economic development strategies, the report calls for scalable programs to address producer reliance on coffee income. Put differently, the report recognized that economic practices differ across people and place, yet a new goal is now to find a solution for one producer group that can be applied to multiple contexts—a universal fix for a diverse set of peoples, places, and production practices. This approach speaks to the geopolitics of knowing how people should live that comes from development paradigms, the idea that there is one right path to development and one right way to live. That the report recognized the importance of place-specific contexts, yet recommends a universal approach, reifies this knowledge geopolitics.

An additional finding of the Fairtrade International report (Fobelets, Rusman, and de Groot Ruiz 2017) that corresponds with the experiences of fair rebels in the highlands was that even though coffee producers adopt the fair trade standards for their practices, they are not able to sell all of their coffee at the fair trade price. The report noted that only about half of the certified producers in the countries surveyed even sold as much as 40 percent of their product at the fair trade price. Yet these are the same strategies that are purported to "lift farmers out of poverty" and facilitate the "improvement of entire communities." Simultaneously, third-party certifiers create standards that govern how these processes unfold, attempting to manage and fix producers. This "fixing" falls into interventions in economic and community development, whereby fair trade "subjects" are viewed as needing to "improve" themselves or be improved through interaction with the market, while simultaneously cementing them in time and place as "fair trade coffee producers." The focus on the market and trade is one manner in which the narratives of fair trade serve to depoliticize and "render technical" (see Ferguson 1994; Li 2007; on fair trade, Dolan 2010; Naylor 2017c) the politicized, racialized, and multiple livelihoods of people producing for the fair trade certified market. Put differently, political and place-specific questions are effectively enclosed by development "knowledge," translating instead to technical problems requiring solutions. Instead of confronting the multiple and diverse, rather than recognizing human beings in myriad place-specific contexts, they created producer-subjects as a problem to be fixed (Naylor 2014). However, as Dolan (2010, 34) argues, drawing on Harriss (2002), the narratives of fair trade, where organizations seek to help people empower themselves through partnership and participation in certified markets and community-led development, mask concentrations of power, which sever it from the "fundamentally politicized field of development." Fair trade is a new thread being pulled through existing development aid agendas and systems of power and knowledge production about how to live and labor. In this way, fair trade draws on and repeats Western-centric and patriarchal development agendas.

How does thinking about fair trade in this way unsettle or disrupt the purported binary of trade not aid? It does so because it untangles the notion that certified trade operates under a different auspice than development aid. They are both programs of development that seek to improve the "other." Although it may be the case that fair trade third-party certifiers sought to distance fair trade from ideas of charity, that does not delink fair trade from past and ongoing forms of development aid; in fact, it repeats them, while using charity-esque narratives of "helping." Setting up a market-based solution to poverty that is grounded in colonial–imperial relations of commodity production and trade that is also tied to "rigorous" standards for production and community development that reflect white, middle-class, eco-conscious desires for "improving the other" does not step outside the basic premises of development aid; it is steeped in it.[5]

Returning to the Fair Trade International *2016 Global Strategy Report*, which was released following the establishment of the Global Goals for Sustainable Development, the five-year plan for mobilizing change via fair trade was introduced in the following way: "When it comes to sustainable development, trade can be the best of servants, but the worst of masters. This is why Fairtrade works within the market, to change the market" (3). Leaving aside the problematic use of master-servant as a way of framing engagement with trade, this particular discourse of working "within and against the market" is at the core of claims that fair trade is both a movement and a market based in broader social justice goals. It is to this narrative that I turn in the following section.

A "Movement and a Market"

In September 2017, Paul Rice, the CEO of Fair Trade USA, wrote a letter as part of the announcement of their 2016 *Almanac*, a report that showcases the annual statistics for certified fair trade products. In his remarks, he recalls the beginning of the organization and the fair trade movement, explaining to readers,

> Some people called us crazy, because we actually believed that rural farmers and workers around the world *could learn to navigate the global market and empower themselves* on a journey out of poverty. We believed that business could be a major force for change, creating "shared value" and a better life for farming families. We envisioned *consumers awakening to their power to choose* a better world through their everyday purchases. In short, we had faith that the Fair Trade movement would become part of a much larger shift toward Conscious Capitalism. (7, emphasis added)

This statement is one of many possible examples of third-party certifiers utilizing narratives of a fair trade movement in the service of the certified (neoliberal) market. This particular excerpt replays the paternalistic development discourses that are deployed as part of trying to create a market-based solution to economic unevenness in the context of ongoing colonial–imperial power relations. Yet the same organizations that deploy these narratives do so in the context of positioning fair trade as a movement and a market, a framing that is readily taken up by scholars and practitioners (cf. Dalvai 2012; Fridell 2007a, 2007b; Hudson and Hudson 2004; Jaffee 2014; Lyon 2011; Raynolds 2012; Raynolds and Greenfield 2015; Rice 2001). In this section, I examine the movement and market narrative that is often tied to fair trade exchanges and consider whether they are more than nominally different. In disrupting the somewhat blurry dichotomy between social justice activism around making trade fairer and the fair trade movement, and how the fair trade market is juxtaposed against them, possibilities for considering fair trade in movement emerge (see chapter 4). Here I argue that there is a discourse of the "fair trade movement" that is the starting place for certified fair trade and the market for certification and that there are broader movements to make trade fairer that are based in enabling radical transformation around economic exchanges. The fair trade market is continually expanding, generating profit and social premiums across the world; it is a regulated market that is presented as an alternative to capitalist markets. The fair trade movement is conflated with the certified market, and its radical potential perhaps peaked in 1988, when the first label was established. In the intervening time, the narratives of the movement opened doors for the logics of the market.

The fair trade market has grown considerably since its inception. As noted in chapter 2, millions of producers generated billions of dollars in the fair trade certified market. In its *2016 Almanac*, Fair Trade USA notes that there were almost one thousand certified consumer packaged goods available on the market (11).[6] The United States and the United Kingdom remain the leaders in fair trade certified sales (Fair Trade USA 2016). Fair Trade USA in particular focuses its attention on mainstreaming and bringing more products to conventional retailers—its website suggests shopping for fair trade certified products at large-scale retailers and box stores such as Walmart and Costco. Coffee remains the flagship fair trade certified product; for example, almost 150 million pounds of coffee were imported to the United States alone under the Fair Trade USA label in 2016 (Fair Trade USA 2016, 19). It is a market built on the back of a movement, which it has all but subsumed.

In the first years of fair trade certification, the labeling initiative was discussed as an antidote to capitalism, a (certified) market that curbed the excesses of consumption and the injustices of production. In many cases, it was (and continues to be) described by scholars as a Polanyian (1957) "countermovement" and a socially embedded market that disrupts the commodity fetish (cf. Jaffee 2014; Raynolds 2000; Raynolds and Greenfield 2015). However, even though fair trade certification has at its origins social justice organizing, the tension between activism around making trade fairer and the market is ongoing. Raynolds and Greenfield argue that this tension is a core piece of how the institutions of certification are shaped: "by translating movement principles into formal bureaucratic institutions and rational rules, and by positioning products in mainstream markets, certification has spurred fair trade's commercial growth" (27). What this translation means in practice is that the market for fair trade requires no alteration of retailing practices and makes very few demands on customers to change their consumption habits.

There is a qualitative difference between activism to make trade fairer and the fair trade movement that is drawn on as part of the certification market. The movements to make trade fairer are attentive to injustices related to the colonial–imperial relations of trade and seek to deconstruct spatially disparate and racialized hierarchies; they are transnational and embodied by multiple actors working together to create sites of interdependence and mutual aid. Whereas the fair trade movement, as described by third-party certifiers and in some scholarly work, is about helping producers reach the market and extending the perceived benefits of market interaction to a growing group of producer-subjects who are characterized as disadvantaged, while people purchasing fair trade certified products perform a form of "buycott" through their everyday consumption. The idea that "conscientious consumers" can "vote with their forks" that is expressed in broader "alternative food movements" discourses, which agitate to change behaviors in the market through economic (rather than political) values (Obringer and Naylor 2018), creates what Holt Giménez and Shattuck (2011, 121) describe as "an uneasy dualism between 'quality food' for higher income consumers and 'other food' consumed by the masses." Furthermore, there is an implicit assumption that there is a cohesive fair trade movement, which emanates from consumers and that has, as its greatest challenge, to work within the constraints of "being in and against the market" (Raynolds and Greenfield 2015, 24–25).

The fair trade movement is emphatically drawn on by scholars and practitioners alike as something that is immediately understood as a movement for social justice that pushes on the capitalist market to create change. It is part of the shifting character of social movements consistent with a neoliberal worldview that the primary actors in the fair trade movement are NGOs. As the state was hollowed out and decentered, the number of NGOs in existence increased and took on statelike roles; as such, groups seeking change had to be institutionalized and formalized to gain efficacy (Alvarez 2009; Harvey 2007; Suh 2011). In contradiction, as Harvey (2007) notes in his discussion of the histories of neoliberalism, NGOs have in many ways created avenues to facilitate neoliberal agendas. Similarly, Dolan (2010) argues that the moral arguments drawn from the fair trade movement make it difficult to critique the fair trade market, which allows it to continue in the service of neoliberalism. Wilson and Curnow (2013, as cited in Wilson and Mutersbaugh 2015, 284) note that in the promotion of certified products, "campaigns increasingly adopted the logics of the market they sought to transform." Indeed, Raynolds and Greenfield (2015) identify this problematic as a split between a fair trade organization model and a fair trade certification model. They argue that "fair trade organizations are deeply mission-driven and devoted to movement principles, yet at the same time they face significant pressure to adopt business practices" (26). The market orientation of fair trade leads to a conflation of the movement and the market (Brown and Getz 2008) and suggests that there are principles drawn from movements to make trade fairer to drive the narrative of third-party certifiers and retailers; nevertheless, action-oriented social transformation is not present. They answer the question of what is fair trade by defining the fair trade movement as working on behalf of "disadvantaged producers" to allow for success in capitalist markets.

A social movement is an effort by individuals or organizations to make change. Drawing on McCarthy's (2009) discussion of social movements, they are organized around particular groups, small producers, for example, or particular goals, such as making trade fairer. Social movements make demands, which might be directed at the state and/or society to activate change. These movements may be local or transnational; where they begin and how they are mobilized are important for thinking about space, place, scale, and who benefits from their mobilization. I argue that the present fair trade movement, which is tied to the fair trade certification market, is not synonymous with organizing around making trade fairer.

In 2004, an informal advocacy network was established by members of Fairtrade International and the World Fairtrade Organization to "speak out *on behalf* of the Fair Trade Movement" (Fair Trade Advocacy Office, n.d., emphasis added). In 2010, just ahead of the split between Fairtrade International and Fair Trade USA, the Fair Trade Advocacy Office (FTAO) was formalized and assumed the role of a legally independent foundation. FTAO describes the fair trade movement in these terms: "the Fair Trade movement today is a global movement *representing* over two million marginalised producers and workers that are organized in nearly 1000 producer organisations across 70 countries in the South" (Fair Trade Advocacy Office, n.d., emphasis added). This statement of the movement effectively demonstrates a group based in Brussels taking ownership over who gets to decide what fair trade is and whom it is for. This so-called movement is not described as a transnational movement of people working together to dismantle the structural injustices of trade and colonial–imperial logics of economic exchange and development; it is a social movement that "represents" those "disadvantaged producers" in need of fixing.

Far from disrupting the structural inequities of the commodity market, those institutions tied to the fair trade movement attempted to shift from working within a context of aid dependency toward a market-focused form of development (Dolan 2010, 35). The institutionalization and mainstreaming of fair trade produced a split in the larger movement–market dynamic, which some see as separate components of the same activity. Raynolds and Greenfield (2015, 30–31) note that the values of the social movement are challenged by market forces and identify issues with operating in a moral economy, arguing that the split created a "market-driven" mainstreaming populated by corporations and conventional market activities, and "mission driven" exchanges that promote "relational and civic values." This narrative aligns with the emphasis on fair trade certification being "in and against the market"; however, as Renard (2015, 481) notes, whatever social movement foundations fair trade certification was built on were demolished in a few short years:

> Fair trade certification has become an extremely technical process carried out by people without any investment in the fair trade

movement.... Fair trade transitioned from a relationship based on negotiation and consensus between Northern and Southern actors to the control of the North over Southern activities.

Claims of empowerment and of benefits to small producers under the banner of the fair trade movement are consistently challenged by the certification market.

The fair trade movement is an imaginary of social justice that allows the market for certification to take on the quality of a moral economy, and a space of ethical purchasing and sustainable development. Here I distinguish the fair trade movement, which is concerned less with social justice than with market inclusion, and instead advocate for considering social justice activism to make trade fairer. Such sites of social justice activism lack the institutionalization/ NGO-ization of the branded movement and potentially have momentum to address the structural conditions of unequal relations. The producer-founders of initiatives to make trade fairer and to create direct networks and personal relationships through economic exchanges do not participate in the certification-based fair trade movement any longer; after building the network collaboratively and successfully agitating for representation in the governing bodies they assisted with creating, the shift in priorities from dismantling unjust systems to expanding the market was made visible to small producers (Renard 2015, 475–76; see also Jaffee and Howard 2016). It is these actors and others who may take up action individually or as part of a larger group or grassroots effort who have at the foundation of their interactions a desire for addressing the root causes of inequality, which extend far deeper than access to the market. Fair rebels as part of their identities as *campesinos/as* in resistance participate in social movements that critique capitalism and demand better conditions for all forms of economic production.[7]

Participating in social justice activism and creating momentum around making trade fairer does not completely distance actors from the problems of the fair trade movement, as participants must traverse the messiness of transnational social movements. In seeking to make trade fairer through social justice activism, there are different power geometries at work, which raises questions about who has the privilege to participate and in what capacity. Such power geometries are tied to time-space compression and the relation(s) of groups and the relative mobility of persons or groups. As Massey (1994, 156) details, people experience these power relations and relative mobilities differently, with some initiating or receiving and others being excluded from or contained within them. However, to participate in movements to make trade fairer is to go beyond the feel-good mantra of certified sales "improving lives" and consider the racialized injustices perpetuated in colonial–imperial contexts. A core issue with the universalizing character of the "producer-subject" that pervades the popular and scholarly discourses of the fair trade movement is the artificial homogenization of the people who are participating in the certified marketplace. A portrait of a "disadvantaged" or "marginalized" producer is meant to stand in for the experience of millions.

There is a paradox at work where the racialized imaginaries that feed the desire to develop and fix the "other" are bound to apolitical and color-blind certification standards and development programming. The bodies of people of color are utilized to sell fair trade products, a strategic essentialism that is part of commodifying the producer-subject (Comaroff and Comaroff 2009; on fair trade, see Lyon 2011, 2015b; Varul 2008). As Lyon (2015b) notes, indigenous people are part of the fair trade imaginary; however, fair trade certifiers do not address their experiences as indigenous peoples, only as "disadvantaged producers." Such a strategy loses the particulars of place and lived experiences of people—the producer-subject is from the "South" and is a person of color. This homogenization simplifies and ignores the complexity and history of multiple oppressions and resistances in the colonial–modern world. Where policies, standards, and programs are the same across peoples and places, not considering their experiences outside of uneven class dynamics ("marginalized producer"), there are few possibilities for activating radical change. Moreover, drawing on images of the producer-subject in favor of the market is potentially damaging for social justice and solidarity efforts addressing the human rights abuses, racism, and gender struggles of indigenous peoples.

The apolitical focus on market access and entrepreneurial success being the outcome of the fair trade movement that is deployed in the service of the certified market not only erases the particulars of place, the colonial–imperial past and present, but also the violence written on the bodies of people of color, in the case of fair rebels, the indigenous Maya. Moreover, the desires to extend "fair trade to all," which overlooks local geopolitics in favor of drawing more producers into the global marketplace, allows for groups with wildly opposing agendas to participate, further diluting the imaginary of the fair trade movement narratives deployed by third-party certifiers. Indeed, as discussed in chapter 2, many *campesinos/as* in resistance left their former coffee-growing cooperative in the highlands because other members of that cooperative had participated in the Massacre at Acteal (and some members continue to receive aid and weapons from the government as part of ongoing paramilitary activities). Members of the paramilitary are also coffee farmers and reside in the same communities as *campesinos/as* in resistance; they participate in the ongoing low-intensity war in Chiapas, and yet at the same time they are part of a different coffee cooperative that also has fair trade certification. The label masks the violence in favor of the market, and this violence is experienced by fair rebels as part of their daily lives. Aggressions against them as part of the low-intensity war take multiple forms from violent attacks on people and the frequent military patrolling of the main roads to theft of coffee equipment and sabotage in the *cafetales* of fair rebels.

The discourses of a "fair trade movement" are mobilized by actors participating in the market that tend to mask the capitalocentric and universalizing discourses of development in which the fair trade certified market operates. In chapter 4, I discuss solidarity relations and focus on the possibilities of interdependence in fair trade exchanges by considering fair trade in movement (something that is constantly undergoing the processes of becoming) and through considering the communities of people in the larger fair trade network. To understand how fair trade might come to be in movement, it is essential to disrupt the idea that there is one movement, one market that is a space for making trade fairer. Seeing beyond the binaries of trade and aid, and movement and market, is an essential component of opening up understandings of commodity exchange; however, it is also crucial to examine universalizing economic subjectivities, such as those of the producer and the consumer.

Producer and Consumer: The Consuming *Campesino/a*

The narrative of producer–consumer linkages that comes from third-party certifiers and fair trade scholars points to fair trade being for the people who are purchasing coffee. Again, Fairtrade International draws discursively on the movement to claim the benefits of fair trade; their strategic plan reminds readers that "the powerful connection between producers and consumers remains a fundamental pillar of Fairtrade" (Fairtrade International 2016b, 14). Consumers are directed to feel as though they are able to impact deeply the lives of people producing coffee and their entire communities—as Fair Trade USA (2012) suggests that they do—and that through their purchase they have broken through the damaging commodity fetish points in that direction. Such framings are deeply paternalistic and draw on the "needy" producer-subject, who is being helped by an "ethically minded," "wealthier" consumer. As Moraga (2015, xvii) observes, such identities are defined less by engaged citizenship and more by consumption, where our political actions are undermined by effectively buying our lives. A *campesina* in resistance remarked to me when discussing certification, "Fair trade is too much and who does it serve? Not the small producer." The imagined linkages between these disparate groups are part of a deeper discussion in chapter 4. In this section, I unsettle the binary between the producer and the consumer by drawing out the clear point that people producing coffee are more than this simplistic, capitalocentric descriptor allows for.

I argue that fair trade coffee producers are more than that labeling affords them (Naylor 2014, 2017c). Third-party certifiers homogenize producers, selling an imaginary of a racialized "other" to consumers purchasing certified goods and creating the producer-subject. A complex and troubling binary within fair trade is the producer–consumer divide. The language of fair trade, being a foundation for producer–consumer linkages, consumers "helping" producers and producer communities with their purchases, and consumer solidarity and social justice, saturates academic and popular literatures. This juxtaposition is, in a word, reductionist, stripping away the complex identities, economic subjectivities, and everyday lives of both groups, but especially those producing fair trade coffee. To draw people into white, Western ontologies (imaginaries of how

Figure 12. Fair trade advertising with consumers and producers juxtaposed (Winborn Minster 2006).

people are to exist based in white and Western experiences being universal), there is a long history of misrecognition, and people are categorized and their experiences and knowledges are excluded to make things more manageable, to affix them to colonial–imperial ontologies and epistemologies. Fair trade certification narratives are only one small example in the multitude that exist; nonetheless, it is an avenue for opening up thinking on economic identities and subjectivities.

More than giving additional shape to coffee producer-consumers in thinking through their economic identities as consumers, I wish to further disrupt the producer–consumer binary through drawing a bridge between decolonial feminist theory and economic difference. If the binary represents a gross oversimplification of the identities, subjectivities, and everyday existences of those people participating in fair trade coffee production, in particular excluding those ways of being and knowing the world for *campesinos/as* through compartmentalizing them in a way that fits Western ideas of what a producer looks like and how they live, then through the colonial difference, we find complexity. As discussed in chapter 1, the colonial difference is a site of othering. Yet to think from the colonial difference is, as I and others have suggested, to acknowledge enduring imperialism and contemporary "othering" and to speak from below or the underside (Naylor et al. 2018, 199).[8] Unsettling the consumer–producer binary is one avenue for multiplying difference and disordering capitalist imaginaries that comes from the *cuerpo-territorio* (body-territory) (Zaragocin, in Naylor et al. 2018, 204) of the everyday practices of *campesinos/as* in resistance—those struggles bound to place, politics, and geohistorical events that come from below as part of efforts to build dignified livelihoods.

The categories that we place on ourselves and others are a relation (on gender, see Probyn 2016). A capitalocentric relation divides and categorizes people into producers and consumers, neglecting our important and multiple roles as political, social, and economic beings. The fair trade market is imbued with this categorical language. To disrupt such simplified framings dislocates capitalist-driven development and the continuous search for peoples and places to exploit (as producers, as subjects of development, as racialized peoples). Drawing on the idea that sexual identity is dominated by an incoherence in our thinking about gender described by Sedgwick (1993, xii), I suggest here that there is an incoherence about the market, which proffers overly simplistic "producer" and "consumer" identities tied to exploitative capitalist relations.

Viewing production and consumption practices through a capitalocentric lens misses the ways that economic processes take place. For example, fair trade advocates might point to the bodega and *abarrote* (small general store) run by the Maya Vinic coffee cooperative as a signal of success in the market. Indeed, the bodega provides steady jobs for multiple people and temporary forms of employment during the processing of the coffee for export, and the *abarrote* provides a permanent job for one person and a place for people to buy food and supplies. At first glance, the Maya Vinic *abarrote* appears the same as any other along the road to Pantelhó: Pepsi, Coca-Cola, and Bimbo products are available; candies, cigarettes, and soap can be purchased. Missing from this initial gaze is the network that made possible the financing for the store, the ways that goods come to occupy the shelves, how people interact with the space, and how goods and services are exchanged. Simultaneously, to view the laborers at the bodega as only wage earners loses sight of who they are, why they are participating in wage labor, and how they participate in the broader economic network that these spaces provide.

At the bodega, people cycle in and out of positions, creating opportunities for earning additional cash income for the extended network of *socios* in Maya Vinic. This practice may not stand out overmuch; however, I draw attention to it because it is a core part of the struggle toward autonomy and forms part of the resistance of fair rebels. Creating opportunities for income earning in the highlands assists with keeping people on the land and with their families, which can be contrasted with other strategies, such as migration to urban areas or to the United States for wage labor opportunities. Additionally, the hire of temporary workers to assist with processing and packaging the coffee for export is a key way that the next generation of *socios* becomes connected more intimately with the cooperative. More than just a job or a training exercise, it is a ceremonial induction passed, in this specific case, from fathers to sons. On the day that they arrived, these teens participated in a candle-lit prayer ceremony in the bodega and then proceeded to a daylong workshop and training on how to process the coffee, how to use the machines, and what happens to the coffee that they grow. One of the members of the leadership of the cooperative noted that they needed more people to know about the processes and to not have "outsiders" running the machines—that it was best to teach the young people.

The *abarrote* was begun with seed funding from the U.S. importing cooperative for Maya Vinic, and it is now self-sustaining. Members of the leadership of the cooperative are responsible for bringing products to the store, and once a month, someone will make the trip into town to buy items in bulk. Bulk items are purchased from suppliers who are also *campesinos/as* and who are also in resistance. Being able to purchase items within the community and to support each other is another piece of living with dignity—not to have to rely on government stores or those run by *partidistas*. Moreover, it saves the cost of travel not to have to go into town to purchase goods. The *abarrote* is more than a place to purchase goods—it is a meeting space, a place to make or receive a phone call; it functions as a waiting room, as people watch for taxis and wait out the rain (as I often did). It is a place where things are bought and sold, yet it is also a space where other forms of exchange happen.

Campesinos/as in resistance are participating in fair trade exchanges and struggling for dignified livelihoods through a diversity of economic practices, not solely as producers of coffee. The fair trade label renders the existence of these producers static, fixing them in place as the personification of a litany of keywords tied to coffee production, capitalist framings of economic improvement, and empowerment. This rendering happens in tandem with the reality that so-called fair trade producers are not even able to sell all of their coffee at fair trade prices. Rereading the economic practices of subsistence and fair trade coffee producers for difference (instead of as capitalist practice) creates a foundation for considering how the resistance being enacted by fair rebels forms the basis of the multiple exchanges (not just the exchange of coffee for money) that take place along the fair trade network of which they are a part. Put differently, it is an opportunity to view practices as driven by the experience of struggle and withstanding suffering, not just as capitalist actors in a marketplace. Here I want to break down the consumer–producer binary so that we deconstruct the producer-subject. One avenue for this project is to expand the economic subjectivity of the "fair trade coffee producer"; if we can understand producers as consumers too, we can see the strategy of participation in the fair trade marketplace and how it is part of building dignified livelihoods on their own terms, not as part of the imaginary of the producer-subject and white, Western desires for development and for "fixing" impoverished peoples and communities.

Fair rebels are not disembodied from the production or consumption of coffee, nor are they defined by it. As *campesinos/as*, they are producers of agricultural products. These performances of production are written onto their bodies in myriad ways, from traversing the miles from their homes to their fields to laboring on the steep slopes to the sweat expressed as part of their daily labors. The products of their labor become a part of the household as corn, beans, and coffee are processed for sale or household use. Women in particular embody this labor as they prepare daily meals and take the coffee out each morning to dry and bring it in each evening to prevent new moisture accumulation. Food is prepared, coffee is toasted, and it is taken into their bodies. These embodiments are a critical piece of reproducing dignified livelihoods in the highlands and are what make possible the struggle and resistance of fair rebels. To talk about fair trade coffee producers is stifling, and their identities are more than what is inscribed onto their bodies by the fair trade label.

We can begin simply by considering the ostensible coffee producer as a coffee consumer. On one of the first days I sat down with producers in a Zapatista support base to discuss my research, we talked generally about coffee and its role in the struggle for autonomy. Coffee was deemed important because "people buy it," which prompted me to ask if they drank their own coffee as well. This question was met with laughter, and one *campesino* remarked that it was "like water." "Yes, we drink our coffee . . . you have to consume it right?" And indeed, I drank many cups of coffee with *campesinos/as* in resistance during my fieldwork; it was often the first thing offered to me by my gracious hosts in the highlands. Mostly this coffee was from microscale production around households and roasting for personal consumption. Many of the homes I visited had a few coffee plants in the immediate vicinity of the household, in addition to their *cafetales*.

To better unlock the imaginary of the fair trade coffee producer, we can then expand to consider coffee producer-consumers as food consumers. Although third-party certifiers cast coffee producers in the narrow light of coffee production, fair rebels are first and foremost subsistence corn cultivators (Naylor 2017a). This point is crucial, because it is the production of coffee that assists with maintaining a subsistence lifestyle (Naylor 2017c). However, coffee production also competes for time-space, making the maintenance of subsistence-based livelihoods not as simple as growing coffee for the fair trade marketplace but a messy negotiation within households. There is great joy and anticipation when the first planting of corn is ready; fresh corn, *elote*, is prized. In some cases, it serves as a delivery mechanism for special treats, such as mayonnaise. Whole corn cobs are steamed, and then mayonnaise is liberally applied with a spatula and salt and lime juice sprinkled over it all. But generally, day-to-day foods are tortillas (or tostadas) and beans with salt and eggs, and *pozol* (fermented corn). In many cases, the tortillas and tostadas are handmade by the women in the family, but when we gathered for larger meetings or during my times at the Maya Vinic bodega, the cooperative leadership would purchase commercial ones from a motorcyclist delivering warm and freshly pressed tortillas manufactured in Pantelhó.[9]

Beyond daily foods, and moving past the myth of subsistence, fair rebels rely on cash income gained from participating in coffee production to purchase medicines, salt, soap, and Western clothing, such as jeans and jelly shoes. Cell phones are ubiquitous, compact discs with new music are cherished and shared among household members, and these are only some examples of personal, material consumption in the highlands. In a place where infrastructure was not constructed to benefit peasants, the warm light of an electric bulb is theft. Fair rebels capture the electric lines that once bypassed their communities; a contribution of the Zapatista rebellion and training was clandestinely acquiring energy resources and distributing them to households in their support bases. And perhaps the image of an indigenous teen with spiky gelled hair, drinking a soda, listening to pop music on the radio, and wearing bedazzled blue jeans does not map onto the smiling fair trade coffee producer projected by third-party certifiers, but such an identity is one of many embodied and lived by fair rebels.

There is a particular way that we expect farmers to live in order to have the products that we want. This is a reality for commodity producers in Chiapas, and for farmers globally. Yet, as Wolford (2010, 71) notes, "the 'peasantry' is not a thing, an 'objective' category with essential unchanging elements"; it is a relation. Yet these problematic imaginaries feed a capitalocentric narrative with images of peasants as inherently noncapitalist. The idea that is often presented is that peasants are eager to be capitalist, that they want access to markets and fair prices, and the fair trade consumer and certifier savior are the ones who can help them realize their capitalist potential. Paternalist and limiting, these narratives lose sight of how much more peasants are. Fair trade is a "window to better money" and functions as *comercio más justo* (as discussed in chapter 2), but the way that *campesinos/as* in resistance identify and participate in fair trade is multiple and diverse, while also being part of their demands for structural change to make livable worlds. Breaking down these imaginaries begins with seeing people producing coffee in the fair trade marketplace not as peasants needing to be fixed and brought into the capitalist fold (producer-subjects) but as humans trying to live well.[10]

Unsettling

The production of knowledge about people and places, about development and economic subjectivities, about life and living, cannot come from one corpus or narrative. There is a monopoly on fair trade narratives that uses the language of empowerment, connectivity, and sustainable development to mask long-standing and ongoing inequities. A capitalist-centered system is one with an amnesia regarding accumulation by dispossession. As discussed in chapter 1, such a centering makes invisible the non-"Western." In practice, this invisibilization allows for universalizing paradigms that foreclose other ways of being and knowing. The geopolitics of knowledge of fair trade today emanates primarily from Western Europe and the United States and is the classification of a group of people, "disadvantaged producers," the definition of spaces (outside of the "West") in need of fixing and economic development, the "South," and the institutionalization of economic exchange that now drives this narrative and makes attempts to control both coffee production and the production of knowledge. These imaginaries are both produced and consumed from the outside, the external.

In thinking through the colonial difference, it is possible to expose the forgetting that has happened through this project, recognize the artificial differences created out of colonialism and made lasting by imperialism, and expose the power inequities that underlie systems of economic exchange. A key component of this reframing is to (re)consider the spaces of knowledge production, including where it "sits" and how it is deployed. Here we can begin to see cracks in the universals that are mobilized as part of fair trade narratives and simultaneously resisted. As Anzaldúa (2015, 82) notes, "navigating the cracks is the process of reconstructing life anew." *Campesinos/as* in resistance producing for the fair trade market are not the subjects of fair trade (see Naylor 2017c); their social and economic practices are everyday acts of decolonization, and their political practices as part of indigenous social movements are part of efforts to dismantle what Daigle, in discussing indigenous futurity and sovereignty, has called "structural and intimate colonial political geographies" (in Naylor et al. 2018, 203). The struggle is not to be part of the system but to deconstruct it. The binaries and universals of fair trade are locked in capitalocentric, colonial–imperial ontologies and epistemologies that must be continuously challenged and unsettled.

Scholars and proponents continue to repeat the same tropes about fair trade. Third-party certifiers advance the narratives of trade not aid, a movement and a market, and the producer–consumer binary and promote the positive impacts that certified economic exchange has on producers and their communities. The impact reports that are provided by Fair Trade USA and Fairtrade International rely on volume of product produced and sold, the amount of money that was distributed as part of the social premium, the increased number of participants, and the increased number of products and retailers. They also discuss the development and empowerment programs that they have designed as part of fair trade, but no data are presented to demonstrate any positive impact based on their metrics. Moreover, when attempting to collect data to show positive impacts, as Fairtrade International did in 2016–17, when it hired TruePrice to conduct a study of income earning, it found that coffee producers in the countries surveyed were in fact not doing much better under the systems of certification, despite their ongoing claims. The measures of "impact" are based in a capitalocentric imaginary whereby the only things that count toward impact are those that are calculable—those activities that are quantifiable and visible through the narrow lens of capital. This focus not only ignores those activities and practices that cannot be counted (such as social reproduction) but reinforces a geopolitics of knowledge about how to live well that comes from so-called consumer countries. That a higher income and larger volume of production are the basis for "improving producer's lives" is a component of the apolitical and ahistorical intervention that "fixes" producers by attempting to bring them into a capitalist fold.

Fair trade begins with the premise that all economic exchanges are capitalist ones. From this premise, third-party certifiers seek to make the capitalist system work for those they identify as marginalized by it. This circular line of reasoning is problematic for two reasons: first, it erases the violence of colonial–imperial capital accumulation, and second, it is based on the assumption that all labor should happen in a capitalist marketplace. Such colonizing and capitalocentric paradigms are limiting. Moreover, they propagate a patriarchal, white, Western idea of development—that to live well, we must move along a capitalist trajectory of so-called sustainable development toward high-mass consumption. "Trade not aid" describes a structured development program with rigorous standards for certification and compliance that allow entry into the certified market. "A movement and a market" provides a platform for "nice neoliberalism" (see

Guthman 2007). Finally, the producer–consumer binary creates the producer-subject. Scholarly work uses these narratives to ask if fair trade is working for farmers and to make a space to ask questions about the inequities in economic exchange, yet this scholarship remains grounded in a universalizing paradigm.

Unsettling these false dichotomies demonstrates that a reframing is necessary. Universalizing paradigms neglect the complex and emplaced lived experiences of people and render people and places as apolitical problems to be fixed. The narratives of fair trade are part of the production of knowledge behind what fair trade is, whom it is for, and who gets to decide. If we look only to the dominant discussion, fair trade will be viewed as a capitalist-focused development program that is directed at "marginalized" producers, and the groups of people who get to decide are the executive boards of third-party certifiers. However, if we take a step back and attempt to decolonize and reframe, we can use fair trade as a lens to see the possibilities of economic exchange and new social relations of trade. In the chapter that follows, I pick up the thread of another key narrative of fair trade, producer–consumer linkages. Building from the discussion in this chapter on troubling binaries and problematic narratives, I use the unsettling of these to push past developing "others" through trade, the movement–market dynamic, and the producer–consumer solidarity narrative toward thinking about fair trade in movement and the possibilities of being in common.

October Is Fair Trade Month

For more than a decade now, October has been celebrated as "Fair Trade Month"; similar to other monthlong campaigns in the United States, it is focused on awareness. It was described by Fair Trade USA (2012) on its website as a time when

> ethically-minded consumers, retailers and brands will unite to celebrate and promote Fair Trade. A variety of education events, in-store sampling programs and online initiatives have been planned to help increase awareness and sales of Fair Trade Certified products, ultimately leading to greater impact for farmers and workers in developing countries.

Fair Trade Exploitation and Empowerment 129

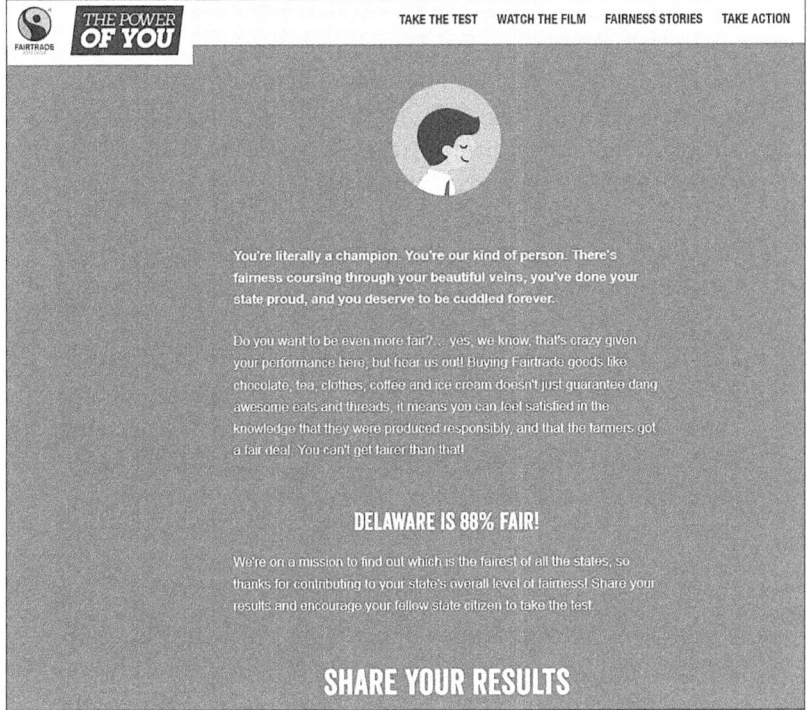

Figure 13. Author results on the 2016 "Fairest of Them All" online quiz.

It is a time for bringing more consumers into the fair trade fold, and third-party certifiers encourage consumers to buy certified products, have fair trade–themed Halloween parties, and engage with fair trade organizations on social media. There are also competitions and prizes for participation.

In 2016, Fairtrade America ran a campaign for fair trade month called "Fairest of Them All," in which consumers were invited to take a test to determine how "fair" they were. The results would then be used to determine which state in the United States was the "fairest" (ultimately, Colorado won). The questions on the quiz were focused, not on equity or just market-based exchange, but instead on etiquette in long lines, how to approach closing subway doors, and whether you might lie about being sick to take a day off of work. Quiz takers were encouraged to take a fair trade pledge, where they could be entered to win fair trade products as prizes.

As I took the quiz, picking out the most logical responses to questions about judgment calls, for example, whether to politely remind someone at the counter of the line behind them when getting breakfast at a coffee shop or upend a granola bar display and storm out in a rage instead. At the end of the quiz, I was applauded on my "fairness" and received a message on my screen:

> You're literally a champion. You're our kind of person. There's fairness coursing through your beautiful veins, you've done your state proud, and you deserve to be cuddled forever.
>
> Do you want to be even more fair? . . . Yes, we know, that's crazy given your performance here, but hear us out! Buying Fairtrade goods like chocolate, tea, clothes, coffee and ice cream doesn't just guarantee dang awesome eats and threads, it means you can feel satisfied in the knowledge that they were produced responsibly, and that the farmers got a fair deal. You can't get fairer than that!

Quiz takers are also reprimanded. I took the quiz again, at the risk of reducing the fairness rating for my state, selecting outrageous responses and triggering a negative result for making "selfish" choices. This time I was admonished for my potential behavior: "You don't believe that the fair way is the right way. You believe there's no 'Team' in 'I.' You're just out to get ahead and you don't care how you do it. That's okay buddy, it wouldn't be 'fair' of us to blame you."

I wondered how this "fairness" metric had any connection with making changes in trading relations and how fair rebels might respond to such inane questions. This kind of advertising prompted me to think about the relationships in fair trade and whom fair trade is for. Fair trade month seems to be a lot of back patting and self-appraisal, which raised more questions than answers for me.

4

Fair Trade in Movement
The Possibilities of Being in Common

The former colonial city of San Cristóbal de las Casas is a rich tapestry of activity and exchange. Quartering the center of the city are two main pedestrian roads populated by shops and restaurants and awash with global expats and tourists. At the conjunction of these pedestrian streets, indigenous men and women traverse the throngs of city-goers, attempting to sell steamed *elote* and *chayote*, handcrafts purchased on credit from larger-scale sellers, and Zapatista dolls, balaclavas, and shirts (whether they are affiliated with the movement or not). At the southern end of the north–south pedestrian walkway sits the Maya Vinic Café. Here coffee that is not export quality is sold. The café (among others in San Cristóbal) is a rare site of local consumption in a coffee-producing region. In this café, in 2012, I sat at a small round table next to a window that commanded a view of both the library and a small church that mark the end of the pedestrian-exclusive component of the street and provided a vantage point of the public area of the café. It was a beautiful space, with a wooden bar and wrapped canvas photos of Maya Vinic members, solidarity delegations, and their roaster partners in the United States.

During that visit, I enjoyed a French press coffee and wondered at any possible discernable difference in the taste of the non-export-grade beans versus the beans from Higher Grounds Trading Company, a single-origin blend called Maya Vinic, that I purchase when I am at home in the states. Reflecting on this experience, I now wonder about who else may come to the café and enjoy coffee; I have a distinct privilege as a researcher who can move in and out of the city fluidly and blend in with tourists. Drinking a coffee in the café, too, is different than the many cups of coffee I'd consumed while visiting *socios* in their homes, enjoying a chat and discussing their participation in various political activities. The coffee I consumed in the company of fair rebels was often roasted *a comal*, boiled over the ever-present cooking fires in the family kitchens, and poured into plastic mugs, often to have sugar heaped in massive spoonfuls thereafter. Throughout my research (and still today), I experience Maya Vinic coffee through multiple forms of commodity relation, participating as a consumer at the far end of the fair trade commodity chain at my home in the United States, purchasing coffee from the café as a participant in the local marketplace, and through a gift exchange as a guest in homes and cooperative offices.

It was at the café that day that I met up with members of Maya Vinic who journeyed into the city on errands for the co-op. They made the hour-long trip in the sole vehicle owned by the cooperative, a rusting and beat-up pickup truck. Together we rode to the main offices of Maya Vinic, and the cooperative members met with the office managers and staff. Following these meetings, I was afforded the opportunity to sit down with one of the city-based staff members to receive an oral history of the cooperative and to discuss fair trade certification and café operations. In the intervening years of fieldwork, I had heard the story of Maya Vinic, of Acteal, of Las Abejas, countless times. However, a bigger picture of the place of the cooperative in their part of a broader struggle took shape through this conversation. Complementing interviews with Maya Vinic *socios*, our conversation began with a discussion of the roots of Maya Vinic, which I was told is bound up in "faith, Christian identity, and peace. You cannot understand Las Abejas without knowing the process of pacifism and evangelization." As discussed in chapter 2, the cooperatives in the highlands grew out of crisis, and it is there that this history was described more broadly and in the context of solidarity connections by the staff member:

> Cooperatives are usually created in the context of a certain future possibility, of a certain hope; the cooperative Maya Vinic was

founded when there was no hope. There could not have been a worse condition and a worse situation than creating a cooperative in a context of war and displacement. . . . There was a desire to form an organization in fair conditions, but then everything else, apart from desire, did not exist. There was no money, there were no resources, there was no room, you did not have anything. . . . It was a very adverse context and, well . . . during the first two years it was a project, it was like a bet, a good intention, but it was not safe, let's say, it was not seen to bear fruit. A lot of it had to do with overcoming the trauma . . . but then, then the fair trade and certifications of organic coffee, we had many solidarity visitors who became clients. . . . And since, there has been great support, and maybe, Maya Vinic, without the fair trade premium might not be able to have such stable relationships.

Maya Vinic, similar to their Zapatista counterparts, maintained solidarity relations through coffee sales. Of course, other solidarity connections exist between the social movements of Las Abejas and the Zapatistas within and beyond Mexico; however, for *campesinos/as* in resistance in the highlands, it is on coffee that long-term relations of exchange are currently predicated.

In this chapter, I discuss the problematic of solidarity and the possibilities of being in common. Producing under the fair trade label assists with establishing important ties to buyers in the United States that allow not only for secure sources of income but also a critical space for information sharing and support for coffee-producing cooperatives, and these relations, I argue, are a critical component of the practice of solidarity in the highlands. Drawing from interviews in the highlands with *socios,* staff of the cooperatives, and U.S.-based coffee roasters, and also from textual analysis of third-party certifier narratives of solidarity, I analyze fair trade relations. I tie these empirical and textual examinations to the efforts of coffee roasters to educate consumers through social media campaigns and a recent documentary. These data sets were transcribed and coded thematically with specific attention to understandings and interpretations of "solidarity" and "ethical consumption." Using the backdrop provided by the previous chapters, here I describe and analyze the ethic of care that is established within the coffee cooperatives and with their U.S.-based buyers. This ethic of care is a key element of fair trade certification that is rarely discussed in the literature and that a diverse economies approach makes space for. Often scholars and activists point to ethical consumption when discussing fair trade economic exchanges, yet the "buy and let live" (Naylor 2018, 1038) foundation for such producer–consumer exchanges is divorced from the goals of movements to make trade fairer, which are concerned with dismantling unequal social and economic relations based in colonial–imperial power dynamics. Here I further explore the idea introduced in chapter 3 of "fair trade in movement," specifically, those processes that have momentum and that take place as part of fair trade economic exchanges but are facilitated by the processes of solidarity and being in common. Inspired by Tyner and Will's (2015) use of Springer's (2012) conception of violence as "moments," I consider fair trade not as a material or singular thing but as a set of multiple and diverse practices and processes that are carried forward by agents in ways that extend from the act of certifying. To identify fair trade as being in movement is to make visible the social relations of fair trade and the actions that take place in excess of production and consumption.

To consider the processes and practices of living well in the context of fair trade exchanges, in the first section of the chapter, I discuss the oversimplification of the fair trade commodity network and zoom out to see the complexity of connection through the exchange of coffee under certification. Understanding that this commodity chain is constructed under the guise of solidarity, in the section that follows, I examine the common trope of producer–consumer solidarity through ethical purchasing and unpack the multiple possibilities of solidarity. In a deeper consideration of the potential contradictions of market-based solidarities, I then delve into the buy and let live of ethically based coffee purchasing, arguing that the articulation of producer–consumer connections is not one of interdependence. Following the longer thread of the fair trade exchange network, I discuss the connections between coffee-roasting cooperatives and coffee-producing cooperatives as possible sites of being in common, and where individual producers fit (or not). Finally, I deliberate the possibilities of fair trade in movement, opening up multiple economic subjectivities and possibilities for interdependence.

Fair Trade Networks

As discussed in chapter 3, fair trade is built on binaries. The strength of the movement–market divide leads many scholars to cast certified trade as "nice neoliberalism" (Guthman 2007) or as a "kinder, gentler form of business as usual" (Lyon 2015a, 162). Yet simultaneously, scholars continue to cast the producer–consumer binary as a form of solidarity relations between a wealthy, ethically minded consumer in the "North" and a poor, marginalized producer in the "South" (Naylor 2014, 2017c). Building on the possible momentum of fair trade in movement, I argue here that these binaries mask the broader networks and social relations of fair trade exchanges and cast a supercilious web of solidarity.

On my first visit to the Maya Vinic bodega in the highlands, I was invited to present my research in a meeting of the leadership with *socios*. On the inside door of the meeting room, I observed a sticker from Just Coffee Cooperative (a U.S.-based coffee roaster) that showed the simplified commodity chain embraced by many fair trade actors. Using pictures from partnering producer cooperatives and the logo of their importing group, Cooperative Coffees, the graphic displayed the following network:

"Just Coffee Product Chain"

Farmer → Farmer Cooperative → Importing Cooperative → Roasting Cooperative → Store → You

Clearly intended for Just Coffee Cooperative's customer (coffee-purchasing) audience, this simplified network diagram shares the same basic story of fair trade.[1] Not only does it leave out additional actors—the chain is shorter, and not just because the *coyote* is absent—but it misses whole nodes in the network and the entanglements of power within the network. My point here is not to suggest any wrongdoing by Just Coffee in their portrayal of the fair trade coffee chain but to address how our thinking more generally on fair trade is simplified through buying into this particular narrative. There is a lack of transparency and democracy within and between the nodes of the fair trade network, something that Mutersbaugh and Lyon (2010) pointed out early on as it relates to so-called ethical commodity chains. This approach speaks to larger debates on the defetishizing and refetishizing of fair trade (see Fluri 2017; Hudson and Hudson 2003; Marston 2013); however, I begin from the premise that fair trade consumption (e.g., for those purchasing fair trade coffee as retail) is not qualitatively different than other forms of consumption, as "looking for the label" requires almost no change in consumer purchasing habits; instead, what I consider here is how we might enlarge our understandings of who participates in fair trade networks and their multiple economic and political identities.

A more nuanced approach shows that under the simplified heading of "farmer," we can enlarge our understanding to consider "farmer" as representing producer households and labor. Generally, it takes a household to produce coffee. While there are restrictions on child labor related to the standards set by fair trade, labor is spread out among family members, and although, in many cases, child labor standards are respected in the *cafetal*, the labor of younger family members is often displaced to the *milpa* or to other household activities, such as gathering cooking firewood or caring for small animals, because the household does not live on coffee alone. In many cases, the more senior members of the family will work in the *cafetal* (and also the *milpa*), and for some families, labor may even be hired during the height of the harvest (although this was less commonly reported among the cooperatives with which I worked). The invisibilization of this labor occurs largely because of the focus on poverty alleviation and the intervention of fair trade to fix producers (Lyon 2015a, 164). However, not only is labor performed across the family unit but the vast majority of this labor is performed by women—an image that aligns imperfectly with those often portrayed by proponents of certification. Such portrayals render static the coffee producer and elide the multiple economic and political identities that may be performed by *campesinos/as* who produce coffee for the fair trade marketplace. Indeed, their labor performed as rebels who have declared autonomy from the state, such as their volunteer work *(cargo)* as members of resistance movements and in rebel autonomous governance, strains their participation in agricultural practices and limits the amount of labor they are able to provide (Naylor 2017a).

The "farmer cooperative" too is not a homogenous entity. In the case of the Zapatista producer cooperatives, their day-to-day practices are mediated by the governing councils of the Zapatista Autonomous Zones (Juntas de Buen Gobierno) and the Rebel Zapatista Autonomous Municipalities (MAREZ), while Maya Vinic may at times be in consultation with the leadership of Las Abejas. Beyond these negotiations, cooperatives have additional levels of leadership, including executive boards, municipal representatives, and staff. The executive board is charged with a number of duties, among them policing their *socios* to determine compliance with the certification standards (both for fair trade and for organic) (on the complex quality of community-based standards policing, see Mutersbaugh 2004, 2005a).

Figure 14. Member of Maya Vinic leadership documenting herbicide use in the *cafetal* of a *socio*. Photograph by the author.

The municipal representatives attend meetings and disseminate information about standards for production and cooperative news. The staff take on various roles, but most importantly, they fill the only paid positions in the cooperatives and wield significant decision-making power; for example, the three *socios* who worked in the Maya Vinic bodega were the gatekeepers for all *socios* delivering their coffee. The intake process for coffee includes determining if it is dry enough to process—any coffee that is not dry will either be purchased at a lower rate (and the bodega workers will use the driveway at the facility to dry it out) or the producer will have to return another day with their dried coffee beans to receive the full price. More than once, I observed *socios* forgo the full price for their coffee and allow the bodega workers to finalize the drying of their beans. Other times, *socios* would dry the beans on the driveway of the bodega using their own labor, raking them out in the morning and returning in the evening to sell them, now dried, at the full price. These power dynamics are driven by standards for fair trade (and organic), which create everyday hierarchies tied to coffee production that did not previously exist, extending the reach of the third-party certifier into the homes and fields of *campesinos/as* in resistance (see also Naylor 2017c).

The importing and roasting cooperatives are also populated by staff and volunteers, who may participate in the fair trade network for any number of reasons and who are also involved in their own social reproduction. Yet they are cast as monolithic entities that exist for the intake, processing, and sale of coffee. It is perhaps this characterization that makes it possible for large corporations, such as Starbucks and Walmart, to sell fair trade coffee and use it as part of their branding but to not claim responsibility for their own workers and labor violations (cf. Wilson and Curnow 2013). By considering any retailer of fair trade coffee as one and the same, the possibility of a community economy forming as part of the fair trade market appears bleak. In the fair trade commodity chain, the roaster and/or retailer is not expected to change its character to participate; the same standards for labor, sustainability, and community development are not placed on the groups in this segment of the commodity chain. Moreover, there is no expectation of performing solidarity or mutual aid beyond the mere purchase and sale of certified goods.

Figure 15. Member of the Maya Vinic bodega staff rakes out and dries the coffee of a *socio* in the driveway of the bodega. Photograph by the author.

Finally, where does the person purchasing coffee fit? This emboldened, ethically minded purchaser of fair trade coffee is portrayed as the actor who provides the glue for the network, who creates the community for the fair trade movement. Yet the coffee purchaser bears the least responsibility for their part in the commodity chain, being told to base their solidarity in the mere purchase of certified, labeled products.

Completely missing from the simplified fair trade coffee commodity chain are the certifiers and governing bodies that set, maintain, and audit the standards for fair trade (and organic) certification. This expansion includes groups such as Fairtrade International and Fair Trade USA as well as FLO-CERT and MAYACERT (Mexico-based organic certifier) but may also extend to other parties. Mutersbaugh (2016) provides a detailed look at these nodes in the certification network, particularly as they relate to the eco-certification of coffee, noting that simplified diagrams mask the dozens of actors, including government and/or financial institutions, that facilitate subsidies or hold accounts for cooperatives (and have their own forms of gatekeeping), and groups that write standards, conduct inspections for entry into the certified marketplace, and hold audits for compliance. As demonstrated in chapter 3, the expanded/simplified network masks significant power geometries at work in fair trade certification. There is a complex set of social relations and different expressions of power that do not flow evenly through this network.

Expanding the simplified fair trade commodity chain assists with showing the distance between the producer of coffee and the so-called ethically minded consumer. Even the portrait that I paint here is incomplete, as other interests (specialty coffee export grading, packaging, shipping, international borders, and so forth) are missed. Nonetheless, zooming out to see what is often missed facilitates deeper considerations of what fair trade is and whom it is for.

The rather messy qualities of this expanded network signal that the ethical spaces of fair trade exchange must be more deeply examined. Often fair trade certified exchanges are offered up as an example of ties that form bonds of solidarity between geographically disparate places and economically polarized groups (such as coffee drinkers in the United States and coffee producers in Mexico). Networks of solidarity that are built through certified trading relationships are critical for fostering long-term connections and knowledge exchange between groups in different places; however, they are also an important site for generating discourse that serves certification narratives of so-called producer–consumer relations. Drawing on the possible forms that solidarity takes in heterogeneous fair trade networks here assists with contextualizing contemporary solidarity in fair trade activism and draws attention to whether fair trade exchanges open up possibilities for being in common.

Solidarity Relations

As discussed in chapter 2, in the same period that Mexican (and global) markets underwent the early stages of neoliberalization, the ICA collapsed, and INMECAFE was dismantled, a "coffee revolution" was under way in the United States. As gourmet coffee consumption was rising in the United States, a growing number of activists were politicizing coffee consumption by advocating for boycotts against oppressive military regimes in Central America and drawing awareness through buying coffee directly from small-scale coffee producers (Bacon 2013). Solidarity networks based in the alternative trade of crafts and coffee (and, later, other commodities) became a critical component of political movements based in the United States working against U.S. imperialism and other unjust political and economic conditions in Latin America (Koopman 2008). Such networks were identified by some scholars as facilitating solidarity not only between producers and political activists (Hudson and Hudson 2003) but also between producers and consumers (Raynolds 2000; see also Arce 2009, who refers to this relationship as commercial solidarity). In chapter 3, I discussed the framing of producers and consumers in a binary that problematically cultivates a "wealthy consumer" and a "needy producer" and urged a rethinking of the subjects of fair trade that is distanced from narratives of marginalization. In making visible multiple economic identities, chapter 3 sets the foundation for having a deeper conversation about the possibilities of being in common and how solidarity relations play out from and through the colonial difference.

Solidarity is a key frame for movements that support alternative trade networks and fair trade in particular. The idea of distributing and purchasing commodities at more equitable prices for the producer was cast early on by many as an act of solidarity between privileged consumers and so-called marginalized producers globally (cf. Bacon 2010, 2013; Hudson and Hudson 2003; Raynolds 2000, 2002; Raynolds, Murray, and Taylor 2004; Raynolds, Murray, and Wilkinson 2007), and this discourse continues to pervade scholarly work on fair trade despite critique (cf. Knapp 2009; Nicholls 2010; Raynolds 2017; Raynolds and Greenfield 2015). Although more recent critiques of fair trade suggest that fair trade standards reproduce consumer interests, early writing on fair trade articulated it as a solidarity network; Raynolds (2000, 306) in particular noted that "by building alternative networks of solidarity between agro-food producers and consumers, fair trade initiatives encourage the participation of disadvantaged farmers." Here it is important to note that the discourses of fair trade deployed by the vast majority of scholars and practitioners are lacking critical geographic and scalar perspectives concerning the place-specific and also multisited fair trade network, instead casting fair trade in those binary terms discussed in chapter 3. To discuss fair trade initiatives for this group is to construct an imaginary of the "disadvantaged producer" and "poor countries" vis-à-vis a "wealthy consumer" and "rich countries." What these discourses and imaginary allow for is a context in which purchasing fair trade goods is described by scholars and practitioners as a wholly positive activity divorced from the complex and messy entanglements of fair trade processes and practices.

In December 2017, I received a holiday email from Fairtrade America thanking me for my support of fair trade, reminding me that "Fairtrade is a global movement that *you* make possible," and encouraging me to visit its website for "ideas for how you can *help* others this season, and facts about how Fairtrade improves lives year-round" (emphasis added). Often consumer interests lie at the center of fair trade, where purchasing practices are based in Western-centric and patriarchal desires for improving the "other" (Lyon 2011; Naylor 2018). These desires stem from fetishized notions that there are forms of consumption that liberate those others (rather than perpetuate alienation and oppression), and largely ignore the colonial–imperial past and present that make possible such exchange relations. Yet, they continue to be described as a way to create links between people and foster solidarity—or at least as a way of portraying to consumers a solidarity economy (cf. Fisher 2013; Polynczuk-Alenius and Pantti 2017; Wilson 2013). But in many cases, solidarity is a foregone conclusion, being described as a way to connect producer and consumer based in ethical purchasing and moral economic exchanges. Furthermore, the market-driven character of such solidarity relations tends to reinforce colonial–imperial tendencies of primary commodity production dependence rather than interdependence and equitable allocation and distribution of resources.

The word *solidarity* is used by third-party certifiers to describe a variety of issues ranging from the social, via interconnectedness of producers and consumers, to the environmental, such as combating climate change (made possible by certification standards), to the intimate, including personal satisfaction in purchasing certified goods and the joy it brings consumers (cf. Gould 2003). Certifiers describe solidarity as a way for consumers to "empower" producers. A press release from Fair Trade USA offered this quote from one of its wholesale buyers: "we are aiming to help people consume healthier, higher quality food while standing in solidarity with the global poor . . . the poor want jobs not handouts"; the CEO of Fair Trade USA concurred, "American consumers have so much power, and they want to use that power for good" (Fair Trade USA 2013).[2] Embedded in the neoliberal market, to purchase a commodity at a higher than market price is devised as a solidarity relationship—even when the price of coffee on the international market is the same as the fair trade price (as it has been for the vast majority of the past thirty years).[3] Fair trade pricing does not represent a substantial burden for the retail purchaser. However, the price for *campesinos/as* in resistance is a critical component of being able to maintain a subsistence-based lifestyle and not be forced to shift to being full-time commodity producers. Yet, certification is formulated as part of an international entrepreneurial and empowerment tool kit that enables farmers to build businesses and develop their communities and this formulation consolidates knowledge about what fair trade is.

To reiterate, fair trade certified exchanges allow for actors participating in retail fair trade exchanges to pay a higher price, which is viewed as being in solidarity with imaginary producers seeking to empower themselves (and their communities) through increased participation in the market. Yet this viewpoint is mismatched with producer desires in rebel autonomous communities, who participate in fair trade markets as part of cultivating dignified livelihoods as subsistence producers and political actors seeking autonomy through resistance. They are not interested in capturing a greater market share or becoming business owners; for fair rebels, the production of coffee is part of earning cash income and, more importantly, a key component of maintaining the visibility of their resistance. The leadership of the coffee-producing cooperatives are clear on this point, as will be discussed in the latter part of the chapter. The transnational networks create a space for dialogue, not just about coffee, but about autonomy and indigenous rights—in one conversation with the leadership, I asked if they saw problems with the struggle for autonomy and whether coffee helped. The treasurer replied, "Yes, it is a connection and a little bit of money and we can drink our own coffee then." The connection is the linchpin of this economic relation, which differs from imaginaries of "helping" "poor" farmers by buying any brand of any coffee at any retailer. Thus what solidarity is and how it is understood differ dramatically throughout the fair trade network.

Such a characterization of solidarity and ethical–moral economic exchanges ignores the entanglements of power and messy realities of "being in common" (Gibson-Graham 2006b) and how the heterogeneous economic and political identities and daily realities of coffee producers limit the forms that this "participation" can take. Drawing on Nancy's (1991) considerations of being as "being-with" and Agamben's (1993) "community as being, as solidarity," Gibson-Graham identify being in common as a path toward multiple and diverse economic subjectivities. More than this, too, being in common encompasses an ethical responsibility for being together, for existing together and occupying the same spaces (from the scale of the body to the global scale), between humans and earth others. Such relations are built from connective ontologies and trusting relationships (see Lawson 2007; Popke 2006). It is a hopeful space that opens up the possibilities for a politics of belonging and mutual aid. For it is not enough to promote economic well-being; we must also consider social (Gibson-Graham 2006b, 83) and ecological well-being, as well as the political practices and ethics that shape it. To be in common requires more from us as citizens of the same planet. A piece of this ontological puzzle is tied to economic exchanges and the outcomes of our decision-making and knowledge production as participants in these exchanges. A fair trade purchase is considered ethical and a way to demonstrate solidarity. Yet, how does solidarity function as a component of economic exchange? Are consumers buying their way into solidarity through ethically minded purchases? Are consumers paying coffee importers and roasters to perform solidarity on their behalf? Such questions raise others about the social spaces that are created through fair trade exchanges, interdependence in economic exchange, and what solidarity means in this context. Fair trade third-party certifiers articulate very particular economic subjectivities that are tied to solidarity, which constrains the possibilities for belonging and mutual aid.

Solidarity is a slippery concept intimately related to concepts of progressive political struggle and activism. Marco Arruda of the

Brazilian Solidarity Economy Network stated at the World Social Forum in 2004,

> a solidarity economy does not arise from thinkers or ideas; it is the outcome of the concrete historical struggle of the human being to live and to develop him/herself as an individual and a collective...innovative practices at the micro level can only be viable and structurally effective for social change if they interweave with one another to form always-broader collaborative networks and solidarity chains of production–finance–distribution–consumption–education–communication. (cited in Warren and Wollard 2016)

Here I am not examining fair trade as a solidarity economy per se but as a potential space of solidarity tied to the social relations of economic exchange. While not explicitly defining solidarity, I am considering it as site of social activism or political participation aimed at creating change, which is often associated with the idea of an individual or a collective movement being "in solidarity with" another group. The preceding quotation illustrates that the practices and processes of cultivating solidarity must be multiple and intertwined and that they are inextricably bound to the production of knowledge and the co-creation of production–consumption networks.

Historically, solidarity movements in the Americas were tied to awareness campaigns and to protesting South and Central American dictatorships and military regimes in the 1960s–1980s, as well as to actions supporting historic grievances regarding land tenure and social inequities in the region (Sundberg 2007). Such groups attempted to give an international voice to those whose voices were being stifled in their own countries (Keck and Sikkink 1998, cited in Sundberg 2007). A number of solidarity movements formed in the 1980s and 1990s in the context of resistance and struggle in places such as southern Mexico and Colombia (e.g., International Service for Peace, the Mexico Solidarity Group, Colombia Support Network) (Sundberg 2007, 148).

Solidarity is practiced in varied ways, through boycotts, sit-ins, demonstrations, being present, accompaniment, and information dissemination, and more recently, it is articulated as something that people can deploy on "behalf" of others through purchasing power. Yet solidarity is also characterized as creating "subject–object relationships," "speaking for others," or taking on the role of a "helper" (Koopman 2008; see also hooks 1992). There is a particular whiteness to "helper" forms of solidarity that entrench the help offered or provided in long-standing and unequal race relations that position white bodies as helping bodies and brown bodies as recipient bodies. Indeed, Koopman (2008) and Sundberg (2007) alike point out the neocolonial tensions in so-called North–South solidarity. Working with anti–School of the Americas activists in North America, both Koopman and Sundberg observe that activism is sometimes understood by activists as being done on behalf or for the benefit of "others" (something that is demonstrated by the statement of the Fair Trade Advocacy Office noted in chapter 3). These solidarity groups are often dominated by white, middle-class women (not unlike me) who exercise their power as "good helpers" (Koopman 2008, 283). Both Sundberg and Koopman argue that solidarity relations may sometimes reinforce existing inequalities and work to concentrate imperial power.

Solidarity (in the context of social movements) is defined as a practice by activists who "seek social change or the transformation of power relations for the benefit of others" (Passy 2001, cited in Sundberg 2007, 147). Scholars seeking to better understand solidarity define it as "political struggle" (Featherstone 2012, 5) or "working for social change" (Scholz 2008, 56) to make visible and mitigate oppression and/or suffering. Koopman (2008, 294) contends that "in the U.S., international solidarity is focused on people particularly affected by U.S. imperialism. Ideally this is so that we can better struggle together, combining our different points of leverage to end U.S. empire and build a better world for all of us." Consistent with the concern that unequal power relations persist even within solidarity networks, Koopman is primarily arguing that activists (and scholars) should not identify themselves as taking on a helping role and as working on behalf of others but instead create a network of mutual support. What I suggest here is that solidarity does not mean the same thing to all actors within the certified fair trade network and that broader research and scholarship on fair trade that focuses on consumer–producer linkages and ethical purchasing falls into

Koopman's critique of "helper solidarity." This helper solidarity is something I call the *buy-and-let-live* mentality of fair trade consumerism, which I argue is not mutual aid, or interdependence, but is instead dependent on the continued existence of disparity.

Although such helper forms of solidarity underlie so-called consumer–producer linkages, as I discuss later in this chapter, fair trade certification offers connections for producers, to a cooperative and potentially to the third-party certifier, the importer, and, in the case of coffee, the roaster. If this economic practice fits in the community + economy model as Gibson-Graham et al. (2017) infer, then how can we understand exchanges of coffee in fair trade certified networks? Ultimately, in cultivating community economies, questions about life and livelihood are intended to prevail over those of wealth and accumulation. If, as Gibson-Graham, Cameron, and Healy (2013, xiii) suggest, "our economy is the outcome of the decisions we make and the actions we take," what manner of relationship are we to have through coffee? In their earlier work on reframing the economy, Gibson-Graham (2006b, 79) point to fair trade networks as sites where economic relations are resocialized. A diverse economies framing recognizes fair trade networks as potential sites of community economies and being in common, yet the interdependence and care among the actors within these sites appear uneven; as argued by scholars critiquing fair trade, these exchanges *are predicated on the existence of a marginalized producer* (cf. Manokha 2004; Naylor 2014). Gibson-Graham et al. (2017, 15) argue that "in a community economy what gets negotiated is how all parties (including nonhuman others) are affected by the process of exchanging goods and services inside the market and out," yet further attention to the messiness of these exchanges and the power imbalances within them is necessary. A community economy is meant to be a space that opens up possibilities for considering how people throughout the exchange can live well. In the following section, I examine the asymmetries at work in cultivating fairer trade.

Buy and Let Live

If fair trade exchanges are cast in a solidarity shape, what does it mean when that solidarity is tied, as in the case of fair trade, to product purchasing and neoliberal market relations? There is a muddled intersection between fair trade activism, individual consumer purchasing of fair trade certified products, and people who straddle the line as wholesale buyers of certified products who are engaging in a market exchange even as they attempt to uphold the ideas and integrity of movements based in social justice organizing and allyship.

Solidarity in certified fair trade coffee networks as portrayed by third-party certifiers is part of an imaginary of so-called North–South relations that unquestioningly situate a "Northern" consumer as the "helper" of a "needy" "Southern" producer (Naylor 2014). Again, where these imaginaries sit is a key component of the geopolitics of knowledge. The buy and let live of ethical consumerism is reliant on the third-party certifier, the label, and the brand. Differences exist between the actors in these exchanges: the community formed between the coffee-producing cooperatives and the coffee roasters—where the roasters and producers attempt to attach a deeper set of social relations to place and to struggles for life and livelihood—and the community created by third-party certifiers that connects them to their "Northern" consumers and encourages them to use their purchasing power for "good."

The argument that the "helper" form of solidarity often leads to neocolonial practices is an interesting jumping-off point for considering the social relations of fair trade. Drawing on Anderson's (1983) concept of the imagined community—where it is "imagined" because it is impossible for everyone to meet, however, everyone feels that they are part of a whole—Lyon (2011, 181) argues that advertising in fair trade "unevenly unites producers and consumers"; such advertising provides a "fair trade mirror in which consumers' fantasies about producers' lives are reflected back to them in their coffee cups." The very images that are linked with fair trade producers, and that adorn the walls of coffee shops or coffee bags, provide a seeming proximity of a community centered on the exchange of coffee, while simultaneously perpetuating an idealized and homogenous group of producers. Fair trade purchases are considered sites of ethical and informed decision-making; however, such sites of consumption effectively romanticize and commodify the producer (Naylor 2014; Varul 2008). Longtime fair trade scholar and advocate Raynolds (2017, 175) perpetuates the mythology of fair trade as an imagined community, arguing that "Northern consumers may come to align themselves with Southern producers creating an 'imagined community' (Anderson, 1983) of 'global citizens . . .' or 'citizen consumers' (Micheletti, 2003) . . . who play a central role in bolstering fair trade's progressive potential." However, Raynolds further notes that the role of the consumer is privileged and that this role can reproduce imbalanced power dynamics unless it is also used to support the desires of producers.

The very existence of fair trade certified exchange is based in cultivating a particular imaginary of coffee production (small scale, sustainable, fair wages, community development, producer empowerment). This imaginary comes not only from advertising but also through price setting and standards for production and community development. The fair trade certification label becomes the site of decision-making for the person purchasing certified coffee, while the practices and performance of this exchange place the burden on the producer and producer cooperatives to meet standards for production and development. Simultaneously, the increased number of third-party certifiers and products dilutes the meaning of the label. As noted in chapter 3, fair trade labels serve to defetishize and refetishize coffee production (cf. Fridell 2007a, 2007b; Lyon 2006; see also, on ethical trade, Freidberg 2003; Guthman 2007; Varul 2008), providing images that allow nonproducers to capture a generalizable idea of what may lie behind their cup of coffee, while also masking the actually existing conditions of production under fair trade standards and the particulars of place where their coffee originated.

Fair trade exchanges are predicated on unequal relations between a "consuming North" and a "producing South," which effectively calls on an ethical commitment by a "wealthy consumer" to purchase commodities from an "impoverished producer" (Naylor 2014, 277; on the "reinforcement of difference," see also Lyon 2011, 181). This practice, too, is tied to specific attempts to manage and control the behavior of producers and their cooperatives through standards for community development (Lyon 2011; Naylor 2014, 2017c). As part of their participation, those purchasing coffee are enfolded into an imaginary producer–consumer community whereby their perceived participation takes place not only through imbibing coffee but also through its purchase, improving the daily life of their extended "community" of producers, which now reaches beyond an individual producer family, across and through the homes and fields of distant others. Simultaneously, and opaquely, *campesinos/as* in resistance push back against the box that consumer imaginaries draw around them, utilizing certified production as one piece of a larger struggle to live well (Naylor 2017c). For example, the fair trade premium may be used in ways that assist with stabilizing efforts for maintaining autonomy, such as financing a community-based shop or water project.

The reality of how exchanges happen disrupts the discursively organized imagined community between individual coffee purchasers and coffee growers. Consumer practices of purchasing and ethical, informed decision-making fall on the margins of fair trade networks. Consumers are not dependent on any particular producer for either their coffee or their ethical purchasing. Their performance is bound to purchasing a gourmet or luxury item that could come from any number of possible producers.[4] Moreover, the "life and livelihood" (community economies) versus "wealth and accumulation" (capitalist) measure within this so-called producer–consumer solidarity is asymmetrical, meaning very different things for disparate groups. As noted in chapter 1, when discussing what *socios* thought of fair trade, we often talked about price. In 2012, one *campesino* remarked to me that "this year it is a really low price. . . . If we need to buy something at the store or medicine the price keeps increasing, but the coffee price does not go up." In the fair trade exchange imaginary, one group is using their accumulated wealth to facilitate the life and livelihood of another group. The purchase of coffee at a premium tends not to create financial strain on the part of the purchaser, yet the greater share of income being retained by the producer tends to allow them to stand in place financially.

If being in common is premised on seeking possibilities for building equity and interdependence, then the asymmetrical relations of fair trade exchanges appear antithetical. This result does not come as a particular surprise but is instead consistent with seeking to understand economic exchange in its multiplicity and fluidity—or how possibilities are opened up (or not) for overcoming uneven relations. Cameron (2015, 54), drawing on Gibson-Graham (2006b, xv), notes that "far from an idealized image of the world, negotiating these interdependencies and building community economies is understood as involving 'struggle, uncertainty, ambivalence, and disappointment.'" Again, this reflection points to there being no one right way to construct a community economy, although it begs the questions, Disappointment for whom? How can we reconcile "helper" forms of solidarity, which require very little action from coffee purchasers, with creating community economies and the possibilities of being in common, which require interdependence and mutual aid? What I suggest here is that the asymmetrical relations between the individuals making an ethical commitment to support fair trade certification through coffee purchases and those who are cultivating coffee and negotiating its sale as part of the fair trade certified marketplace point to these struggles, uncertainties, ambivalences, and disappointments. At the same time, these relations also demonstrate multiple meanings and understandings of being in common and broaden the foundation for rethinking power relations within sites of diverse economies. So, even as I critique the so-called producer–consumer solidarity relations of fair trade and raise questions about fair trade as a form of community economy, I want to simultaneously open up the opportunity for thinking about different communities and power relations that exist on the fair trade spectrum. This opening up is an important component not only of thinking from the colonial difference and destabilizing the geopolitics of knowledge but also for recognizing praxis. To do so, it is critical to consider, as Walsh (in Mignolo and Walsh 2018, 28) notes, "embodied practice from the ground up" by those "who live the colonial difference" and how they understand their own practice and participation. Returning to the discussion in chapter 1 on "withstanding suffering" is one way to think against the imaginaries of solidarity that reinforce unequal power relations. To be a *campesino/a* in resistance, a fair rebel, is an embodied practice that is firmly grounded in ontologies and epistemologies otherwise. The varied economic identities that are taken up by *campesinos/as* in resistance are one avenue for reframing (which will be expanded on in chapter 5). To identify difference and praxis is to undertake the challenge to think with (not just about), to be in solidarity with (not just to "help"), in such a way that reduces the limiting forms of knowledge production that are constantly at work (Wynter 2003; see also Mignolo and Walsh 2018) while also moving from reflection to action.

Concentrating on how producers experience solidarity is an important distinction, as many scholars and activists in the wake of the 2011 Fair Trade USA–FLO split and the mainstreaming of fair trade were concerned with how to maintain consumer solidarity. Such concerns are matched against attempts to "stay true" to the core values of movements to make trade fairer despite the changes in standards and the growing corporate involvement in fair trade commodity networks (cf. Dolan 2010; Getz and Shreck 2006; Howard and Jaffee 2013; Jaffee 2014; Jaffee and Howard 2010; Low and Davenport 2007; Wilson and Curnow 2013). To understand the contrast between the relations of economic exchange in the fair trade certified network and building solidarities and possibilities for being in common, in the next section, I analyze the efforts of the cooperatives that are connected through coffee-based economic exchanges.

Connected by Coffee

In considering who constitutes the community in the community economies at work in fair trade exchanges, an examination of multiple sites of solidarity is key. If the solidarity that is generally celebrated as part of fair trade exchanges is that between producer and consumer, yet it is mediated through the third-party certifier and the contradictory character of buy-and-let-live purchasing, then how are we to understand activism against "unfair" forms of economic exchange? I suggest that other nodes in the network provide an opportunity to consider community and the possibilities of being in common. In attempting to understand what it means to build solidarity or to create economies predicated on interdependence and/or being in common, it is important to examine who is being enlisted in these projects and how. While there exist tensions and entanglements at each node in the larger network, the messy reality of building community + economy is also a hopeful space, as relations predicated on social justice activism and solidarity continue to be generated through knowledge exchange. These exchanges make evident that groups of people are actively considering the exchange relations that they want to foster, yet power dynamics still exist, and the processes of being in common take work. The relations between fair rebels, coffee-producing cooperatives, and coffee-roasting cooperatives provide a space for opening up some of the bigger questions on fair trade and assist with further identifying cracks in the fair trade model.

Following the divorce of Fair Trade USA and Fairtrade International, a growing concern of fair trade coffee roasters was how to distinguish themselves from "business as usual." A number of groups, including small-scale coffee roasters, members of producer cooperatives, and advocacy organizations (such as the Fair World Project), attending the Specialty Coffee Association of Americas Meetings in 2012 explained that they wanted to emphasize and publicize their commitment to the "real fair trade" in the immediate aftermath of the split. There were a series of responses from groups in the United States that remained committed to the principles of making trade fairer (e.g., addressing structurally uneven relations of trade). One such response was a reflexive moment on the part of two coffee roasters who launched a one-thousand-mile tour through Central America. This journey, called the Fair Trade Chronicles, was driven by the question, "has our work really helped coffee farmers?" (Earley 2013). The two representatives were Matt Earley, cofounder of Just Coffee Cooperative (Madison, Wisconsin), and Chris Treter, cofounder of Higher Grounds (Traverse City, Michigan); both of these roasters purchase coffee from the cooperatives with which I worked in the highlands.

When asked about their connection to coffee, both discuss social justice and solidarity. In the case of Treter, Higher Grounds was begun explicitly out of a desire to create what was envisioned as a solidarity network with Maya Vinic. Likewise, Just Coffee Cooperative, where Earley is based, was founded to purchase coffee grown by Zapatistas in Chiapas. Neither roaster existed until a partnership was struck in the highlands to create a connection through the exchange of coffee. I focus on these relations as they tend to resemble exchanges that appear differentiated from singular capitalist exchanges. The relationships forged between the roasters and producer cooperatives cannot possibly reach every coffee producer, as the producer cooperatives have members across dozens of community locations; however, the Chronicles were an attempt to extend personal relationships beyond the leadership of the coffee-roasting and coffee-producing cooperatives. It is already custom that the leadership of the cooperatives (producer and roaster) work closely together throughout the year, creating sites of economic, educational, and cultural exchange, which may take many forms beyond establishing a sales contract, such as facilitating visits to the United States for coffee producers, negotiating a price bump in addition to the market or fair trade price, providing information and on-the-ground observation of diseased coffee plants, and providing opportunities for diversification of production.

The Chronicles, which feature Earley and Treter, were the site of blogging, social media posts, and short videos, and their culmination was a documentary film, *Connected by Coffee* (Dennis 2013). As I detail more in the sections that follow, in these spaces, stories were told by the roasters and the cooperative producers, hardships of fair trade certified cooperatives were examined, and hard "truths" about the reality of fair trade certification were confronted by the coffee roasters. The Chronicles and the documentary follow Treter and Earley as they travel to meet cooperative leadership and dialogue with producer members on a trip from Chiapas, Mexico, that extended into Estelí, Nicaragua. The documentary promises to show how coffee changed from "a tool of oppression to a tool of empowerment" (Dennis 2013). The start of the journey in the highlands of Chiapas showcases Maya Vinic and begins by introducing the audience to a *socio* and his ten children. The case of Maya Vinic is then used to explain the benefits and drawbacks of cooperative smallholder production and coffee production practices under fair trade certification. It is a story told from the perspective of the filmmakers and through the eyes of the coffee roasters. The outputs of the Chronicles and the documentary were ultimately directed at the people purchasing coffee, as a way to distinguish the differences between those groups who are committed to making trade fairer and to establishing lasting relationships built on trust and toward mutual aid and those who participate in market-based relations, which rely on the narrative of the certification-based fair trade movement. Yet these sites of storytelling were also potential sites for reclaiming interdependence along different nodes in the coffee network by confronting the messy realities of fair trade coffee exchanges.

For the roasters who participated in the Chronicles, it has "never been about coffee." It is about building long-term relationships based on respect, dignity, and equality and forging solidarity between grower cooperatives and roasters. What came from this trip, from their conversations with coffee producers, was an acknowledgment that fair trade does not work as it was intended to (Earley 2013). It has not "lifted people out of poverty," facilitated "community-wide development," or "connected producers and consumers." It does not address the very agenda that is continuously heralded by proponents of fair trade. If fair trade exchanges have not met the broader goals of the movement, why continue to have such exchanges? Why continue to participate? If we only look to fair trade certified exchanges as regulated commodity sales in a capitalist market, if we do not look past wealth and accumulation, if we only rely on a "helper" form of solidarity, then fair trade will always fail to meet the expectations that have been set; it will always be—harkening back to Gibson-Graham's discussion of alternatives—a "disappointment."

Both Earley (2013) and Treter (2013) contributed social media posts reflecting on their experiences. While they both consider their positionality and their intent, it is important to acknowledge that not unlike myself (an educated white woman), as educated white men with funding/salaries and networks of care at home, they are both in a privileged position to be able to travel in and out of the communities from which they purchase coffee. The ability to make a documentary to capture their stories alongside producer stories and the ability to shape the narrative are also important (if uncomfortable) positions of power. In a follow-up conversation reflecting on the Chronicles, Earley reiterated to me that it was not always a "feel good story." He explained that the impetus for the Chronicles was

> having been in the industry for almost ten years and really wanting to do a qualitative assessment of the work. When I would visit farmers and it was disappointing to see that there weren't major changes in terms of how farmers were living and it didn't match up with pulling farmers out of poverty.

What he and Chris began to see was that they could pay double or even triple the market price for a pound of coffee and it would not change the structural conditions that delegitimized the lives and livelihoods of *campesinos/as*. I also spoke with Treter after the release of the documentary, and he concurred, offering that "no matter how much coffee we sell for Maya Vinic they are still going to be in poverty." The thinking they established during that trip was not new—both Higher Grounds and Just Coffee made the choice not to be certified fair trade in the mid-2000s because of the lack of representation by producers and, as Treter remarked, because they found that "fair trade was nothing but a capitalist structure that placed constraints on grower groups and gave opportunities for capitalist companies to sell a product, not to change the world." Although both Treter and Earley purchase their coffee through Cooperative Coffees at prices at or above the fair trade minimum, neither roaster works with third-party certifying agencies. The ultimate impact of the trip for Earley was the recognition that what they were doing beyond purchasing coffee from these groups, the relationships they established and the friendships they continue to make had become a crucial piece. Earley related this, saying,

> What we came away with was, it's not that farmers are getting so much more money, a fair price, because as an objective measure it is not a fair price—every farmer said that to us—but there are other merits that are part of how we're approaching our relationships and the partnerships we have with the farmer cooperatives we visited and that led to the strengthening of the On the Ground Initiative. That trip was important because we still have these connections, even if the coffee goes away.[5]

What fair trade coffee exchanges highlighted in the Chronicles demonstrate is that in an effort to create more just forms of exchange, it cannot just be at one site (e.g., coffee, a label, a project); there must be a set of multiple and diverse interactions. Treter believes that the time for market differentiation is now. He explained,

> Right now we live in a moment in time where storytelling that ties back to farmers is a huge piece. . . . The inspiration and the

struggle, it is something that people would be riveted by, but there is so much more that we need to be doing to tell an authentic story. I think this is where the opportunity lies, but only when you have authentic relationships.

These ideas suggest that we must ask questions about the type of economic exchanges in which we want to participate, about how we want to bring meaning or not to our economic practices and performances. The economic exchange that prioritizes life and livelihood over wealth and accumulation is more likely the one between the coffee-growing cooperatives and the coffee roasters. These groups establish relationships, co-create knowledge, tell stories, and share food and, of course, coffee. Although power and privilege still create distance between these groups, these exchanges speak to a politics of the possible and provide an opportunity to consider what being in common could start from. As the producer cooperatives struggle to remain visible under threat, sharing their stories through the sale of coffee is one strategy. As the coffee roasters seek to participate in a movement for change and justice, they also build relationships with coffee-growing cooperatives. Their reflexivity points to an identification of the failures of both free and fair trade, and rather than a romanticization of certification as it is used as a platform to facilitate solidarity relations, rather than being bound to the market for fair trade, they articulate a fierce activism around making trade fairer. Although these actors may not describe themselves as enacting economic difference, I argue that these exchanges suggest, at least, a possibility for thinking through fair trade differently and, at best, a recognition that there is no one right way, no universal solution, only multipronged strategies for trying to create livable worlds.

As the Chronicles unfolded and were shared by Just Coffee and Higher Grounds, the importance of the connections between Maya Vinic, as an organization seeking recognition not solely in the marketplace but more importantly in the human rights arena, was discussed (see Treter 2013). Following the Massacre at Acteal, international human rights activists descended on Chiapas, and over time, coffee growers in Acteal were accompanied into their fields so that they could harvest their coffee with less fear of violence. This was a part of "overcoming the trauma" discussed by the Maya Vinic staff member at the start of this chapter. Similarly, as the Zapatistas became connected with human rights activists during the period following the uprising, and especially as part of the negotiations of the failed San Andrés Accords, they maintained the possibility of growing food and harvesting coffee. Eventually, with the creation of coffee-producing cooperatives in the late 1990s, *campesinos/as* in resistance found a space for their product that was more secure than selling to the *coyote* or enabled them to depart from cooperatives populated by *partidistas*. Following the trade relationship initiated with the U.S.-based importing group Cooperative Coffees, rebel coffee became available to roaster members in the United States. Both Higher Grounds and Just Coffee bought Maya Vinic beans as part of their initial purchases through Cooperative Coffees and continue to be the primary purchasers of Maya Vinic coffee. Both roasters also purchase coffee from cooperatives run by Zapatistas. All three U.S.-based organizations maintain websites and social media outlets, which privilege the stories of the producer cooperatives and make visible the everyday threat that exists for fair rebels in the highlands.

In the past, both roasters have branded and sold in packages blends such as Just Coffee's Mexican-origin Solidarity Blend and Maya Vinic exclusive packages, including Maya Super Dark and Higher Grounds's Mexican Maya Vinic. Maya Vinic's coffee is not blended into obscurity; it is placed front and center for retailers and coffee purchasers. In the years following the uprising, there were coffees available as Zapatista Coffee, and such roasts can still be purchased through NGOs such as Schools for Chiapas. That their coffee is being sold not with a story of better wages and livelihoods but with a story of resistance and struggle distinguishes it. It is not generalizable and made homogenous with other coffees sold under the fair trade label but instead connects the coffee to a specific place and a specific group of people. This relation is what motivated the *campesino* to tell me that their "coffee sends a message" (see chapter 1). Contemporary exchanges originating in rebel Chiapas are not unlike early exchanges within the fair trade movement, where groups such as Equal Exchange and other independent/small roasters imported Nicaraguan "solidarity" coffee (see Bacon 2013). As detailed in chapter 3, there is still a strong emphasis on making trade fairer, and that traces of early origins of the movement for fair trade linger within the fair trade marketplace demonstrates that there are multiple ways of being in common within the world and that they persist.

The recognition that connecting through coffee makes their struggles to build livable worlds visible speaks to a process of becoming, of being in common and opening up economic identities. The connection here is not simply between a buyer and a seller but between groups in the United States that are attempting to disrupt conventional trade relations and make trade fairer and groups in Chiapas seeking visibility and security to sustain their lives and livelihoods. Treter believes that through storytelling, the commodity chain narrative is flipped on its head. For Higher Grounds, the producer is the guide through the messy and entangled relations of the commodity network. These narratives take a step away from what Treter called "victimizing the producer." He continued, arguing,

> If we can tell the story in an inspiring way then we are all inspired. We all go through struggle, each and every one of us at some point, our lives take a turn. Everyone has hardship and pain and everyone struggles and has resilience. From this standpoint these stories can contribute to everyone's well-being.

At a time when violence continues to displace people and when international interest turns to other places, the connection to the coffee buyers in the United States is deemed crucial to producer cooperatives for maintaining the visibility of their struggle. The production and sale of coffee is a critical link in international solidarity networks.

Another component of solidarity experienced by producer cooperatives connected to Higher Grounds and Just Coffee through their broader fair trade network is the facilitation of *campesino/a*-led projects. As discussed in more depth in chapter 2, a development plan is a requirement for fair trade certification with Fairtrade International. This plan is intended to improve producer organizations and their surrounding communities. Yet it is difficult for fair rebels to put into practice because of the fractious and oftentimes violent politics in their communities (Naylor 2017a, 2017c); the relationships with the coffee-roasting cooperatives provide an alternate means for facilitating projects, such as infrastructure projects.

Projects that are successful, such as the Chiapas Water Project, are those which are facilitated through outside donations (not from the fair trade premium) gathered by Just Coffee and Higher Grounds and disseminated through the nonprofit On the Ground Initiative.[6] These projects are considered successful largely due to their development in conversation with producers and completion in communities that have a majority membership of coffee producers who are aligned with Las Abejas and the Zapatistas. For example, in a project designed and completed in a community north of Chenalhó called Aurora Esquipulas, which is featured in the documentary *Connected by Coffee*, the nonprofit assisted one hundred families (sixty claiming membership in Las Abejas) in gaining access to spring water through a system of water tank reservoirs (Dennis 2013; Treter 2013).[7] The fund-raising for this $7,000 project was done in the United States, and according to the nonprofit, the story of Maya Vinic and Las Abejas was told and retold as a way to solicit donations. However, consistent with the ongoing politics in rebel Chiapas, Earley explained to me that there have been tensions around the use of the water and who is responsible for upkeep. Nonetheless, he further commented that the model for On the Ground is that the project must come from the people and as part of community dialogue. He continued, "We don't want a bunch of gringos to go down and build something that will fall apart in a few days; it has to be a groundswell from the community." Members of producer cooperatives can put in applications for funds, and then there are meetings to receive community buy-in. A favorable scenario is not striving for an idealized community development project but one that Earley states is an opportunity to bring community members together in spaces that are "otherwise separated by politics, economics, or religion." Such relations are not experienced evenly across communities, in producer spaces, or by those purchasing coffee. Solidarity between the coffee-roasting and coffee-producing cooperatives extends well beyond the buy and let live of coffee purchasing; however, as I stated earlier, there are still power relations at work. The ability to make funding, contract, and other decisions that impact producer cooperatives establishes a hierarchy—that it is done in consultation with producer cooperatives, though, is an important component of establishing possibilities for interdependence. Another tension is the experience of the coffee producer and/or coffee-producing household, who may never come in contact with roasting cooperatives and who rely primarily on relations with their cooperative, as *socios*.

Producer Cooperatives: The "Window to Better Money"

Solidarity relations between the cooperative and the roaster/retailer are generally only visible to producers through the tangible benefit of income. While fair trade certifiers extol the solidarity relationships facilitated through certification, the producers' connection within such relations is obscured. In interviews with cooperative leadership and with *socios*, price and availability of money was consistently referenced as the most important part of fair trade.[8] The (then) president of Maya Vinic explained to me:

> When Maya Vinic was first started there wasn't any money, it was just a place to sell your coffee. Now there is a fund, which allows us to pay when coffee is delivered. Before, if we didn't have the money right then, sometimes people would go and sell to the *coyotes* so that they could get cash right away.

The price and money relation remain a key part of the connectivity between many producers and the cooperative. When asked about the benefits of belonging to a fair trade cooperative, the responses I received from the *socios* were generally tied to the price. One *socio* claimed, "Fair trade is good for the *socios* because it is *más tranquilo* [calmer], you don't have to go and look for a buyer, the cooperative buys and the price is better than the *coyote,* who robs you." Critical to gaining a better understanding of farmer relations to fair trade solidarity is that the overall connection expressed by the *socios* is with the cooperative, not with their buyers or, as some scholars argue, with consumers. In this estimation, fair trade certification is not part of the equation. Put differently, the meaningful relations and exchanges detailed in the previous section are largely between the cooperative leadership group (the five democratically elected positions) and the coffee roasters (in this case, Treter and Earley).[9] For the nonleadership *socios*, the relationship is not with the roaster but with their production cooperative. Not only does this create an additional breakage in the producer–consumer linkage imaginary but it demonstrates the messy relations of fair trade exchanges and where power imbalances lie in the broader fair trade "community." As stated earlier in this chapter, certification and cooperative structure create power relations within the producer cooperatives as the leadership make decisions on behalf of, and police, cooperative members.

One afternoon when returning by truck to the bodega after a meeting in town, the leadership of the cooperative stopped to pick up a *campesina* and her children who were walking along the road. In the course of the conversation held in the back of the truck, I learned that she was a member of Maya Vinic and that she had hoped to receive an early payment for her coffee because her family needed money to buy medicine. Her husband was diabetic, a chronic condition requiring medicine year-round. When we arrived at the cooperative, she received a small amount of cash from an emergency fund the cooperative has set aside for such purposes. This incident speaks to the connections that *socios* have with the cooperative (and not with certification per se), yet it also points to the struggles of trying to live well while producing coffee, which is seasonal. Fair trade certification, and the sale of coffee more generally, does provide a safety net for producers; however, it does not provide a year-round, stable income and instead acts as more of a seasonal stopgap measure.

Other year-round needs, such as educational opportunities, are also more likely to be linked to the cooperatives or the political movements that *socios* are a part of (rather than expressed as an outcome of fair trade certified sales). An ongoing discussion during the years of my research focused on the desire of Maya Vinic to open their own education facilities to serve their members. There are very few schools in the highlands, and the schools that do exist are run either by the government (although they are understaffed and often closed) or by the Zapatistas. Some are able to travel to Zapatista centers to attend school; however, as part of their practice of resistance, families (for the most part) do not send their children to the government schools. Many *campesinos/as* in resistance are able to send their children to school at some point, but going to school is expensive and often requires travel costs. In a visit with a family who are members of Maya Vinic, I had a chance to discuss this reality. In this family, the elder son was currently in school, the second son was working in the *milpa*, and the eldest daughter had just finished primary school (in her teenage years) and wanted to continue to secondary school but had to wait until her brother had finished because there was not enough money to send them both at the same time. The leadership of the cooperative is well aware of these issues, and the establishment of a school is something that the leadership of the cooperative began to discuss with their members in 2012.

Other *socios* highlighted the importance of the cooperative, especially in the aftermath of the height of violence in the highlands. Following their experience under threat and as refugees, one *campesino* in particular noted, "We were displaced people, my family between 1998 and 2001 because of the violence, but we came back to our place and we joined our organization [Maya Vinic] and began producing again." The principles and solidarity connection of fair trade does not factor into the importance of the cooperative for the majority of the *socios* with whom I spoke. The existence of the cooperative is the main concern of the producers:

> Our organization is good, because even though the price changes in the world we have our price of Maya Vinic and we have the cooperative and the organization, which is better and it is much better than the *coyotes*.

When discussing coffee production under fair trade certification, it often came to price and the ability to have someone to whom to sell. The coffee-growing cooperatives may have solidarity relationships with the coffee-buying cooperative and their member roasters, but for the most part, the *campesinos/as* have a relationship to their cooperatives and to a consistent price—the "window to better money" discussed in chapter 1. This distinction is important because *socios* see the trade-offs in entering the fair trade marketplace as a change in labor, trade, and community relationships as they relate primarily to price and the ability to receive cash on delivery of coffee. The ability to sell at the price set for the season is directly connected to their ability to embody a fair trade certification performance, whereby, based on fair trade standards, for example, they exert more labor in the daily maintenance and upkeep of their *cafetales*, they must bring their coffee beans to the bodega for inspection and sale, and, as members of a certified cooperative, they must participate in the "betterment" of their product. Most of these demands do not exist for producers *libres* (independent), who sell to the *coyote*. The connections forged through fair trade relations are less of a focus for producers; their connection is more to the cooperative to which they sell.[10] Notwithstanding this relationship, still many *socios* are unable (or unwilling) to meet the requirements of the standards.

On the day that I took the photograph of a member of the leadership documenting the use of herbicides in a member's *cafetal* (see Figure 14), I asked questions about why producers would not follow the fair trade standard. On our way to investigate the coffee plot that was reported to the leadership for being in violation for using chemicals, I learned more about Maya Vinic's policies. If *socios* are found to be using chemicals, they will have to wait two years before they can sell to the cooperative again and then three more years before they can sell at the organic price. After walking around the plot and taking photographs, we discussed why some families may undertake this practice even if it is against cooperative policy. "Maybe they don't want to clean [weed] the *cafetal* or they don't have time, or they have more chemicals left after using them in the *milpa* and decide to use them here." Another *socio* who joined us for the inspection made a similar claim: "there are many who use chemicals, maybe because they don't want to use the machete or because they don't know that it's bad. Or it was given to them and they were told to use it." As part of what became a larger conversation about member practices, we also considered why independent producers might not join a cooperative. A leading reason is that Maya Vinic and the Zapatista cooperatives are exclusive to members of their rebel movements (although this changed for Maya Vinic, which currently also welcomes Zapatista members and others not affiliated as *partidistas*). Yet other cooperatives selling under fair trade certified labels exist in the highlands (as noted in chapter 3) that producers not affiliated with the autonomous resistance movements could join.

The *socio* who had documented the policy-infringing plot surmised that *campesinos/as* who chose to be *libres* did so because of the trade-offs around labor and policing: "maybe because they don't like the regulation, or maybe because they don't want to do all of the things you have to do to be part of a cooperative." While cooperatives may be a space for establishing sites of mutual aid, fair trade complicates this relation.

Producers are not unaware of what fair trade certification is—in fact, some producers told me that fair trade was not something that they generally concerned themselves with; for example, one *socio* noted, "We don't think about fair trade, we don't talk about it very much"—and across my discussions, *campesinos/as* in resistance often lamented to me that fair trade is not really "fair." Indeed, it seems that the claims third-party certifiers make about improving the lives of farmers are not, in reality, tied to fair trade certification but to their participation in a cooperative. Being a *socio* has historically been beneficial for producers in Mexico more broadly and is not a unique claim for third-party certifiers in this case (cf. Jaffee 2014; Martínez-Torres 2006; Stephen 1997). Additionally, *socios* describe the hardships endured as part of participating in the fair trade certification system, such as the additional labor and time needed to comply with standards—hardships that beget very little return.[11]

The processes of being in common continue to be messy. There is an inherent and deeply ingrained idea of development, of "improving the lives of producers," that is perpetuated through fair trade discourses. Evidenced in recent communiqués from Zapatista leadership, such discourses are examined in Zapatista cooperatives (coffee and otherwise) as they seek to challenge capitalist unevenness and power relations head-on. Since the establishment of the Escuelitas (Little Schools) on autonomy and resistance (2013), a new examination of what the Zapatistas call the "capitalist hydra" is under way. This investigation is part of thinking from below about economic instability and corporate power, never-ending war and violence, as well as the environment and ecological destruction. It is an attempt to struggle against the many-headed monster depicted at the end of the introduction to this book (see Figure 3). However, such resistances and processes of tearing down and rendering visible multiple economic subjectivities remain imbalanced. There continue to be relations of power and privilege that infiltrate and filter through the nodes of the certified coffee network that constrain and complicate producer efforts to build livable worlds. The market for fair trade emerged in a neoliberal context that signaled troubled times for small-scale commodity producers—neglecting that troubled times for indigenous groups are ongoing and tied to the five-hundred-year war on indigenous people. That the impact of a neoliberal restructuring began to permeate communities that had not been "withstanding suffering" for more than five hundred years further demonstrates that advocacy and allyship on the part of those who may be the beneficiaries of white supremacy and the patriarchy (of which white women are a significant group; see hooks 2000) is a "helper" form of solidarity that perpetuates colonial–imperial relations. The market for fair trade is an unlikely space to create interdependence and dignified livelihoods, something that activism and solidarity toward fairer trade are poised to address.

Fair Trade in Movement: Toward Diverse, Secure, and Dignified Livelihoods

As Borowiak et al. (2018) note in their study of solidarity economies, when moving beyond localized and grassroots efforts to networks that cross social divides, solidarity can be hurtful if it is not inclusive and tied to mutual aid and action. It is not enough to make claims of empowerment and interdependence without directly addressing the systematic, structural oppressions and deeply entrenched racial and class inequities. However, even when solidarity organizing attempts to be attentive to such issues as part of participation in broader fair trade networks, in some cases, it is compromised. Wilson and Curnow (2013) conducted research with student activists who participated in the Fair Trade Campaign on college campuses and who reported that their efforts to work in solidarity with producers ended up being used as free labor by third-party certifiers to recruit more potential fair trade consumers. After months and years of organizing and running awareness campaigns, many students began to see troubling paradoxes in the certification market, as third-party certifiers such as Fair Trade USA urged their student activists to promote new partnerships with Walmart, Coca-Cola, and McDonald's (Wilson and Curnow 2013, 575–76). Such reflection underscored important questions scholars have asked about the efficacy of market-based solidarity relations (see Guthman 2007; Lekakis 2012; Low and Davenport 2005). Arguments that fair trade purchases do not nominally stand outside other market interactions (Naylor 2018; Polynczuk-Alenius and Pantti 2017) and instead serve to commodify producers and facilitate "helper" forms of solidarity require a rethinking of social justice activism and the movement to make trade fairer. As Koopman (2008) articulates, drawing on Lorde (2003), solidarity activists have used "helper solidarity" as a master's tool to attempt to bring down empire; however, she states that "this master's tool is toxic. When we use it we may appear to take tiles off of the master's house, but we unintentionally reinforce the foundations, the systems of domination that prop up empire" (299). Fair trade certification as a market-driven approach to address the failings of free trade emulates the incisive critique of solidarity relations Koopman offers. Yet, consistent with Koopman, I do not intend to identify a right or wrong way to *do* solidarity but instead point to the possibilities of solidarity in economic exchanges. Moreover, opening up this possibility is a way to identify difference across and within space and to break down global-scale hierarchies that position a "wealthy Global North" and a "needy Global South" and recognize multiscalar privileges. There remains the danger of romanticizing and even fetishizing the resistance of fair rebels if deeper inequalities are not addressed, however.

What if we were to consider activism around being in common and solidarity through interdependence and mutual aid? Looking to the failings of solidarity and activism through the lens of fair trade, it is crucial to step back and reflect on what the perceived underlying foundation for solidarity is/was. Although messy and uneven, the solidarity project of coffee roasters was clearly delimited by seeking peace and justice in cooperation with fair rebels and has perhaps transitioned to a more brand-focused "solidarity in difference" (see Goodman and Herman 2015, 142) in the wake of the changes made by third-party certifiers and the mainstreaming of fair trade products. In reflecting on fair trade solidarity more generally, it falls cleanly into universalizing and capitalocentrist projects of development. A reconsideration of movements to make trade fairer outside of universal narratives of capitalism is crucial.

As discussed in chapter 3, there is a significant division between capitalist, market-oriented fair trade certification and social justice–focused movements to make trade fairer. It is important not only to move beyond the problematic binary of movement and market (or the imaginary of fair trade being in and against the market) but to push against the paranoia of neoliberalism and universalizing tendencies of being subsumed under or organizing against a monolithic capitalism. Fair trade exchanges began on the premise that trade was unequal and that the unevenness of trade exchanges disproportionately impacted particular groups of people—primarily raw material and commodity producers. Fair trade, thus, assisted with raising questions about the form and function of economic exchange and opened up spaces for establishing an ethic of care in trade and attempting to be in common as humans and consumers of global, environmental resources. However, setting up fair trade as alternative or in opposition to capitalism reduced its radical potential and allowed market-driven certification initiatives to exploit movement-based discourses of social justice and equity. I suggest that we begin to see fair trade "in movement," recognizing the multiple and diverse identities of actors throughout the nodes in the larger network and allowing for a divorcing from the ideas of fair trade as alternative to capitalism. Instead, seeing movements to make trade fairer as connected to pluriversal ideas about how to live well and build dignified livelihoods creates possibilities to understand and support the economic difference that Gibson-Graham and other scholars point to as already existing and, in some cases, thriving.

In identifying fair trade in movement, I intend to imply a momentum for change. The idea of cultivating fairer forms of exchange seems to have become stalled by universal ideas of development that place people on a similar trajectory toward high mass consumption. Such universals are mired in contradiction, as they are deployed to fix people in both time and space, rendering them static on this trajectory, even as they are exploited to fuel the movement of privileged others along a narrowing capitalist consumption path. A diverse and community economies approach to making trade fairer does not obviate the need to engage those messy and entangled power dynamics that exist within these larger networks. But even as multiple economic identities are recognized, it must additionally be recognized that we are all also in the process of becoming. This piece is crucial. It is a demand that we must make upon ourselves and others so that we stay in movement and do not affix an identity to others but instead allow such identities to be fluid—to break away from the notion that fair trade activism means promoting and consuming products made by "poor and powerless" people in some arbitrary regional/global space—on the edge of being pejorative—called the "South." Instead, we can consider fair trade as a site of mutual aid and interdependence whereby we work in solidarity "with" to challenge inequities, which may be tied to any number of oppressions (not neoliberal capitalism alone). In undertaking this task, the difficult work of recognizing the ways that the economic subjectivities written onto bodies reinforce oppressions and colonial–imperial power relations and the everyday complicities of some groups is essential (see Naylor et al. 2018). Fair trade in movement means not just breaking down inequitable systems of trade but breaking down universalizing systems of economic exchange and opening up to multiple and diverse economic exchanges and identities.

For social justice activists attempting to be in solidarity with *campesinos/as* in resistance, such as coffee roasters Treter and Earley, this means gathering others into the fold. For Earley, it is not just about getting people to buy and consume the coffee sold by Just Coffee—that is simply a way to start the conversation. The certified market has simplified so-called fair trade so it can be distilled to a label, but Earley argues that this oversimplification relieves the customer from having to think about their purchase. He explained, "If we're really interested in changing the detrimental things about commodity exchange, we have to ask people to change their behavior, and just looking for a brand is not changing their behavior." Fair trade in movement means drawing others into the social relations of economic exchange; it proposes enlarging the community of people and earth others in the community economy. As St. Martin, Roelvink, and Gibson-Graham (2015, 9) note, "community economy refers to a praxis of coexistence around which economic decisions are negotiated and made." To think about fair trade in movement as a possibility for building community economies means to move away from the institutionalization and possible co-optation that many groups experience as they try to gain legitimacy while filling in the hollowed-out state.

To recognize already existing practices of fair trade in movement, I spoke with Earley about how Just Coffee attempts to negotiate the privileges and power that their roasting cooperative has vis-à-vis their customers and the producers from whom it buys. The self-reflexive moment of the Chronicles and the work with On the Ground is one aspect, but Earley expanded on these activities, arguing that the exchange of coffee (whether certified or not) had to be about more than a brand or a certification label:

> [We] have to find ways for the consumer to engage in more meaningful ways than just seeing the symbol—it can be a way to interact, not just with the product but with the place and doing information gathering about the projects and making actual connections to farmer communities and having relationships with the farmers. That way the community we are in here [Madison] isn't so disconnected. A bag of coffee can't stand for what they wish commodity exchange looked like, there has to be more. It's not some nebulous decision here, it is directly affecting these people, directly. We create opportunities for customers to visit farming cooperatives and we also bring farmers to Madison and we go all over town in the community to build the connection. There are different ways to do it—they are all still a little bit messy and awkward, but . . .

Such activities and considerations for how to live well form a critical component of the ethic of care that is necessary in practicing a community economy and making attempts toward being in common. It provides an avenue for considering social relations and the character of the interactions we want to have in economic exchanges. Additionally, it makes a space for opening up economic subjectivities and identities. Fair trade in movement implies working toward equity in socioeconomic relations at multiple sites. It is also a space of reflection—for Earley at Just Coffee, it is about "critically examining what we're doing; this isn't failure, it's a success, to reassess and think about how we can do better." For him, the idea of fairer trade is not to put all people on the universal trajectory to high mass consumption; it is about addressing imbalances in economic exchanges and about "shifting resources around." Treter, at Higher Grounds, sees an opportunity to transform the supply chain, to "actually make it a *value* chain." And this signals possibilities for working toward interdependence and mutual aid.

Considering fair trade in movement shines a different light on the questions of what fair trade is, whom it is for, and who gets to decide. If we critically reflect on economic exchanges as potential sites of solidarity and ask difficult questions about what it means to be in common, we open up sites not just of disappointment but also of hope and possibility. Querying what fair trade is through the kaleidoscope of fair trade in movement makes it multiple and pluriversal—it means that it is defined by the way it is practiced. It also enlarges the community of participants by reflecting on how we might participate in the market and considering whom fair trade is for—if it is about changing the social relations of trade, fair trade in movement diverts us from the universalizing narrative of fair trade being for "disadvantaged producers." To think about fairer trade and social justice activism aimed at creating equitable exchanges is to reconsider fair trade outside of universals and binaries. To consider fair trade in movement is to consider multiple ways of knowing, practicing, and performing economic exchange. In the next chapter, I examine the different ways that *campesinos/as* in resistance are creating livable worlds through embodying and practicing multiple economic identities as part of their pursuit of autonomous resistance.

"Organized Coffee against the Wall"

The U.S. presidential election of 2016 reinforced a heinous truth: that the country remains deeply divided and that for all apparent victories in celebrating difference, racism, sexism, heteronormativity,

Figure 16. Interzone Collective Coffee, March 16, 2017. Published as part of a Zapatista communiqué "La primera de varias" (The first of many) and featuring artwork by Chilean painter Beatriz Aurora. Screenshot by the author. http://enlacezapatista.ezln.org.mx/2017/03/16/la-primera-de-varias/.

and the consolidation of class power remain strong. In one of the most visible affronts captured by the reality television show that masquerades as the forty-fifth presidential administration, the president promised a border wall at the southern border of the United States. And in 2017, he promised that Mexico would pay for it. Never mind the fact that there are already substantial border barriers constructed strategically along the border and their uses are few—yet, they serve as a reminder of the racist and xenophobic tendencies of U.S. immigration enforcement and as a way to direct would-be immigrants into more dangerous sites of crossing. At the end of February, there were clashes between the presidents of Mexico and the United States over the financing of the wall. In early March, the Zapatistas responded.

A communiqué, "La primera de varias," was released on their website on March 16 declaring the new campaign of "Facing the Walls of Capital: Resistance, Rebellion, Solidarity, and Support from Below and to the Left." Subcomandante Galeano (née Marcos) and Subcomandante Moises issued a joint statement explaining that the *campesinos/as* in resistance in coffee-producing areas across Chiapas were pooling together their coffee and that they would process, roast, and distribute it to solidarity groups to assist with the struggle of immigrants in the United States and those fighting the border wall. They organized to bring the coffee together, and they urged those who are organizing in the United States to use the coffee to finance their efforts.

They reminded those who are working in solidarity to "always remember that one must resist, one must rebel, one must struggle and one must organize," and they ended by making their meaning plain with a very simple "Fuck Trump!" This original communiqué emphasized organization and solidarity, and it explained the impetus behind creating a mutually supportive network. A second communiqué on April 30, 2017, "Café organizado contra el muro" (Organized coffee against the wall), drew out the campaign more clearly. In the words of Subcomandante Moises:

> So we started to remember the year 1994, 1995. . . . At that time we asked civil society, in Mexico and around the world to help us. So we started to say: we think that now it's our turn, that we have

to support them, just like the people in solidarity who helped us because they saw we were in struggle. It's also up to us to support these communities, to tell them to struggle with resistance and rebellion. Because they have no other option. . . . So we began to shake out our pockets: we don't have euros, we don't have dollars, we don't have anything. But we discovered that we do have the results of the collective work of the communities.

According to them, "this Zapatista coffee has the best taste if you drink it struggling."

5

Resistance as Agricultural Practice
Rethinking Food Sovereignty

Sometimes the complexity of activities, affiliations, and solidarity relations felt to me as though they were vast and stretched over an endless network in which *campesinos/as* in resistance maintained nodes. Although I went to the highlands to learn about fair trade coffee production as a site of indigenous resistance, what I continued to learn about were the processes of building dignified livelihoods and sites of mutual aid. In 2012, I participated in a meeting of Maya Vinic members and a group that was visiting from Europe to learn more about the coffee-producing cooperative and provide support for the struggle of members of Las Abejas. Over the few years I had been in the highlands conducting research, I saw the cooperatives of fair rebels receive many guests from outside of Chiapas. In most cases, the encounters would begin with coffee—whether it was a tour of a *cafetal* or, in the case of Maya Vinic, the bodega, where they store and process coffee for export. However, the sharing of coffee and coffee production served solely as a beginning point as guests were taken to visit other sites of cooperative production, such as honey, or shuttled through the *milpa*. On one occasion, I sat at the end of a table set for twenty and shared soup, handmade tortillas, and sweetened coffee while members of the cooperative explained how they were organizing to build livable worlds. They described the violence, their displacement, their desires to have many hands to move forward and to have justice.

Speaking in Tzotzil for the benefit of the group and translating to Spanish for the guests, one *socio* explained,

> Here, our community has had much history of conflict and problems, and it is too long to tell the whole history. We have had many difficulties, but the support of organizations and solidarity groups and the church has been important. Our brothers and sisters have helped us to be a cooperative. We have our papers and our certification of organic and fair trade and they exist because of the hands of many and the support of many. We work collectively.

It was during this meeting that members of Maya Vinic reflected on the start of the cooperative, explaining their displacement and the need to exit from other coffee-producing cooperatives (as described in chapter 2). As signaled in many other conversations, the start of Maya Vinic was not an easy process: "There was much that was needed, there are problems with production and it can be difficult to be a producer at times . . . the conflict makes things a little complicated to discuss." But in this meeting, *socios* continued to exhibit the importance of their collective efforts and resistance:

> They say that it is with the support of many hands that things are made better. We are always working and we are glad to tell you about it. We are working in our production and with the cooperative and we are glad that people are listening and that we are not alone. It takes many hands to move forward, but we want to work on our land and maintain our families. We have risen from being a displaced people. With this word, we will move our hearts to do the things we need.

As they continued to discuss their work, they did not idealize their struggle, instead noting that "there is a lot of sadness here. . . . After 1994 it became more complicated because of the violence." Always, though, it came back to working together and struggling for solutions.

After that meeting, I spent time traveling around with a U.S.-based NGO that had brought a group from the United States to visit

Zapatista support bases. Each of these visits made visible the multiple activities undertaken in the highlands, embodied practices (from making tortillas to weeding *cafetales*) to social performances (from cultivating new forms of solidarity to having an audience with the Zapatista government council). I reflected on these activities, and in conversation with one of the NGO staffers, I remarked that the most radical thing about *campesinos/as* in resistance is that they want to maintain a subsistence lifestyle and largely disassociate from the high mass-consumption way of life that is associated with so-called developed countries. One of the NGO staff responded, highlighting the less visible aspects of rebel autonomy: "and the government is actively and violently trying to keep them from doing so." Yet, if I reconsider my earlier thoughts, it seems less a radical act of resistance than the practice of an economic identity that is not captured by neoliberal capitalist paradigms of development.

Campesinos/as in resistance are reclaiming and redefining their economic identities through their struggle. Although fair trade coffee production is a key site of cash income, it is not, as discussed in earlier chapters, the way that fair rebels define themselves. To resist, to "withstand suffering" (as discussed in chapter 1), is to co-create economic exchanges in ways that support struggles for autonomy and the right to live as indigenous peasants. Again, this points away from capitalocentric narratives of development and progress that rely on universal paradigms of how to live well. As noted in chapter 3, the struggles of *campesinos/as* in resistance are complex, and the practices that are pursued in the highlands bring potentially contradictory and competing strategies for building dignified livelihoods. A core component of the efforts of fair rebels toward autonomy is cultivating the *milpa*, however, producing coffee under fair trade standards creates competition for labor, land, and other resources (Naylor 2017c). Fair trade production complicates the daily activities of *campesinos/as* in resistance; however, it also creates sites of solidarity and knowledge exchange that are important for generating momentum around change, such as making visible multiple economic identities and practices that are being deployed, not in the service of a universal paradigm of development, where producers are expected to use commodity trade to "lift themselves out of poverty," but instead in the service of their struggle.

Participation in the fair trade marketplace is one component utilized by *campesinos/as* in resistance in efforts to build livable worlds. As noted earlier, participation in the fair trade market provides cash income and connections to the cooperative and transnational solidarity networks, and through these activities, other possibilities for building dignified livelihoods emerged, such as the shop run by Maya Vinic and the opportunities for training the next generation of fair rebels at the bodegas. While there is no one right way to live or to build these worlds and knowledges otherwise, a core component for fair rebels is their agricultural practices and the ability to grow the food they need to have secure livelihoods. In many cases, scholars might refer to this practice as striving for "food security," which is generally defined in terms of economic access to food. However, in the context of resistance in the highlands, I examine the efforts of *campesinos/as* in resistance as potential sites of food sovereignty, which is more concerned with rights to land, resources, autonomy, and food. In chapter 2, I discussed the discourses of development that position indigenous peasants as "backward" and in need of "improvement"; here I analyze the role of the peasantry in enunciating multiple and diverse economic exchanges as a way to deconstruct this narrow framing of the "peasant" and create possibilities for thinking about multiple economic identities and practices that may be tied to a range of places and scales.

As detailed in chapter 2, if fair rebels are defined solely as peasants, this framing renders them static. Moreover, it limits *campesinos/as* identities emplacing them in their subsistence livelihoods as a site to be fixed by the capitalist marketplace. However, the diverse and multiple identities of peasants cannot be reduced to noncapitalist and subsistence practices; the peasantry is a relation (see Wolford 2010). Fair rebels offer an example of how peasants globally are always in the process of becoming. The experiences of *campesinos/as* in resistance shed light on how, through struggle, people build and sustain economies within and across scale, ranging from the household to the international coffee commodity market.

In this chapter, I make a departure from the zoomed-in focus on fair trade economic exchanges by zooming out to the other activities and struggles that *campesinos/as* in resistance face as they assert their autonomy from the state and state-led development, while also attempting to maintain their subsistence-based livelihoods. Resisting universal (and neoliberal) paradigms for how to live well is, in many cases, tied to the agricultural production practiced by fair rebels. For this reason, I attempt to read the diverse practices and knowledges at work in the highlands through the lens of food sovereignty in this chapter. It is important to note that although I use the term *food sovereignty* to describe the actually existing (see Gibson-Graham 1993) practices of negotiating multiscalar food systems from self-declared autonomous spaces in the highlands, this term is not one that I heard used by *campesinos/as* in resistance. Instead, I reflect on observations and discussions with fair rebels about efforts to build secure livelihoods, the forms that these efforts have taken, and how their experiences might be drawn on to better understand the possibilities of diverse economic exchanges as part of working toward food sovereignty. Drawing from food sovereignty literature, with a particular focus on practice, and using interview data and notes from extensive participant observation in the highlands, I examine new ways of thinking about food sovereignty and resistance. These data sets were transcribed and coded thematically with a specific focus on "resistance," "autonomy," and "food sovereignty."

Fair trade and food sovereignty, as discussed by scholars, may in practice contradict each other as fair trade certification continues to support neoliberal markets and development and food sovereignty is tied to a democratization of the food system (see Bacon 2015). Yet, drawing from chapter 4, the possibility of fair trade in movement presents potential sites for "being in common," which incorporates multiple forms of exchange, livelihood, and mutual aid. A key thread that ties this chapter to the others in this book is in reframing the way that we think about economic exchanges and identities. In this case, I pull this thread through the book in considering what it means to live well, through practicing agriculture and other cooperative activities as part of resistance. To ground this conversation, I begin the chapter by examining why thinking through food sovereignty assists with breaking down universal forms of knowledge. To facilitate this analysis, I discuss the issues identified by fair rebels in their agricultural practices, as participants in the fair trade market, and within their struggles to resist. A deeper discussion of how food sovereignty is articulated follows this section, beginning by examining struggles to build secure food systems with scarce resources. I then reread these practices through an analysis of food sovereignty as a mechanism for creating livable worlds. After considering the possibilities of food sovereignty, the section that follows provides a closer look at the economic identities of *campesinos/as* in resistance that extend beyond their subjectification as fair trade coffee producers. Finally, I return to where fair trade production fits (or not) into these attempts to build dignified livelihoods.

Building Food Sovereignty?

In the previous two chapters, I described the complicated and messy character of fair trade exchanges highlighting the neoliberal and universalizing role of certification and the market for fair trade coffee, while also underscoring the solidarity relations and processes of being in common that the relationships built in the contexts of fair trade exchanges can foster. Again, I reiterate that coffee remains an important agricultural product for *campesinos/as* in resistance; however, as one *campesino* described it, "you can't eat coffee." And, so while I focus much attention on what forms participation in fair trade exchanges takes, it is important to flesh out the underlying food production that makes possible the resistance of fair rebels, because ultimately, the identities of indigenous *campesinos/as* are shaped by being producers and consumers of corn.

The leading reason that I identify fair rebels' agricultural strategies as both multiple and competing is largely due to articulations of resource scarcity made by *campesinos/as* with regard to land and labor. A key issue that fair rebels face as peasants seeking dignified livelihoods and secure access to food and agricultural resources is land—something that is not unique to them but that is faced by peasants globally. However, in the case of the highlands, the struggle for autonomy vis-à-vis government efforts to privatize peasant lands (namely, through PROCEDE) is a distinguishing factor (see chapter 2). Land is a significant issue for *campesinos/as* in resistance, and to understand how fair rebels are moving toward dignified livelihoods, it is crucial to recognize the way that they have gained access to and maintained their territory. As discussed in chapter 2, one of the main outcomes of the 1994 uprising by the Zapatistas was widespread land seizures.[1] The invasions by Zapatista supporters (and other nonaffiliated peasants) were met with great protest on behalf of wealthy landowners, and many people who had seized land were duly evicted between 1994 and 1998 (Bobrow-Strain 2004). However, a number of *campesinos/as*, both Zapatista and otherwise, managed to maintain their claims to territory, and the negotiations that took place between the government and indigenous leaders in 1996 (San Andrés Accords) assisted with a large-scale and unprecedented redistribution of land in Chiapas. As Bobrow-Strain (2007, 4) explains in work examining landowner responses to land invasions in Chilón, Chiapas, as a redistribution that was aimed at reducing conflict in rural areas of the state, "land tenure in Chiapas underwent a rapid repeasantization and reindigenization rather than privatization and concentration." Invasions and subsequent land redistribution assisted *campesinos/as* with maintaining communal forms of production through newly established (or enlarged) *ejidos*, gaining access to key resources, and provided a territorial basis for their resistance against (some) neoliberal reforms.[2]

However, access to scarce material resources, such as land, water, and tools, continues to create conflict in self-declared autonomous communities (Naylor 2017c). When discussing the efforts of the government to privatize *ejido* lands and what it meant for the communal production of corn, one *campesina* disclosed to me that despite the redistribution of land in the 1990s, "the government still attacks us in many ways, through our resources, through the schools, in the fields, in many ways." She reflected on these attacks as another component of efforts to "withstand suffering" that have been ongoing for five hundred years but that are punctuated by the lies of the state. The redistribution of land was premised on uneven access to resources and a long history of indentured servitude and violence against indigenous peasants on large estates; PROCEDE and other forms of government intervention in the highlands were rather a reinstatement of colonial–imperial relations within Mexico. While fair rebels had originally worked to persuade the state to guarantee their rights to land and resources, they now work peacefully to ignore state and market processes that seek to remove them from their land and ways of living. Their declaration of autonomy is one piece of this, but their continued designation of land for coffee production, participation in global markets through fair trade, and subsistence corn production cannot be dismissed.

While *campesinos/as* have long recognized that there is a finite amount of land, after declaring autonomy from the state, access to land has transitioned from being a demand on the state to a critical component of maintaining their resistance. As I discussed in chapter 2, the distribution of land continues to be unequal in Chiapas, with the vast majority concentrated in large landholdings held by individual landowners or corporations. In an interview, a *campesino* who is a Zapatista agroecology promoter (educator) for the autonomous municipalities in the highlands remarked to me that a key problem in the highlands with growing food was that, as he described, "there just isn't a lot of land . . . and so we have to be careful with the land and with the water, we have to conserve the water, the forests and the land." Not unlike other *campesinos/as* in the region (regardless of political affiliation), many *campesinos/as* in resistance with whom I spoke relied on the millennia-old polycultural *milpa* production system involving corn, beans, and squash. In the highlands, there is only one harvest per year, yet *campesinos/as* work most days in their fields maintaining their most important staple food, corn (except Sundays, which are "for rest"). Successful and self-reliant agricultural systems are a critical component of resistance for fair rebels, and as a result, gaining access to and maintaining productive land is a way to "withstand the suffering" that is described as part of the "war of five hundred years" for their right to exist as indigenous peoples. To use their land well, *campesinos/as* adopted agroecological methods in both the *milpa* and the *cafetal*. These practices tend to be organic and range from individual plant management and successional cycling of crops and forest to composting and complex intercropping of plants, trees, and woody perennials. These are radically different approaches than the methods deployed to gain efficiencies in monocultural production of corn and coffee, which is chemical dependent and reliant on government subsidies. In discussing how an agroecological approach was practiced in the highlands and in the context of resistance, I asked questions about daily practices. These questions prompted answers about agroecology being an approach of "daily work." In one case, it was explained to me that the daily work of agroecology was work "toward the land and the house." This *campesino* explained that the house was not just about the structure but, more holistically, was "a concept that is bigger than you and where you live. It is your family, your water, your food, your land." For this *campesino* and others, it was about using the land well to give and take, to provide and replenish.

These methods form part of the sustainable and organic agriculture that continues to be developed within rebel networks; production practices established throughout the network are exchanged and filter from global fair trade solidarity networks into the *milpa* and *cafetal*, and back again. These sites of production (and also food storage) are also sites of knowledge production, as are the networks in which fair rebels participate through their fair trade exchanges. Discussing how these knowledge exchanges take place as part of participation in cooperatives, *socios* in Maya Vinic pointed to their new macadamia trees and their *colmenas* (bee boxes for honey production). The impending threat of *La Roya* (the rust) and the possible damage it may wreak in *cafetales* prompted the coffee growing and roasting cooperatives to discuss ways to diversify production.[3] Interchanges between *campesinos/as*, with agroecology educators (both within and outside the Zapatista and Las Abejas movements), and with solidarity groups are places where knowledge about production is exchanged and co-created. Ultimately, though, many *campesinos/as* with whom I spoke agreed that without corn, there is no life, no resistance (see Naylor 2017a). The ability to grown their own corn is an essential element of their autonomy and indigeneity. It is not only a matter of not having to purchase corn; it is more than a financial issue. Family- and communally grown corn is food, but it is more than that to the "people made of corn." For fair rebels, corn, and native seeds, are multiple.

These agricultural production and knowledge exchange systems demonstrate that not unlike elsewhere, peasants forge creative local and transnational mechanisms for asserting their right to a livelihood within the constraints of a neoliberal marketplace that views peasant production as a barrier to economic development (see also Akram-Lodhi and Kay 2010a, 2010b; Martínez-Torres and Rosset 2010; Ploeg 2008).[4] That this work to diversify production and develop life-sustaining forms of agriculture is done in the context of struggle is something that is made more visible by thinking about agricultural production outside of capitalocentrism. Food sovereignty narratives draw attention to imbalances in food and agricultural systems from the site of the body to the global, while also making visible peasant and smallholder production. Attention to food sovereignty has accelerated over the last decade, yet mobilizing it proves to be messy. Here I draw on food sovereignty to reread the agricultural practices of *campesinos/as* in resistance and consider how we might understand food sovereignty through alterity and grasp its "ways of knowing" (Trauger 2017, 32).

Articulating Food Sovereignty

As noted earlier, food sovereignty is viewed as a potential site for resisting neoliberal capitalism. However, in considering putting food sovereignty in practice alongside fair trade, the governance systems, market mechanisms, and push for growth within fair trade certification run contra to the principles in food sovereignty, which are tied to a radical agenda for change (Bacon 2015, 485). Returning, though, to the idea of fair trade in movement (see chapter 4), the processes and practices of being in common potentially align with the broader goals of democratizing food systems and facilitating opportunities for peasants to be more food secure. In this section, I consider a holistic approach to understanding how food sovereignty might be practiced in this context. Trauger (2017, 17) notes that "food sovereignty narratives identify modern notions of property rights and global capitalist markets as the source of problems in the food system." This assessment highlights the need for thinking differently about how land is accessed and about how agricultural resources and knowledge are allocated, distributed, and exchanged.

The concept of food sovereignty has been taken up by social movements, state governments, nongovernmental organizations, and civil society more broadly, becoming a critical narrative for assessing the global politics of agriculture. For advocates, the promise of an alternative food system is especially provocative at a time when food is identified as a major factor in global geopolitics (Brown 2011; Essex 2012; Trauger 2014, 2017). Food-related riots and violence reaching from Egypt to Haiti in 2007–8 exposed long-standing problems with industrial–capitalist production–consumption systems.[5] Arguing that democratic control of the food system is an important step in constructing viable alternatives, many posit food sovereignty as a promising solution (Desmarais, Wittman, and Wiebe 2011; Rosset 2009). Desmarais, Wittman, and Wiebe (2011, 19) argue that recent crises "result directly from an industrial, capital-intensive and corporate-led model of agriculture and that the time for 'food sovereignty' has come." The concept of food sovereignty is now widely used by scholars and activists, yet it emerged in the early 1980s as part of an attempt by the Mexican state, which was losing corn autonomy, to achieve greater self-sufficiency in food production (Edelman 2014). However, it was not until the mid-1990s that the concept of food sovereignty gained traction as a social movement agenda through appropriation by the international peasant movement La Vía Campesina (The Peasant Way) (Martínez-Torres and Rosset 2010).

The definition of food sovereignty has been fluid since the 1990s, changing as groups adopt the terminology while developing and building new alliances (Patel 2009). The first definition put forth by La Vía Campesina in 1996 articulated food as a basic human right ensured by the state:

> Food sovereignty is the right of each *nation* to maintain and develop its own capacity to produce its basic foods respecting cultural and productive diversity. We have the right to produce our own food in our own territory. (emphasis added)

In highly politicized language, here food sovereignty is a petition to the state to shift its focus to small producers and away from a global–industrial food production and distribution model, which tends to privilege large producers, corporations, export-led growth, and imports of scarce food items. However, in 2007, a new definition was put forward by La Vía Campesina that shifts away from the state as the focus of action toward food sovereignty:

> Food sovereignty is the *right of peoples* to healthy and culturally appropriate food produced through ecologically sound and sustainable methods, and their *right to define their own food and*

agriculture systems. It puts those who produce, distribute and consume food at the heart of food systems and policies rather than the demands of markets and corporations. It defends the interests and inclusion of the next generation. It offers a strategy to *resist and dismantle the current corporate trade and food regime.* (Nyéléni Declaration; emphasis added)

As Patel (2009, 666) pointed out, there are some contradictions inherent in this definition, as it encompasses *all* producers and consumers while failing to articulate who is the guarantor of such rights, although in many cases, the state is implicitly articulated as the guarantor (Trauger 2017).[6] Beyond issues with establishing a concrete definition of food sovereignty, struggles over how to enact food sovereignty are directly related to different understandings and strategies concerning how to achieve it and at what scale, whether through international agreements, national legislation, regional methods, or small-scale, localized efforts. The food sovereignty movement agenda is used to expose the power relations at work in the global food and agricultural system; advocates argue that it is a call for a democratic redistribution of power and more equitable access to food as a basic universal human right (Wittman, Desmarais, and Wiebe 2010).

Food sovereignty is mobilized by La Vía Campesina, both as a response to neoliberal globalization and as an attempt to address the shortcomings of previous frameworks, which focused on increasing national food supplies (right to food), and an individual's economic access to food (food security) to ameliorate the problem of hunger (Fairbairn 2010, 27). Broadly speaking, efforts to gain food sovereignty are attempts to disrupt the global–industrial–capitalist food and agriculture system and are thus viewed as more radical than previous approaches, including the humanitarian-focused "right to food" and the more neoliberal "food security."[7] Food sovereignty proponents envision a democratized food system that operates differently from the neoliberal model, which positions small-scale producers at the bottom and corporate entities at the top of a hierarchical system. This positioning of peasant production systems in the neoliberal market neglects the important role of 2.5 billion small-scale producers who have developed sophisticated systems that promote polyculture rather than monoculture and are more productive than conventional systems (Altieri 2009; Altieri and Nicholls 2008; Gliessman 2007). Equally important, many scholars who promote the concept of food sovereignty highlight small producers as the population most consistently at risk of hunger and malnutrition (Pimbert 2009, 2–3; see also Rosset et al. 2006). Thus food sovereignty advocates call for the support, protection, and expansion of small-scale, localized agricultural systems, which put the needs of the local population first.

Although initial scholarly engagement with food sovereignty was overwhelmingly positive, as part of a critical dialogue initiated in 2013, important criticisms of food sovereignty advocacy emerged (cf. Akram-Lodhi 2013; Bernstein 2014; Burnett and Murphy 2014; Edelman 2014; Hospes 2014; Jarosz 2014; Trauger 2014).[8] Many agree that at first glance, food sovereignty is a desirable goal. However, even those who recognize its potential offer important critiques: Akram-Lodhi (2013, 4) argues that "as a concept its depiction of an alternative is not a depiction grounded in the messy compromises of the here and now but rather in a fully-fleshed-out depiction of another world . . . which is possible to build, and now." Explicitly stating that, although "another world" is appealing, simply offering an outcome or potential end point is an incomplete account. Missing from such accounts is how to use food sovereignty efforts to deconstruct colonial–imperial systems that are at the root of unevenness in food consumption–production systems.[9] Additionally, discussions of the pursuit of food sovereignty in accounts from the global core alongside accounts from the global periphery tend to conflate the objectives, desires, needs, and obstacles to making systems of production and exchange of food and agricultural products more just. Demands from groups in the global core, while no less important, are often focused on retaining autonomy over rights to produce and consume foods (cf. Alkon and Mares 2012; Kurtz 2015; Trauger 2017; Wittman, Desmarais, and Wiebe 2011).[10] Demands from groups in the periphery are more often focused on visibility, survival, and reclamation of not only land and resources but also worlds and knowledges otherwise. Again, such conflation between core and periphery efforts (and possible cooptation) potentially points to a perpetuation of a geopolitics of knowledge over what systems of production and consumption should look like (cf. Naylor 2017b).

This critique raises significant questions about how food sovereignty is deployed. As an agenda for social movement action, food sovereignty is an important rallying point for exposing problems within the contemporary food regime and responding to the regulation and control of agricultural resources under the World Trade Organization (cf. Martínez-Torres and Rosset 2010; McMichael 2009). However, as a concept, food sovereignty is often positioned in a capitalocentric way, as a radical alternative to neoliberal capitalist food and agricultural systems where the state is seen as both the problem and the solution (Trauger 2017, 35; see also Wittman, Desmarais, and Wiebe 2010).[11] Trauger (2017, 34) distills the larger body of work on food sovereignty into three "orientations": "national food self-sufficiency, rights-based resistance to the status quo, and autonomous food production." It is portrayed in a powerfully hopeful way as an approach to creating food relations built on love and friendship (Trauger 2017), transforming food systems education (Meek and Tarlau 2016), forestalling knowledge enclosure (Naylor 2017b), and reclaiming food as a social relation (Wittman 2009; Wittman, Desmarais, and Wiebe 2010, 2011). Indeed, Handy notes,

> Capitalism was dedicated to divorcing producers from any right over the goods they produced and encasing those goods in ever larger, ever more disconnected, ever more monopolized and ever more destructive markets. Food sovereignty challenges all of that because it demands that we rethink what was at the very centre of this transition; it demands that we treat food not simply as a good, access to which and the production of which is determined by the market, *it demands that we recognize the social connections inherent in producing food, consuming food, and sharing food.* (cited in Wittman, Desmarais, and Wiebe 2010, 4; emphasis added)

Handy's argument is common among scholars and advocates promoting food sovereignty—they position smallholders and peasant producers against an absolute capital. This capitalocentric approach, even as it aims to make visible multiple forms of consumption–production, dangerously obscures systems in existence currently that navigate impersonal and far-flung marketplaces while simultaneously activating social connections within food production as part of resistance and survival. Paradoxically, such an approach neglects the diverse food consumption–production strategies of peasants in particular, which may actually emulate the core ideas of food sovereignty, while negotiating relations within the conventional marketplace. It additionally occludes the efforts of peasants who may depend on export markets—such as the fair trade coffee market—and who strive for fairer trade relations as part of their politics (cf. Bacon 2015; Burnett and Murphy 2014). Moreover, a viewpoint couched in the primacy of capitalism renders invisible the solidarity relations that can be built through international networks that may (or may not) be premised on economic exchange, such as fair trade coffee exchanges. Put differently, articulating food sovereignty as a way to radically disrupt neoliberal capitalist systems reinforces the hegemony of capitalism, while simultaneously simplifying diverse economic exchanges and efforts to build livable worlds. If food is a critical linchpin of autonomy (and autonomous resistance), we might consider applying the ideas of food sovereignty, yet setting it alongside fair trade exchanges sets up a tension due to capitalocentric framings. What I suggest here is that reframing economic exchanges to remove the primacy of capitalism and instead looking at the multiple (if competing) economic practices opens up possibilities for examining and practicing livelihoods that are not exclusive to capital.

Underlying many of the arguments found in the rubrics of food sovereignty is a tendency to romanticize peasant production as operating against the capitalist marketplace (cf. Wittman, Desmarais, and Wiebe 2010). For Baviera and Bello (2009, 74), the resurgence of peasant production (cf. Ploeg 2008) was created by "the negative dynamics of global capitalism and empire and seeks to reverse them." These types of approaches speak to the pitfalls of capitalocentrism articulated by Gibson-Graham ([1996] 2006a), as food sovereignty efforts are measured against capitalism instead of as economies in their own right (cf. Gibson-Graham, Cameron, and Healy 2013). This approach to food sovereignty creates a dichotomous arrangement in which food sovereignty is either encapsulated by the neoliberal capitalist market or fundamentally restructuring noncapitalist market relations. Even as movements toward food sovereignty make visible peasant food and agricultural production, they promote a vision of the practices of food sovereignty as an alternative and anticapitalist practice, which has to some extent romanticized an ongoing struggle to create more secure and just food systems, potentially rendering food sovereignty a black box. Moreover, the positioning of food sovereignty as radically anticapitalist dismisses the everyday realities of producers who may engage in multiple markets and economic practices.

Investigating spaces where the friction of "compromise" within economic exchange is occurring as efforts to build dignified livelihoods is key to fleshing out how narratives of food sovereignty may play out differently over space. As fair rebels renegotiate their economic subjectivities, they do so, not in a way that places the state as guarantor of their rights or as the vehicle for creating more secure food systems and/or development, but through their resistance. Although *campesinos/as* in resistance do not explicitly articulate food sovereignty as a goal, their experience in building community economies across scale assists with making visible some of the tensions of actualizing the goals laid out by broader efforts for food sovereignty. Indeed, what others might call food sovereignty is expressed by fair rebels as autonomy.

Early in my fieldwork, I discussed with *campesinos/as* what it meant to work with international networks for coffee and how that might change the way that their political agendas could be realized. One *campesino* responded to me that capitalist systems insist on people buying food,

> but within our economic system production is the base. If a family can produce more than they can eat then they can sell it to maintain the family and here in the struggle there are other types of jobs that have to be worked, it is a process.

It is not an anticapitalist or antineoliberal approach as much as it is a community + economy approach to livelihoods "with dignity." The economic activities that are put into practice in the highlands are consistent with smallholder "plural economies," which Pimbert et al. (2001, 17) articulate as a combination of subsistence and market-based activities. Nonetheless, the economies of *campesinos/as* in resistance are diverse and are not referent only to capitalist economies but to considerations of what it means to build livable worlds.

Fair rebels use food and coffee production as a way to maintain claims to communal and productive spaces and to gain access to resources, and through this approach, they have established new political, social, and economic relations that assist with attempts to remain autonomous from the state and to withstand suffering. Within these communities is a multidimensional expression of the ideas that ground food sovereignty, such as rights to land and resources and pushes for fairer forms of economic exchange (cf. Edelman 2014), which is put into practice by actors at the local level while simultaneously connecting up to regional and international networks. If we consider Mencher's appraisal of food sovereignty as a set of ideas that embody new approaches to knowledge production, an examination of consumption–production in the highlands assists with considering what resistance as an agricultural practice looks like and what economy can mean. Mencher (2013, 10) notes that

> food sovereignty can be thought of as a concept having implicit roots in the life and struggles of peasant *campesinos/as*, and even small and medium-sized family *campesinos/as* in the west for many years. But today its political implications can be seen as part of the politics of knowledge.

Framing food sovereignty in opposition to neoliberal systems is not useful to discerning the ways that the ideas ensconced in food sovereignty narratives can be practiced and unnecessarily romanticizes the struggle to be food secure, to have control over productive resources, and to resist universalizing paradigms of development. In the case of *campesinos/as* in resistance, food sovereignty is not limited to food and agricultural production but is a form of a community economy, where men and women as political, social, and economic actors work for themselves, their families, and "the *pueblo*." Simultaneously, a reframing offers avenues to break down the geopolitics of knowledge by reclaiming and reasserting economic subjectivities that stand outside Western ways of knowing and understanding production and exchange. These practices are happening in the context of resistance, are formed within rebel autonomous spaces, and are not clearly defined but are messy and co-constituted by existing frictions and politics in place.

Much literature on food sovereignty is squarely focused on "working against" the neoliberal food system and reconfiguring capitalist political-economic relations (see Akram-Lodhi 2013). Yet, even if hopeful visions of food sovereignty are realized, how is food sovereignty to be maintained? Even while food sovereignty discourse and scholarship point to examples of how groups are enacting food sovereignty in both the global core and the periphery (cf. Alkon and Mares 2012; Block et al. 2012; Boyer 2010; Daigle 2017; Desmarais and Wittman 2014; Desmarais, Wittman, and Wiebe 2011; Fernandez, Mendez, and Bacon 2013; Kurtz 2015; Trauger 2015, 2017; Wilson 2016), the compromises and friction that exist in building secure and economically varied food systems are many times elided. Fair rebels are putting a number of the ideas embedded in food sovereignty into practice, and this is done in the context of hardship, struggle, and resistance. The diverse economies of *campesinos/as* in resistance are an example of how the friction of participating in a number of different economic activities takes shape and illuminates the multiple and competing ways that they seek to withstand suffering in the context of universalizing paradigms.

In the self-declared autonomous communities in the highlands of Chiapas, *campesinos/as* in resistance are harnessing multiple methods to exercise rights that have been long denied them by the state. The postcapitalist politics and economic practices that are experienced at the community level are struggles for diverse economic spaces. They are not islands of production, isolated from international, regional, or even neoliberal exchanges, yet they have cultivated localized, community resource bases and collective workspaces while also harnessing an international marketplace through coffee production. In Zapatista support bases in particular, fair rebels participate in collective production that ranges from corn and coffee cultivation to bread making, steel working, weaving, and boot making. The labor is conducted collectively, and items are produced for laborers and their families, for visitors, and for the marketplace. In one of my first visits to a self-declared autonomous community, I met with a weaving cooperative that was run by women in the community. They explained that they worked together a few days a week, weaving items for personal use and for sale in shops in San Cristóbal de las Casas. Any money earned is used to purchase new materials and also to buy items such as soap and salt in bulk, which are then distributed among the members of the collective. They also began a fund for emergency use—"in case someone needs medicine." The work in the collective is one site of labor, however, each participant also cultivates the *milpa,* and the collective reduces the hours worked on weaving to prioritize the corn harvest. This work is part of the mundane everyday struggle for autonomy in resistance.

The resistance being practiced by *campesinos/as* resonates with the discourses of food sovereignty as it is directed at the persistence of the peasantry as well as the powerful impact that repeasantization is having on a global scale (cf. Ploeg 2008, 2010). *Campesinos/as* as political actors in their everyday lives signal that they want to continue subsistence-based production and that, to do so, will appropriate and incorporate agroecological methods, forge collective cash economies, and pursue autonomy and nonuniversalizing ways of living well. In many cases, *socios* pointed to autonomy as a way of life that is a form of self-sufficiency, but one that goes beyond subsistence. As Gibson-Graham, Cameron, and Healy (2013, 198) note, creating diverse economies "is not about producing communities that are the same everywhere." Communities in the highlands struggling for autonomy are not representations of what the highly acclaimed food sovereignty concept looks like in practice but instead are places where questions can be generated about what kind of economic exchanges, social relations, and political processes can be had that promote secure access and more egalitarian distribution of food and agricultural resources.

Diverse Economies and Livable Worlds

If, as scholars, we view the economic activities of *campesinos/as* in resistance as valuable only if they are diametrically opposed to the capitalist market, we reinscribe a capitalocentric logic that limits our analysis. Most importantly, we foreclose understanding how a range of productive practices can be transformative even as they are part of diverse economic spaces shared by neoliberal capitalism.

These conceptual blinders thus make it difficult to produce a fine-grained analysis of the implementation of a variety of strategies as well as producer practices and interpretations of economic activities. As one *campesino* remarked to me when discussing the meaning of *comercio más justo*, "there are many who think that money is the answer, but we are looking for another way." Fair rebels perform wage-based work, they produce commodities for the capitalist marketplace, and they participate in a range of economies and economic exchanges alongside these more formal, quantifiable, and conventional practices. If we consider diverse economies—as discussed in chapter 1, those spaces in which concrete economic identities, activities, and narratives are being produced in ways that destabilize the knowledge of a singular capitalist economy—different ways of knowing and understanding economic practices are made apparent. How people create, interpret, and mobilize economies helps us to understand dynamic approaches to cultivating secure and just food systems.

One of the major critiques leveled against food sovereignty is that its proponents articulate a radical alternative without specifying the concrete changes necessary to achieve it. Akram-Lodhi (2013) made such an argument through pointing out two fundamental contradictions made visible in trying to build food sovereignty within a capitalist system. First, there is a contradiction between articulating food sovereignty as predicated on local control of resources by peoples while ignoring the power relations that make possible structural control of land, water, and other key resources (5). Second, even as food sovereignty is offered as a critique of the existing political economy of food production and distribution, it does not address the political conditions needed to "exercise the autonomy to build food sovereignty" (6). These contradictions point to problems with positioning food sovereignty as way to reconfigure market relations when equating the market economy only with capitalism. It is also, as Daigle (2017) argues, mired in Western-centric ideas of sovereignty tied to property rights over land and resources rather than indigenous ontologies of human–land–earth–other relations. I address each of these contradictions in turn through a discussion of how *campesinos/as* in resistance have approached establishing a resource base and also how they have cultivated diverse production systems.

It should be noted at the outset that I am not holding up the experience of *campesinos/as* in the highlands as an accurate portrayal of food sovereignty; instead, I am highlighting concrete practices that can assist with considering both how we want to think about economic practices and creating secure spaces of agricultural production and food consumption, which may help us better understand the diverse ways that food sovereignty is already under way. This section addresses two ways that *campesinos/as* in resistance are attempting to realize and reshape existing forms of economic exchange, first through subsistence agricultural production and second through economic networks that range from household to global scales. What is made evident by the practices of *campesinos/as* in resistance in the highlands is that there are different understandings of what economies are and that through a diverse approach (one that is not based in capitalist or noncapitalist divisions), *campesinos/as* in resistance continue to withstand suffering while also creating dignified livelihoods.

The difference between *campesinos/as* who have declared themselves in resistance and those who have not is evident in strategies undertaken to survive the "lean months." In many coffee-producing areas, families who are not part of the rebel autonomy movements may seek income through sending a family member to an urban area, or *al norte,* or rely on government programs (such as Prospera) or even short-term, high-interest money-lending arrangements.[12] However, fair rebels tend to focus on economic activities that are intended to keep their young and healthy population in residence, maintain their separation from the government, and reduce unequal labor relations. In one interview, this strategy was explained as an important part of the struggle: "we need people to stay and be productive in the community. . . . The coffee cooperative, for example, it stops migration and it helps with the family and helps to fortify the family base and the economic base." Such community-based economic interactions help set *campesinos/as* in resistance apart from their *partidista* counterparts. In particular, they help create cohesiveness among political actors and also assist with ameliorating economic-related issues of food access.

Importantly, *campesinos/as* in resistance explained that they were creating new ways for accessing resources and building autonomous, democratic networks of production, such as exchanging seeds. Strategies to maintain secure food resources by fair rebels are also consistent with demands made within the context of food sovereignty, which articulate a system that is democratically controlled and is attentive to the social conditions of production and consumption. Collective efforts to create food-secure communities as part of diverse economies also highlight why it is problematic to conceptualize a food sovereignty that is either/or. To do so discounts the struggle of *campesinos/as* who embody the resistance outside, alongside, and from within economic exchanges that are used toward building dignified livelihoods. Furthermore, it neglects the character of resistance in place. Where the resistance is located matters.

Part of creating such self-reliant systems includes the cultivation of coffee for income, and many *campesinos/as* also divide their time working in their *cafetales*. Both the *milpa* and the *cafetal*, which are rain-fed, demonstrate a remarkable diversity of plants and growing methods.[13] For example, in one *milpa*, a *socio* would plant a number of varieties of corn (generally varieties of white, black, and yellow), some that mature faster and others that are better for storage. Alongside that corn, different varieties of climbing beans would be planted. A *socio* explained, "When you grow the beans and corn together the organic material gets turned back in, the bean has much nitrogen, this is basic, this, the corn and the beans is the basic *milpa*, so it is." In the *cafetal*, two to three different types of coffee plants (which are perennial) might be planted among a variety of shade- and food-providing trees.

At the border of the *milpa* and within the *cafetal*, I was shown sunflowers, weedy edible greens, banana palms, peaches, and macadamia. A number of *campesinos/as* keep bees in their *cafetal* as well, providing a source of honey. Outside of their fields and dotted around household buildings were spaces of coffee processing, but also coffee plants for household consumption; small vegetable plots; tangles of the climbing vine squash called chayote; and, in many cases, chickens.[14]

All of these agricultural goods are produced at a micro-scale and are primarily for household consumption. These products also serve as a basis for barter or a small stream of income. In some cases,

Figure 17. A young climbing bean ascends a corn stalk in the *milpa*. Photograph by the author.

Figure 18. *Colmenas* in a *cafetal*. Photograph by the author.

households would make prepared foods and sell them on busy days at the coffee cooperative (e.g., tamales). Additionally, these biodiverse and economically diverse agricultural production practices are foundational for the diverse economic spaces that *campesinos/as* in resistance are co-creating. Knowledge sharing with regard to production practices and seed saving assists with the maintenance of secure sources of food, which form a core component of what we might point to as food sovereignty measures. Fair rebels are not in isolated areas of production or homogenous communities but instead form part of a network of struggle.

The cultivation and preservation of their native corn are of particular importance in the pursuit of a secure resource base (Naylor 2017a). A leader in one of the communities explained to me, "Our self-sufficiency is through our seed saving and through maintaining the diversity of our seeds."[15] There is a great deal of conversation around climate change and genetically modified seeds throughout the network of communities in the highlands, and households continue to seek ways to protect their seeds and to experiment in their fields. Through their global and regional networks, there are dialogues about the risks associated with climate change. In a conversation with a group of *campesinos/as* in resistance, we discussed efforts to adapt and improve corn; a collective answer (after discussion in Tzotzil about the question of climate change and how to respond) was "here we talk about climate change and we are trying to figure this out because there could be droughts or hurricanes that could wipe out our seeds." Another *campesino* added, "Yes, so it is, but also the climate [temperature], and so we talk with the *campesinos/as* in other regions and we exchange seeds." When I asked about how this worked, they laughed and said it was a very slow process—"we are doing experiments with the seeds, but the climates between regions are still very different." But they noted that they had built knowledge about the seeds and that the exchanges with other *campesinos/as* in self-declared autonomous communities are important. Additionally, knowing that families could not dedicate scarce land to experimenting, communal land was used to test the seeds. Communal land is increasingly used this way by *campesinos/as* in resistance who live in Zapatista support bases.

Even with agroecological methods and careful storage, however, the corn does not last between harvests, and *campesinos/as* experience this lack differently. One *campesino* explained this lack of sufficient food to me as a problem of land: "it [hunger] is a problem of land because there are very few pieces. There is little land and what land there is, is very small because there are a lot of people." Other *campesinos/as* argued that it was a problem of fertility; for example, "the problem when the corn doesn't last all year and we have to buy corn is because the earth doesn't produce as much and because the fertility is still being improved." Beyond issues with land scarcity and reduced fertility, many *campesinos/as* felt there was a problem of not being able to let the land "rest" long enough to recover its fertility. They associated the declining fertility of the soil with increased problems with insects, which significantly reduced the amount of corn that they were able to harvest and store. Furthermore, families lose a significant amount of harvested corn, as stored corn is subject to frequent problems with rodents. For coffee-producing households, the decision to prioritize the storage of coffee—keeping dried beans dry ahead of selling to the cooperative is essential to receive the full price—led to many sacks of corn being left in more precarious storage sites. Such issues have led to community-based experimentation with new storage methods as well as idea sharing between Zapatista support bases.

In one example from a Zapatista collective effort in an experimental shade coffee plot, a corn storage container (nicknamed for this project a "mini-bodega") was constructed to test different pest abatement strategies. This project tapped into a broader network of support: these Zapatistas received assistance from a U.S.-based NGO to purchase wood, neem leaves from *campesinos/as* in resistance in the regional network in Chiapas, and volunteer labor from within their immediate community. Neem is a tropical tree that cannot grow in the cloud forest environment of the highlands, but it is being grown in the tropical areas of Chiapas. It is a natural insect repellent often used as an organic application in small-scale and agroecological farming and also in nonchemical, personal-protection bug sprays. On the day of the project, *campesinos/as* arrived early to the experimental *cafetal*. Some pulled unripe peaches off of trees and handed them around for people to enjoy a tangy snack, and others hauled wood off of a truck. The entire morning

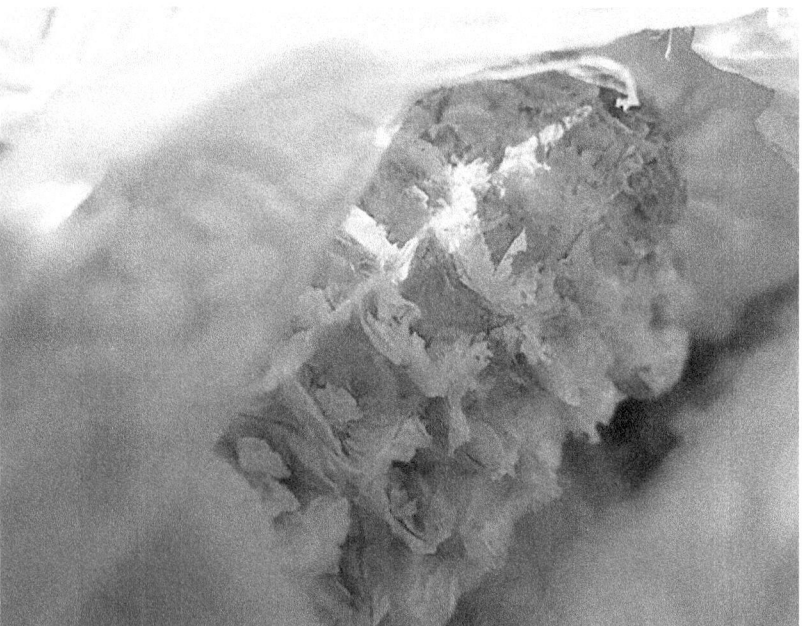

Figure 19. Bags of corn for storage *(above)*, and rodent-damaged corn. Photographs by the author.

was spent digging holes, securing posts, and constructing a small shed that was raised from the ground. The shed was then lined with neem leaves and stocked with dried corn. The corn was weighed ahead of being stocked and will be weighed again at the end of the season to see if there is a change. The overall goal is to see if this approach can be used by other *campesinos/as* in resistance as a sustainable storage strategy that will assist with minimizing losses to both insects (neem deterrent) and rodents (enclosed storage shed).

Shortages in corn are seasonally predictable and pervasive in coffee-producing communities in the highlands and for smallholder producers in the region more broadly (see Bacon et al. 2014). As a result, *campesinos/as* must turn to income-generating activities to be able to purchase basic foodstuffs in lean times, and in the case of fair rebels, this income generation largely takes shape through collective activities. Such collective economies not only serve economic goals but are important sites of political and solidarity organizing. Even as *campesinos/as* in resistance challenge how their resource base is accessed and controlled—a key component of Akram-Lodhi's

Figure 20. Mini-bodega in a communal experimental plot. Photograph by the author.

(2013) vision of building food sovereignty—they seek additional mechanisms for asserting their rights to productive spaces.

As political actors affiliated with multiple movements operating at distinct scales, the networks established through solidarity, knowledge sharing, and political action create a foundation for collective production of goods for cash income (including collective agricultural production on communal plots, individual coffee production for cooperatives, and weaving for example). Consistent with the situation of peasants globally, fair rebels seek income for the purchase of items that they cannot produce at home (such as soap, salt, and medicine) and for the lean months. However, such interactions bring *campesinos/as* in resistance in the highlands into new negotiations of power within the marketplace. While not immune from such power struggles, *campesinos/as* in resistance use their position as political actors to work collectively toward dignified livelihoods.

Cooperative production of resources and community economies form an important spectrum of resistance for fair rebels. A *campesina* conveyed the importance of the collective economic practices to me, stating, "To resist is to work beyond your home in the collectives, that is a way to get some money and it is not like the *partidistas* who have, for example, the bad government program of Oportunidades [Prospera]." The collective work for *campesinos/as* in resistance draws on long-standing community labor arrangements to democratically distribute responsibilities within and between community members. These are community-based initiatives that take many forms. Some communities have a wide range of activities (this is more common among Zapatista-affiliated *campesinos/as*), including weaving, metalworking, bread making, gardening, and agroecology experimentation; other communities were limited to one or two activities, such as bread making and coffee production for the organic and/or fair trade market.[16] One of the critical components in the creation of the diverse economic spaces of highland communities is their recognition that to build self-reliant community economies, they cannot leave out a significant portion of the population, and so men and women alike participate in cooperative production.

The use of *ejidal* community spaces to conduct experiments that could otherwise be costly and risky for peasant families is an important site for addressing issues in corn and coffee production; any produce from this communal area is distributed among the community. Overall, the collective economic practices make up a critical component of community self-reliance, where the burden of economic interaction and the cultivation of secure access to food and income are shared. In conversations about these practices and how they work, a *campesino* remarked, "If we work collectively in our communities we maintain the right to land and to resources. So it is. It is the best way to organize and work." Through cooperative work, *campesinos/as* are able to put their politics into practice on a day-to-day basis. Such activities make up community economies that transgress scale (tapping into regional and global networks) and disrupt monolithic understandings of economic activities that are attached to neoliberal capitalism.

The community economies form the base of support for subsistence production and also for participation in fair trade coffee production. These differing forms of production and economic exchange allow for more consistent forms of income and to extend their community to an international scale (as noted in chapter 4). It also means that they have cast the net of "self-sufficiency" somewhat wider (see Stahler-Sholk 2007, 57); rather than relying on lower coffee prices through community- or regionally based *coyotes*, *campesinos/as* in resistance chose a consistent buyer through accessing international networks. The connection to fair trade cooperatives for *campesinos/as* in resistance forms an important part of creative livelihood strategies and diverse community economies. When discussing the practices of collective work and their importance to autonomous resistance, one *socio* noted, "We resist the programs of the bad government because it is a lie, like the capitalist system. Instead, we have the collectives and do work together. Neoliberalism attempts to reconstruct our culture; this is bad, and it does not serve us." It is in these diverse economic spaces that *campesinos/as* in resistance continue to struggle against neoliberal development and the subsuming of their cultural autonomy. And although *campesinos/as* told me that they are resisting neoliberalism, they have harnessed programs that are firmly embedded in the neoliberal market: organic and fair trade certification. This resistance was not described as a complete noninteraction with the neoliberal market (e.g., boycott) but in the context of recognizing the power differentials in the market, while withstanding them and negotiating their participation.

In examining postcapitalist politics (or political practices), the focus is often on localized responses to globalization. But what does it mean when these practices are based in community interdependence in subsistence and collective work as well as globally networked interdependence through the fair trade movement and market? A community economy is not restricted to any one place. If the idea of community is teased apart and detached from Western-centric notions of community—which is juxtaposed with individualism and difference (Young 1990, 302, as cited in Gibson-Graham 2006b, 85)—the economic interdependence practiced by fair rebels is a function of their resistance. As these economic identities are performed and practiced, *campesinos/as* in resistance are participating in a continuation of being in common (see also Gibson-Graham 2006b, 85–86). It is through this mix of activities that dignified livelihoods are built while withstanding suffering. It brings together autonomy, self-sufficiency, diverse production, and ecosystem management (Gibson-Graham 2006b, 192) at multiple scales and in the context of a pacifist struggle against state and market violence. Decoupling economic development from growth and economy from capitalism allows for a more nuanced approach to examining livelihoods in the highlands. Gibson-Graham suggest "four coordinates" for considering the active ethical and political decision-making spaces of community economies: necessity, surplus, consumption, and commons (193). Here, using my collected field notes, observations, and interviews, I evaluate these spaces at local, regional, and global scales with particular attention to subsistence and coffee production.

Figure 21 hints at building livelihoods through prioritizing people. And although *campesinos/as* in resistance are engaging the fair trade market, it is not with the stated goal of making money, as the quote that leads this section suggests ("we are looking for another way"). It is a multifaceted social interdependence (see Gibson-Graham 2006b) where indigenous peasants are agents in cultivating and continuously remaking their political, social, and economic identities. Communal and collective production is a key way that fair

Figure 21. Four Coordinates Chart

	Local	Regional	Global
Necessity	Dignified livelihoods, peace, native corn, reduced pests, better harvests, a way to address the 'lean months,' cash income, a better price for coffee, a healthy and stable population, opportunities for youth	Social, political, and economic networks, knowledge sharing, peace, cooperative production, transportation networks for coffee	Solidarity, social, political, and economic networks, knowledge sharing, a better price for coffee, representation
Surplus	Appropriated via: self-exploiting and volunteer labor, some wage work; Distribution: replenishment of communal resources, toward building dignified livelihoods (maintaining subsistence)	Appropriated via: self-exploiting and volunteer labor, some wage work; Distribution: collectives, communal land and knowledge sharing	Appropriated via: self-exploiting labor in for-profit market, marketing of history and resistance; Distribution: static price and price premium to coffee cooperative and farmers, profits to coffee roasters
Consumption	Basic household maintenance; clothing, consumer durables, other material possessions	Communal supplies and experimentation	Bettering production, the product and the processing of coffee
Commons	Collectives, *milpa, cafetal*, nature and earth others, knowledge, seeds	Collectives, knowledge, seeds	Knowledge

rebels embody and enact their resistance. It is a political engagement that disrupts a universal language of resistance, development, and economy. Most importantly, these relations, processes, and practices happen in place. Being in common is not something that happens "out there" but is place-specific and sits in and between actors as part of the co-creation of sites of interdependence and mutual aid.

What Is Fair Trade, Whom Is It for, and Who Gets to Decide?

In the context of fair trade certification, narrowly reading the landscape of the highlands as a capitalist space locates *campesinos/as* as a site in need of "fixing." However, rereading the landscape for economic difference and viewing multiple forms of economic exchange work toward decolonized knowledges and a reframing of geographical imaginaries of place. It is an entangled and messy process underlined by friction and compromise, as well as hope.

If we return through the avenues of building secure livelihoods, in ways that are attentive to creating secure access to food and resources (articulations of food sovereignty), different answers are possible to the questions of what is fair trade, whom it is for, and who gets to decide. If we consider it from the perspective of striving toward livable worlds and as a component of building secure foodways based on indigenous knowledge and ways of being, these answers do not come from the certification market or third-party certifiers. Such answers may align with social justice activism and participating in keeping fair trade in movement, but here I look to the producers, to the *campesinos/as* in resistance. Over three years, and many cups of coffee, I learned that fair trade agricultural production was just another part of everyday life. The connection to fair trade is part of a broader commitment to struggling for autonomy: "we are coffee farmers who became organized so we could work on our own and better, and so we could feed our families." Fair trade is an afterthought, followed by the importance of the cooperative; one *socio* expressed this while we were discussing the fair trade price for coffee that year: "Through Maya Vinic we sell the coffee and through them we get the best price, a better price. We agree to be here and produce certain ways, if there is a drop in the price . . . before it would hurt our families, before we couldn't help our families." Simultaneously, *socios* reflect on the fair trade price not being a "living wage" and the sorrow of not having "enough land" to produce corn, and having to purchase corn prior to the harvest. Fair trade does not fully insulate *campesinos/as* in resistance from the vicissitudes of everyday life.

What is fair trade? Something that is really not that different, a window to better money, and a way to create and maintain solidarity relations between growing and roasting cooperatives; it is one part of a multipronged strategy to maintain subsistence-based livelihoods. Whom is it for? In this case, it is for those people struggling to live well on their own terms. Finally, who gets to decide? The participants. And here is a key way in which we might think about multiplying and diversifying knowledge: *campesinos/as* in resistance are not the subjects of fair trade (Naylor 2017c); throughout their cooperatives, they make decisions about life and livelihood that form their interactions and understandings of fair trade, pushing back against the capitalist logics of the market through practices that are multiple. As one *campesino* explained, "it's a future we construct to counter the deconstruction and it's a way to get respect."

Other Worlds Are Possible

I began this book with a Zapatista mural, and it seems appropriate that it should end with one too. I think this mural speaks for itself. But I want to draw your attention to it to provide a space of hope at the end of this book. Not a glimmer, or a straw to grasp at, nor a silver lining, but a stalwart space from which to escape narratives of there "being no alternative" to the violence of capitalism.

When I discuss the research that I conducted with fair rebels in Chiapas and the complex realities behind the fair trade label, I am often asked by people, "What coffee should I buy?" From their perspective, I imagine I am giving a very unsatisfying answer when I respond, "What kind of economic exchanges do you want to participate in?" Their potential dissatisfaction likely stems from my attempts to encourage them to have more engaging forms of economic exchange. I tell people to look behind the labels, not rely on branding, and think about the type of interactions that they want to have in the marketplace. I answer their question with a question, knowing that it is a request to undertake the difficult task of learning about production and production practices, while holding

Figure 22. Mural in the Zapatista Caracol of Roberto Barrios: "Entonces el rebelde en vez de angustiarse busca otros caminos para construir otro mundo que es posible" (The rebel, instead of being anxious, looks for other ways to build another world that is possible). Photograph by the author.

themselves responsible. It is a hopeful request that we, as human beings, will participate more deeply in making the world a better place in inclusive and equitable ways.

However, as someone who is rethinking, reframing, and rereading economic exchanges as sites of difference, I recognize the hard work that this participation will take. It means confronting the structures that give power to particular groups of people—white supremacy and privilege, the hetero-patriarchy and colonial–imperial geopolitical relations. For some of us, it means recognizing our place(s) in broader structures of oppression and relinquishing power and/or using it differently. It is not up to the people you see on your bag of coffee to do this work for you.

We are constantly in the processes of becoming, of learning, of seeking mutual aid. We do this from different geographies. But we are all citizens of the earth. We cannot face our roles anxiously; we must face them from places of strength, together.

Conclusion
Other Worlds Are Possible

The twenty-fourth anniversary of the Uprising of the Zapatistas was celebrated on January 1, 2018. Incidentally, 2018 is the thirtieth year since the first fair trade label was put into place. The close proximity of these events is not coincidental. They were, among many others, an outcry that the system is uneven, that colonial–imperial relations of power are violent and ongoing, and that there are other ways to know and understand the world. They shouted truth to power. The dissonances between these moments more than two decades on are deafening. I went to Chiapas in an attempt to understand the chasm that grew and how bridges were being built and by whom.

In 2012, I watched as five young men carried export-ready, seventy-kilo (~150 pound) bags of coffee beans from where they had been stacked in the bodega following their dry processing and onto a container truck. They were hired by the cooperative to assist with the processing of the coffee, another way to bring in some cash income for their families. More than this, however (as noted in chapter 3), they were becoming part of the next generation that will take on the mantle of participating in larger networks for coffee that eschew the *coyote* and practice rebel autonomy. These labors were performed as another node in the coffee chain but also as part of the formation of economic identities for indigenous youth, who were born in a time of autonomous resistance and struggle.

In *Fair Trade Rebels*, I attempted to examine the complex and

Figure 23. Coffee bags filled, sewed, and ready for export to the United States. Photograph by the author.

messy realities of participating in diverse and community economies and make room for pluriversal ontologies and epistemologies. To undertake such a task, it was necessary to begin in place—to consider how diverse economic identities and ways of living are sedimented in political and geohistorical contexts that are not contained by their place-specific settings but extend across space and scale. It is an ongoing project to decolonize development and recognize that there is not one right way to live and labor. The colonial–imperial relations of economic and knowledge exchange are pervasive, yet they are not absolute.

Reading and reframing economic exchange and knowledge production through a fair trade lens requires unsettling the long and tired tropes deployed by third-party certifiers and other proponents of fair trade certification, who seek to facilitate market access and "fix" "impoverished producers." In deconstructing dichotomies and rethinking the practices and possibilities of economic exchange through fair trade networks, the essentialized producer-subject fades from view. The label of "fair trade coffee producer" is singular and limiting—in discussing the multiple economic practices of *campesinos/as* in resistance, the character of economic exchanges and efforts to build dignified livelihoods are made more visible.

Although I write this book from a space of hope, I do want to thread through to the very end the caution that simply pointing to sites as multiple and diverse does not solve the problems of capitalocentrism or the geopolitics of knowledge. "Other worlds are possible," but while they exist all around us and always, in some spaces, there are significant and sometimes violent struggles to maintain them, which can sometimes be neglected when imagining diverse and community economies. The experience of one group to cultivate sites of economic alterity does not always map onto the racialized, gendered, and classed experiences of many who as part of their daily existence rely on multiple forms of economic exchange. Although we are always in the process of becoming, it is essential to deeply reflect on what it is (who we are) that we are becoming. A component of this reflection is the acknowledgment of uneven power relations that are part of colonial–imperial multisited and multiscalar core–periphery interactions and the privilege (or lack thereof) that exists along a continuum of exchanges and identities.

A Window on the World

This book began with a description of fair trade as a "window to better money" for fair rebels in Chiapas. In this concluding segment, I seek ways to keep the window on the world open and transparent and a community economy, of which fair trade exchanges are a part, animated and in movement. Much of this book trespassed over the different vantage points of the fair trade "window." The universalizing narratives of poverty and development provide an outside-in view of how third-party certification acts in apolitical, ahistorical, and ageographical ways to mold and shape peasants into "rational economic actors." An inside-out view shows political struggles grounded in place and based on historical and continuous colonial–imperial violence(s); it further shows fair trade production not as the panacea for development but as an economic activity taken up with a suite of other forms of economic exchange. Using fair trade certification as a window on the world opens up possibilities for heterogeneity as expressed by the diversity of experiences and possible trajectories of fair trade more broadly. It is seeing fair trade through a pluriversal lens and from a space that recognizes difference that can illuminate the possibilities of cultivating more just economic exchanges.

Thinking about fair trade certification is nothing if not messy. Yet, there is a necessary messiness that comes with making things multiple and diverse rather than universal and similar. When asked whether we should have fair trade if it really has not accomplished what it set out to do, I always say that fair trade provides opportunities to ask questions about the economic exchanges we want to have. I am an opponent of unjust and universalizing systems, and in seeking to expose and reframe economic exchanges, an examination of the fair trade certification system and efforts to make trade fairer assist with making visible how far we must yet go to address the centrality of capitalism and neoliberal–capitalist forms of economic development in contemporary economic imaginaries. It signals that we need to recognize existing and build new knowledges about what it means to live as citizens of the world who have diverse and multiple identities.

While recent work on fair trade certification presaged that global capitalist processes, universal economic principles, and "Global North" consumption patterns will shape the future of fair trade, making it a milder form of "business as usual" (cf. Lyon 2015a, 162), I want to urge a rethinking of fair trade in movement. An ethic of care written across the movements for fairer trade creates possibilities of dignified economic exchanges across space and scale. It is an opportunity to "be in common" and to share stories of people, place, life, and livelihood. The case of *campesinos/as* in resistance demonstrates that fair trade certification is just one component of a diverse livelihood strategy and larger political struggles. The large- and small-scale networks that are built by participants form a critical piece of resistance to the idea that "there is no alternative" to neoliberal development and economic activities.

The experience of fair rebels does not exist in isolation;

campesinos/as in resistance are renegotiating and reframing their identities not through dismantling or deconstructing but through existing place-based and political identities. They deploy their struggle not from an "island of resistance in a capitalist sea" but through working at multiple sites along transnational networks. Moreover, they point to a "world in which many worlds fit," not as a fantastical possible future but as a site of indigenous alterity and futurity that exists here and now and always.

Acknowledgments

I first acknowledge the importance of geographic knowledge. I came to geography by a meandering road, and I found my place. Geographers examine and produce "earth writing." We strive to understand and explain difference across the globe, from the subterranean to outer space. I can think of no better place to have difficult conversations and to provide outward facing scholarship that I hope inspires people to seek deeper meaning and change. Change is not easy, and celebrating difference has proven difficult for humanity, but I write from a space of hope, and I invite others to participate in the project of writing and rewriting the earth in profound and meaningful ways.

There is a large community of people that I would like to thank for the day to day that makes possible this kind of scholarship. But I cannot begin to thank the people by whom I am surrounded without first acknowledging those who embody and make up the struggle that I attempted to portray within these pages. I am humbled in the presence of the rebel peasants of Chiapas. Without their time, energy, and struggle; without the ongoing dialogue and push to unlearn; without them, nothing. I returned from "the field" at a loss, and putting these words to print is but one way that I am trying to struggle with, and adhere *a la sexta* and to strive for peace, justice, and pluriversal worldviews. This book is not intended to give voice or make visible but is for listening and learning to shout and walk with the indigenous peoples of the highlands of Chiapas.

Being cheeky, I want start by saying that I published this book to put to print my gratitude and to thank the great many people who enrich my life and my scholarship. I take great joy from reading the acknowledgments printed in books. Every time I read the outpouring of affection, love, and strife in writing that is expressed by an author, I imagine the web of support surrounding the author, and I feel hopeful. A book, or any writing for that matter, does not get produced in isolation. My experience of writing proves this conviction to me again and again.

I didn't think I would write a book, but it turns out that this format is a strong medium for listening, thinking, and writing new spaces, and I'm thankful to a number of people who helped make that space with me. I am grateful to Kath Gibson and Kevin St. Martin for taking me to coffee and encouraging me to propose a book in their series. I also want to thank the faculty and graduate students at Rutgers University who kindly let me try out these ideas on them first; the broader network of CERN and the CEC, especially Kelly Dombroski and Jenny Cameron, who encouraged me to develop these ideas around diverse economies and saw the glimmer of this book in its first form; and the series editors, who saw its shape and helped me think through it in a constructive and meaningful way. I have much gratitude for the support of Jason Weidemann, my editor at the University of Minnesota Press, who held my hand through being a first-time book writer. Gabe Levin at the Press provided fabulous behind-the-scenes work with much patience. I'm indebted to the broader team at the Press who worked behind the scenes to turn a messy document into this beautifully formatted book. I also want to acknowledge Mick Gusinde-Duffy and Sapana Doshi, who offered early encouragement and provided helpful feedback on my proposal.

Aaron Bobrow-Strain offered my first connection to Chiapas; I'm grateful for time spent sharing Chiapas and food stories, which started with that first cup of coffee at AAG Las Vegas. I thank him for the mentoring on fieldwork and also on book writing and navigating presses. I feel incredibly fortunate to have had his informal read of the first full draft of the manuscript—I thank him for pushing me on the tough things, but also for a kind and energizing review. I also appreciate the informal mentoring space that we've opened up; it's teaching me every day.

At the University of Delaware, I am surrounded by fabulous colleagues, mentors, and friends. I knew I was gaining colleagues when I took my position in the Department of Geography, but I had no idea what I was in for. I am deeply touched by the example of Tracy DeLiberty, a most generous mentor and selfless friend, to whose level of collegiality I aspire. I also thank Sara Rauscher: the cat-o-grams continue to fill me up alongside learning about supercomputing power and regional climate models. I am so glad to be able to share all kinds of things with you (kitties notwithstanding). My weekly coffee and catch-up with Dana Veron is one of the most fulfilling parts of my week. I cannot possibly explain how much I enjoy the meandering rivers of our conversations—flitting from research ideas and department goings-on to family life. I extend that joy, too, to time well spent with Fabrice, Camille, and Noah. I am so glad to have met Emerald Christopher-Byrd, who is my kind of nerd. I am deeply indebted to Paul Jackson, who came up with the phrase *fair rebels* during a writing group review of my first proposal draft—originally called "A Window to Better Money," a title that caused many a grimace around the table—and also for pointing out what I had long overlooked: that the "monster" had a heart. I am grateful for our spaces of co-advising and for having another brain to pick next door. Finally, thanks go to Nathan Thayer, who read and reread diverse economies literature right alongside me and provided much-needed discussion, and who also made the lovely maps at the start of the book.

The duration of fieldwork that allowed for the conversations and observations that are contained herein was supported by a number of units at the University of Oregon, where I completed my PhD. I must acknowledge the Center for Latino/a and Latin American Studies, the Center on Diversity and Community, the Department of Geography, the Global Oregon Institute, a Graduate School Public Impact Award, and the Oregon Humanities Center. Additionally, the one-semester research leave for pretenure faculty at the University of Delaware allowed me to finish the manuscript in a timely fashion.

My colleagues at the University of Oregon had a profound influence on my writing and my academic training overall, and although I did not even have an inkling of this book while I was in residence, the people there with whom I had the honor of working are not missing from its pages. The department doesn't look the same to me anymore, but I hold Condon Hall in my head and my heart always.

Faculty as well as former and fellow students from my graduate work at Oregon provided support during fieldwork and saw the first bits of data and analysis on which I draw in this book; my thanks go to Didi Martinez, Laurie Trautman, Easther Chigumira, Innisfree McKinnon, Ingrid Nelson, Leslie McLees, Emma Slager, Matt Derrick, Corey Johnson, M Jackson, Thomas Nail, Dan Buck, Lynn Stephen, Allison Carruth, Margaret Hallock, Stephen Wooten, Alejandro Vallega, Shaul Cohen, Andrew Marcus, and the late Susan Hardwick. I especially want to give a warm hug and reach out from these pages to Nate and Jenn Bellinger, Derek and Rachel Miller, Ian David Crickmore and Emily Smith, and Dave Fisher for being the kind of people with whom you can always pick up the threads. As we all moved on from UO, I appreciate that we still find time to spend at least, as ID put it, "1 percent" of every year together. I continue to be grateful to Lise Nelson, who advised my PhD, helped me find my footing as a scholar, and provided a strong foundation for me from which to work. Finally, Alec Murphy provisioned a long-lasting question that I have revisited over a decade of work on fair trade: "should we not have fair trade?" I have gotten significant mileage out of that question. I am deeply grateful for his time, energy, and expertise, and I thank him for teaching me how to wave the flag for geography. I've said it before, but it I will put it to print now: I have never met a more curious and giving person in my academic life. He is a lifelong mentor; I will never be able to repay what I have gained, but I try every day to pay it forward. Thanks to him for always having an open door and for inspiring me to do the same.

As I alluded to at the beginning, a wider web of support is present at many times in the production of scholarship, and my support network breaks institutional bounds. I must also thank Marie Price, who gave me my first faculty job and who continues to allow me "mentoring moments" as needed. She is a true champion of the early-career faculty member, which I see especially in her efforts with the AGS. I also thank the extended Price–Crandall family for taking me in and caring for me when I was in residence in Washington, D.C. I'm not sure I would have emerged from the basement if it wasn't for those wonderful dinners (and beer). I hope to trade stories over hops for many years to come. I also thank my Chiapas support network, which extends from the folks at the coffee cooperatives to those at EcoSur and CIESAS—many thanks, too, to Maria Elena Martínez Torres and Peter Rosset for providing local resources and for allowing me time at their table.

David Meek's and my books are siblings. It was amazing to write alongside him and to negotiate the presses together. I think due to new project fieldwork, our chapter drafts are among the best-traveled papers in the world. I cannot possibly thank him enough for the time, energy, and effort that he put into his reviews of my work. I thank him for constantly reminding me of the spatial aspects that I may have otherwise neglected, and I look forward to exchanging ideas over the next round.

Other people who have provided invaluable advice and space for thinking include Josh Inwood, Sofia Zaragocín, Jessie Clark, Ali Alkon, and Ryan Galt. Sarah Lyon continues to be a most supportive colleague, and her review of the full manuscript was among the most giving and thoughtful responses to my work I have ever received.

I also appreciate the support of my extended family during fieldwork and relating to academic life more generally, as well as during the long silences taken while I produced this book and other academic outputs. I promise I am not trapped under something heavy and therefore unable to take your call—I'm probably lost in a book.

Walking and talking with Joe Jasper in the Cascades and then later on other, flatter surfaces remains one of the most important idea-generating and problem-solving spaces I could ever hope for. I continue to marvel at his generosity of spirit—living and working at life, the universe, and everything alongside him feels as though we exist within a love letter that we are constantly writing together.

Notes

Introduction

1. For the purposes of this narrative, I use the terms *campesino/a* rather than *campesin@* or *campesinx* to recognize gender difference. I made this choice based on the use of *campesino/a* by the social movement actors who participated in this research.

2. This is not a diagnostic text; therefore I do not seek to define what it means to live well or build dignified livelihoods.

3. It should be noted that the Zapatista support bases are free of weapons (as well as drugs and alcohol); only the military arm of the EZLN, sequestered in the southeast of the state, maintains weapons. Additionally, there is a well-established body of literature that engages the broader groups of indigenous peoples in Chiapas who are part of, or directly impacted by, the Zapatista rebellion; see, for example, monographs or edited volumes by Baronnet, Mora, and Stahler-Sholk (2011), Collier and Quaratiello (2005), Eber and Kovic (2003), Harvey (1998), Hernández Castillo (2016), Mattiace (2003), Mora (2017), Moksnes (2012), Nash (2001), Pérez Ruiz (2004), Rus, Hernández Castillo, and Mattiace (2003), Speed (2005, 2008), Speed and Reyes (2002, 2005), Stephen (2002), and Tavanti (2003).

4. It should be made clear at the outset that although this is not a book about the Zapatista movement, there are very pragmatic reasons for the use of *in resistance* for Zapatistas and their support base members. For these groups, it takes on a political character to refer to their declaration of rebel autonomy and official policy of refusal of government aid or programming. Additionally, the use of *in resistance* by non-Zapatistas who are in solidarity takes on a distinct, but similar character.

5. In 1974, in collaboration with Catholic bishop Samuel Ruiz García, the First National Indigenous Congress in Mexico was convened. Held in the city of San Cristóbal de las Casas, Chiapas, the Congress marked the five hundredth birthday of Bartolomé de las Casas, and thousands of indigenous delegates (Tzotziles, Tzeltales, Ch'oles, and Tojolabales) representing 327 communities attended (Harvey 1998, 77–78). The meetings were focused on four areas of appeal to the state, specifically, land, commerce, education, and health (Stephen 2002, 117). Many have identified the Congress as a turning point (cf. Collier and Quaratiello 2005; Harvey 1998;

Mattiace 1998; Stephen 2002), as it brought together representatives of the four major linguistic groups and called for unity among the indigenous groups in the state. Stephen (2002, 118) argues that this pointed to "the possibility of a new concept of ethnicity that does not focus on individual ethnic traits but is rooted in a common sense of struggle."

6. Much training was done in the Lacandón Jungle and also in the northern areas adjacent to Agua Azul and the ruins of Palenque.

7. Additionally, as Nash (2001) argued, the state has never fully addressed gender inequities, especially in the cases of landownership and voting rights (see also Speed 2006).

8. While the official Chiapas Project ended in 1980, its legacy remains through other research labs on Harvard's campus, which as recently as 2015 still described their work as "the quest for the causes underlying Chiapas' backwardness" (CID, n.p.).

9. When I arrived in the highlands in 2010, I was acutely aware of social, political, and economic differences in my daily interactions. My race, gender identity (cis-woman), educational attainment, economic status, and U.S. citizenship (settler-colonial) influenced the way that I was able to interact with people and the way they interacted with me.

10. In discussing the politics of representation, I am referring to the problem of "speaking for others and the practice of speaking about others," critical issues that Alcoff (1992) suggests reinforce hierarchies in research. Alcoff notes that "where one speaks from affects the meaning and truth of what one says" and critically that "the practice of privileged persons speaking for or on behalf of less privileged persons has actually resulted (in many cases) in increasing or reinforcing the oppression of the group spoken for" (6–7). Throughout the researching and writing of this book, I have participated in an interpretation of my needs, goals, and situation as well as those of others, which creates the potential for exploitation and ownership over translation and interpretation. One of the ways I sought to ameliorate the problem of "speaking for/about others" in practice is through cultivating a dialogue and attempting to "speak with others" (Alcoff 1992; Spivak 1988) as the research process unfolded; this approach, however, does not obviate the processes of writing and analyzing, and I fully acknowledge the difficulties of speaking "with others" while writing. Similar to Walsh, I do not see myself as "studying or reporting on social movements and actors, but thinking with and theorizing from" the events and daily activities in which I engaged (Mignolo and Walsh 2018, 85).

11. One of my attempts is to maintain my connections with the cooperatives through their extended networks in the United States, and I continue to be in contact with the coffee-roasting cooperatives that purchase coffee from the producer cooperatives with which I worked in the highlands.

12. I would also add gender to this, as my experience as a woman and female-bodied person in the field differs greatly from those experiences reported by my male-bodied colleagues.

13. This idea of "what it is and who it is for" is drawn directly from work

by Leslie McLees (2012), who asked these questions in conducting research on urban agriculture in Dar es Salaam as they related to who and what the city is for.

1. Fair Rebels, Fair Coffee?

1. I use a variation on world systems theory advanced by Immanuel Wallerstein (1974) because it allows for examining core–peripheral relations at multiple scales (and simultaneously). I reject the idea that there is a "developed/undeveloped" or "developing" world, as there are cores and peripheries from the scale of the household—where reproductive labor is extracted—to the global. I also eschew the common bifurcation of the globe into the less derogatory "Global North–Global South" because of its association with the Brandt Line (Brandt 1980), which unhelpfully generalizes an "industrialized North" and "impoverished South" (see Naylor 2014; see also on grand narratives Murphy 2013).

2. For example, see the work of Buttle (2008), Cameron, Gibson, and Hill (2014), Cameron and Wright (2014), Diprose (2016), Dixon (2011), Dombroski (2016), Dombroski, Mckinnon, and Healy (2016), Foley and Mather (2016), Gibson-Graham and Roelvink (2011), Healy (2014), Hill (2011), Hosking and Palomino-Schalscha (2016), Krueger, Schulz, and Gibbs (2018), Lepofsky (2007), Little, Maye, and Ilbery (2010), Morrow and Dombroski (2015), Naylor (2018), North (2015), Oberhauser (2005), Roelvink, St. Martin, and Gibson-Graham (2015), Shear (2010), Smith (2004, 2007), and St. Martin (2007).

3. This discussion of power was part of the conversation between panel and audience at the 2017 American Association of Geographers conference.

4. Although I would argue that fair trade does "work" for some (largely consumers in the United States and Western Europe), a point to which I return in chapter 3, when I discuss "who benefits" from fair trade.

5. In the heyday of the ICA, INMECAFE provided technical assistance, research findings, and export permits and purchased and processed coffee grown by small producers.

6. It is important to note that no new empirical research on the Zapatista movement has been approved by its members since 2003 (see Giovanni 2014, 95; Mora 2008, 2017; Newdick 2012).

2. Coffee "Fixes"

1. The use of balaclavas and handkerchiefs to cover their faces is a key element of embodying a Zapatista identity. It was explained to me as a way to stand out—without the covering, they are "just another Indian."

2. NAFTA, which received renewed attention as part of the incoherent platform of the forty-fifth U.S. president, was negotiated between the United States, Canada, and Mexico in the early 1990s. As part of a global project of economic development, through the negotiations, Mexico made

a number of changes to political–economic policies to adhere to systems set up in the United States and Canada. NAFTA entered into force on January 1, 1994, and has had polarizing results.

3. In anticipation of the competition from NAFTA and the probable decline in prices for Mexican producers, PROCAMPO was introduced in late 1994. Sadoulet, de Janvry, and Davis (2001, 1044–45) note that the "program was introduced when NAFTA started (the Winter of 1994) as a compensatory income transfer targeted to these crop producers. The objectives were political (to manage the political acceptability of the free trade agreement among farmers), economic (to provide farmers with liquidity to adjust production to the new set of relative prices), and social (to prevent an increase in already extensive levels of poverty among smallholders and a rapid process of outmigration to the cities and the border in the North). The program was designed as a 15-year transition toward free trade."

4. Hobsbawm's (1994) argument has been widely contested (cf. Kay 2008; McMichael 2006; Watts 2002).

5. The INEGI criterion for the category of "indigenous" is residents older than the age of three who speak a nationally recognized indigenous language; this figure in 2015 was 28 percent.

6. Mora's (2017, 161–81) discussion of Oportunidades is the study of the fifth chapter of *Kuxlejal Politics*, which I do not seek to replicate; however, it is important to note that 20 percent of the Mexican population benefits directly (cash payment to women) or indirectly (their families) from enrollment in the program. Oportunidades is also critiqued by *campesinos/as* in resistance (and scholars) as a program that does not get at the root causes of structural inequality (Moksnes 2012, 262).

7. The importance of religion and religious organizing cannot be ignored. For an in-depth discussion of the religious roots of indigenous organizing in the highlands, see Moksnes (2012).

8. Land reform redistributed thousands of hectares of land to peasants in a communal form called the *ejido*. Bruce (2016), in discussing such forms of production, argues that the history of fair trade exchanges more broadly needs to be rewritten to account for the power of agrarian reforms demanded by peasants against the hegemony of landowners and unwilling governments, in making possible the forms of production on which certified trade relies.

9. Land invasions were widespread and continuous in twentieth-century Chiapas and are part of a violent history between large-scale landowners and peasants as well as the politics of maintaining claims to invaded land through clientelistic relations (for a more in-depth history, see Bobrow-Strain 2007).

10. The historical roots of contemporary indigenous mobilizations in Chiapas, although embedded within the five-hundred-year history of resistance, can be traced back to organizing in the 1970s by indigenous communities in collaboration with Catholic clergy members who sought to lay the groundwork for self-determination in religious base communities

(known as *comunidades eclesiales de base*, CEBs) (Nash 2001). Although the coffee crisis and neoliberal reforms were watershed moments for indigenous groups, the ability to mobilize around these events was only made possible through the grassroots groups that had been established in conjunction with religious organizing that happened earlier.

11. Bobrow-Strain (2005) notes that this led to extreme violence between *ladinos* and indigenous land claimants.

12. Chiapas has the lowest rate of adoption of PROCEDE in Mexico (Mora 2017, 117).

13. In the case of the Zapatistas, this was expressed in the Aguascalientes political centers that were the forerunners to the *caracoles*. In 2003, the military arm of the Zapatistas retreated into the southeast of Chiapas, and five civilian government centers called *caracoles* (literally, "snail shells") were established (Stahler-Sholk 2007).

14. Both groups do participate in the meetings of the National Indigenous Congress (CNI) and were supporters of the CNI independent candidate in the 2018 national race for president, María de Jesús Patricio Martínez (known informally as compañera Marichuy). The CNI is a group established following the 1996 observance of Columbus Day and is a place for representation and decision-making for all indigenous groups in Mexico (https://www.congresonacionalindigena.org/what-is-the-cni/).

15. Zapatista government centers are open to all indigenous peoples, regardless of affiliation. Both Mora (2017) and Stahler-Sholk (2010) note, for example, that non-Zapatistas utilize the governance structures available for dispute resolution more often than their Zapatista counterparts.

16. The Bartolomé de las Casas Center for human rights reported twelve active paramilitary groups by 1998 alone (Stephen 2002, 172).

17. This experience correlates strongly with antiracist struggles globally—most recently, the example of the premature death from a heart attack of twenty-seven-year-old, U.S.-based Black Lives Matter activist Erica Garner (Elizabeth 2017).

18. Café Zapatista, https://www.highergroundstrading.com/products/cafe-zapatista?variant=31285328518.

19. Gerber (2005) discusses the formation of this first cooperative as a site of indigenous autonomous practice and a practical expression of their political affiliation with the Zapatistas.

20. In 2009, twenty-nine men who had been arrested in connection with the massacre were released, and by 2011, fifty-four of the eighty who had been sentenced were released (Moksnes 2012, 229–30).

3. Fair Trade Exploitation and Empowerment

1. The OECD reported that Official Development Assistance from OECD members (DAC) in 2016 (combining bilateral and multilateral aid) was more than US$143 billion. Development aid may take on any number of forms, including direct payments, social/economic programs, or

infrastructure development. On a linked note, Ferguson, who has critiqued development programming and aid (Ferguson 1994), more recently argued that some of the more successful forms of assistance are state-led efforts to put money directly into the hands of their citizens (Ferguson 2015).

2. I owe an intellectual debt here to Probyn, whose work on gendered dimensions of fisheries prompted me to consider similarities in the fair trade market. In this work, Probyn discusses in particular the gender myopia of human-caused climate change and the framing of women as "vulnerable" or "virtuous" in relation to the environment, finding comparative thinking in "North–South" binaries, where she notes that "women in the Global South [are portrayed] as victims of poverty and so-called natural catastrophes and those in the North [are portrayed] as virtuous ecoconsumers" (Probyn 2017, 105).

3. I have written elsewhere about the trade-offs in producing under standards for the market, in which producers struggle to maintain their autonomy and their own projections of living well while simultaneously negotiating the standards for production and development, as well as the annual audit that fair trade certification requires (see Naylor 2017a, 2017c).

4. The producer networks are regional stakeholders, including Coordinadora Latinoamericana y del Caribe de Pequeños Productores y Trabajadores de Comercio Justo (CLAC), Fairtrade Africa, and Fairtrade Asia Pacific. The National Fairtrade Organizations are the regional groups that license the certification label in their respective country or territory; currently twenty-one such organizations are working with Fairtrade International, all based in the territorial Global North, with the exception of Australia and New Zealand.

5. Indeed, some fair trade third parties receive grants from development agencies, such as the U.K.-based Fairtrade Foundation, which receives grants from the Department for International Development (Dolan 2010, 35); Fair Trade USA, which receives funds from the U.S. Agency for International Development (USAID); Fair Trade New Zealand, which receives funds from the New Zealand Aid Programme; and different outlets at the World Bank, such as the International Finance Corporation, which funds a number of different fair trade certification programs. This flies in the face of "trade not aid" and is instead a new mechanism for funneling aid money through NGOs.

6. Fairly traded products now range from commodity goods, such as coffee and bananas, to composite products, which are made up of multiple ingredients (including ice cream and nonfood products such as clothing and home goods). Composite products must have 20 percent of their content made up by a certified ingredient to be able to display the Fairtrade International or Fair Trade USA label (Jaffee and Howard 2016).

7. The Zapatistas in particular are vocal in their critique of capitalism and in 2015 announced a new campaign against the "capitalist hydra," which critiques the hegemony of capitalism and the power relations that it infiltrates, while offering new paths forward.

8. Another potential site of bridging is through queering. Queer theory is usually a space to examine gender and sexuality, but as a social theory, it represents a form of deconstructing the geopolitics of knowledge formation on identity and subjectivity that assists with disrupting, being transverse, across (see Sedgwick 1993), or queering the normative. Although, Marcus (2005, 196–97) cautions, continually drawing on queerness may render it as a "transgression of any norm," which neglects violence against queer bodies.

9. There is a larger story about commercial tortillas that does not fit in this chapter but is important to note for scholars studying changes in corn consumption in Mexico. It is not hyperbole to state that the entirety of the commercial tortilla market in southern Mexico is now dominated by one group, called Maseca. All of the tortillerias manufacture tortillas from this masa flour from Azteca Milling, which has trademarked and made opaque the ingredients and processing of the masa. In informal discussions with professionals in the city of San Cristóbal, many remarked that Maseca tortillas did not undergo a nixtamalization (soaking with lime) and that after decades of relying on commercial corn, they were seeing health consequences, such as increases in colon maladies.

10. This is especially important as development and capitalist narratives attempt to enclose peasant farmers and plantation laborers as part of fair trade certification (as discussed by Wilson 2017).

4. Fair Trade in Movement

1. Reflecting on this depiction of the commodity chain in an email dated January 16, 2018, Earley (of Just Coffee) observed, "The sticker is a conundrum in itself—in order to speak to consumers in a consumer setting (grocery store, co-op, market, café, etc.), we have to be able to abbreviate these complexities into bite-sized pieces of information that people can digest. However, in doing so, we are by definition dumbing things down to the point of gross oversimplification. It is the tension we have felt in this market from the beginning, and the questions remain of how to bring people to the point that they will engage without either losing interest or becoming intimidated by processes that seem overwhelming."

2. Never mind the fact that the "people" who get to consume "healthier" food in this case are inherently the "wealthy" customers.

3. Over the past thirty years, the fair trade price floor turned into a ceiling. The fair trade price is intended to act as a safety net in the event of a market price dip; it is not a premium price point. The fair trade guaranteed price protected small producers during periods of oversupply, such as in 2001 and 2013, but producers are otherwise paid at the market price, which fair trade matches.

4. In the case of coffee, through the new Fair Trade USA campaign "Fair Trade for All," this community now extends from democratically run farmer cooperatives to laborers on coffee plantations.

5. Outside of the experiences with the cooperatives in Chiapas from which they purchase, during the Chronicles, Treter and Earley also had exchanges with producer cooperatives in Central America. The story of Las Diosas Cooperative provides an additional example of the connections forged through thoughtful exchanges. In 2012, the cooperative was not going to be able to deliver on their contract because they had lost the majority of their coffee to rust (La Roya), resulting in almost an 80 percent reduction in their expected harvest. Earley related to me that the cooperative explained that they were afraid that because they were losing their coffee, the roasters would not come back. Instead, Just Coffee Cooperative decided to take the money that they would have paid for the coffee and invest in the recovery and diversification of the cooperative's crops. In the intervening time, both Just Coffee and the On the Ground Initiative have injected thousands of dollars into beekeeping and honey production as well as hibiscus cultivation; in the meantime, their coffee production has rebounded. Additionally, Just Coffee worked with Las Diosas to extend their organic practices to make their plants stronger and more rust resistant.

6. A joint initiative of Outside the Bean (nonprofit arm of Just Coffee) and On the Ground started in 2005.

7. It is important to note that this impact is significant for the sixty farming families in this particular community, yet they make up less than 10 percent of Maya Vinic's total membership.

8. Earley reported to me that because Just Coffee and Higher Grounds are among the only purchasers of Maya Vinic coffee, they are able to have more earnest negotiations and are willing to pay more (beyond the market or fair trade price floor). They often do direct price negotiating with Maya Vinic and can give a better price, and sign guarantees for prefinancing, which enables the cooperative to obtain cash earlier in the season.

9. The *socios* featured in the documentary *Connected by Coffee* are almost exclusively members of the Maya Vinic leadership (or are former leadership members) at the time of filming.

10. This finding is consistent with results from research conducted with fair trade coffee producers in Nicaragua (see Wilson 2013).

11. In 2013, the price of fair trade coffee was the same as the world market price; for certified organic fair trade coffee, the price was thirty pesos per kilo (a reduction of sixteen pesos from 2012).

5. Resistance as Agricultural Practice

1. Roughly thirteen hundred privately owned estates amounting to more than one hundred thousand hectares were seized during the uprising—about 6 percent of private agricultural property in Chiapas (Bobrow-Strain 2004, 887). It should be noted that these seizures were the work of Zapatista and non-Zapatista *campesinos/as* alike. For a more detailed account of the invasions and the government response, see Bobrow-Strain (2004, 2007).

2. Mora's (2017) discussion of the advance of PROCEDE demonstrates that although the government successfully introduced land titling in Chiapas, it has not succeeded in eliminating the *ejidos* there.

3. Both Chris Treter (Higher Grounds) and Matt Earley (Just Coffee) described these exchanges to me and especially their efforts to work with cooperatives south of Chiapas, which are already experiencing significant coffee losses due to rust (see also chapter 4).

4. The formation of La Vía Campesina in 1992 created an important social movement to oppose the corporate food regime that has displaced small-scale producers (Fairbairn 2010; Martínez-Torres and Rosset 2010; McMichael 2014). Peter Rosset (2011, 22) has argued that food sovereignty moves past other strategies that focus solely on food supply, which disregards "where the food comes from or how it is produced." Focused on reducing the threat of hunger for those who are at the greatest risk—smallholder producers—this idea has been important in emphasizing the limits of existing market-based strategies (such as food security) to improve food supply and access.

5. In 2008, it was reported that global food prices had risen 83 percent in three years (Wiggins and Levy 2008, cited in Holt-Giménez and Shattuck 2011, 111).

6. This raises a host of questions as to what the *sovereignty* in *food sovereignty* means, which I will not address here, but a few have raised this issue (cf. Akram-Lodhi 2013; Edelman 2014; Hospes 2014; McMichael 2014; Naylor 2012a), and it is a line of inquiry that political geographers might explore. Related to such questions, Trauger (2014, 2017) offers insight into how food sovereignty might function (or not) in the context of the neoliberal sovereign state.

7. Although Jarosz (2014) and Clapp (2014) both argue that pitting food sovereignty as the alternative to neoliberal food security sets up a false binary.

8. The Yale University Program in Agrarian Studies and the *Journal of Peasant Studies* together sponsored the conference Food Sovereignty: A Critical Dialogue between September 14 and 15, 2013. The event resulted in a number of professional papers by scholars and activists on the intellectual and pragmatic future of food sovereignty.

9. Giunta (2014) addresses the issue of how food sovereignty is to be pragmatically realized in a recent discussion of Ecuadorian attempts to institutionalize the constitutionally guaranteed right to food sovereignty.

10. I do not mean to suggest here that Native American, First Nations, and Aboriginal groups fall into the same category as settlers, although they reside in the global core in sites of regional and national peripheries.

11. Food sovereignty is often identified as a "radical alternative" to a neoliberal capitalist food system (cf. Ayres and Bosia 2011; Beuchelt and Virchow 2012; Burnett 2013; Desmarais, Wittman, and Wiebe 2011; Fairbairn 2010, 2012; Holt-Giménez 2009; Hospes 2014; Martínez-Torres and Rosset 2010; Massicotte et al. 2012; Rosset 2009, 2011; Schanbacher 2010;

Trang 2012; Wittman 2009; Wittman, Desmarais, and Wiebe 2010). Additionally, questions about who benefits from food sovereignty are being raised as alternative food movements in the United States take up the cause (cf. Alkon and Mares 2012). Furthermore, Jarosz's (2014) argument about the relational and competing discourses of food sovereignty and food security provides an entry point to considering the friction of cultivating more egalitarian access to food at different scales.

12. Prospera (discussed in chapter 2) is a government welfare program that makes cash payments to women in exchange for changes in cultural habits (on its predecessor, Oportunidades, see Mora 2017). Additionally, it should be noted that participants in autonomous resistance are not always cohesive family units within the resistance; for example, in one of the Las Abejas households I visited, one of the older boys was a Zapatista. Likewise, as Mora (2017) points out, sometimes people are incentivized away from the resistance, and the younger members of the household may leave to find wage-labor opportunities.

13. For a more in-depth study of *cafetal* diversity in smallholder plots in Central America, see Méndez et al. (2010).

14. *Campesinos/as* with more income tended to have more *animalitas* (little animals, as they were referred to). Such *animalitas* included chickens, ducks, turkeys, and small pigs. Husbandry of cattle was less common in the highlands—I only met one *campesino* who had a small herd of cattle. This contrasts with strategies elsewhere, as Mora (2017) has documented.

15. Another *campesino* considered importance beyond daily life, telling me, "Here we try to keep variety in the seeds, we men and women, we talk about the different seeds, the varieties here are many.... These seeds have been around for a long time and the seeds from past generations must be conserved, it is part of the culture."

16. Bread-making activities were largely contingent on community agreement to dedicate communal land to wheat cultivation.

Bibliography

Abu-Lughod, Lila. 1990. "The Romance of Resistance: Tracing Transformations of Power through Bedouin Women." *American Ethnologist* 17, no. 1: 41–55.

Agamben, Giorgio. 1993. *The Coming Community.* Minneapolis: University of Minnesota Press.

Aguila-Way, Tania. 2014. "The Zapatista 'Mother Seeds in Resistance' Project: The Indigenous Community Seed Bank as a Living, Self-Organizing Archive." *Social Text* 32, no. 1 (118): 67–92. https://doi.org/10.1215/01642472-2391342.

Akram-Lodhi, A. Haroon. 2013. "How to Build Food Sovereignty." In *Food Sovereignty: A Critical Dialogue.* New Haven, Conn.: Yale University. http://www.iss.nl/fileadmin/ASSETS/iss/Research_and_projects/Research_networks/ICAS/15_AkramLodi_2013-1.pdf.

Akram-Lodhi, A. Haroon, and Cristobal Kay. 2010a. "Surveying the Agrarian Question (Part 1): Unearthing Foundations, Exploring Diversity." *Journal of Peasant Studies* 37, no. 1: 177–202. https://doi.org/10.1080/03066150903498838.

Akram-Lodhi, A. Haroon, and Cristobal Kay. 2010b. "Surveying the Agrarian Question (Part 2): Current Debates and Beyond." *Journal of Peasant Studies* 37, no. 2: 255–84. https://doi.org/10.1080/03066151003594906.

Alcoff, Linda Martín. 1992. "The Problem of Speaking for Others." *Cultural Critique*, no. 20: 5–32.

Alcoff, Linda Martín. 2007. "Mignolo's Epistemology of Coloniality." *New Centennial Review* 7, no. 3: 79–101.

Alkon, Alison Hope, and Teresa Marie Mares. 2012. "Food Sovereignty in US Food Movements: Radical Visions and Neoliberal Constraints." *Agriculture and Human Values* 29, no. 3: 347–59. https://doi.org/10.1007/s10460-012-9356-z.

Altieri, Miguel. 2009. "Agroecology, Small Farms, and Food Sovereignty." *Monthly Review: An Independent Socialist Magazine* 61, no. 3: 102–13.

Altieri, Miguel, and Clara I. Nicholls. 2008. "Scaling Up Agroecological Approaches for Food Sovereignty in Latin America." *Development* 51, no. 4: 472–80.

Alvarez, Sonia E. 2009. "Beyond NGO-ization? Reflections from Latin America." *Development* 52, no. 2: 175–84.

Anderson, Benedict R. 1983. *Imagined Communities: Reflections on the Origin and Spread of Nationalism.* London: Verso.
Antillón Najlis, Ximena. 2011. "El territorio del alma: Una experiencia de acompañamiento psicosocial en la zona norte de Chiapas." In *Luchas "muy otras": Zapatismo y autonomía en las comunidades indígenas de Chiapas,* edited by Bruno Baronnet, Mariana Mora, and Richard Stahler-Sholk, 299–316. México, D.F.: CIESAS, Centro de Investigaciones y Estudios Superiores en Antropología Social: Universidad Autónoma Metropolitana UAM-Xochimilco/Universidad Autónoma de Chiapas.
Anzaldúa, Gloria. 1987. *Borderlands: The New Mestiza = La Frontera.* San Francisco: Aunt Lute Books.
Anzaldúa, Gloria. 2015. *Light in the Dark/Luz en lo Oscuro: Rewriting Identity, Spirituality, Reality.* Durham, N.C.: Duke University Press.
Arce, Alberto. 2009. "Living in Times of Solidarity: Fair Trade and the Fractured Life Worlds of Guatemalan Coffee Farmers." *Journal of International Development* 21, no. 7: 1031–41. https://doi.org/10.1002/jid.1634.
Asher, Kiran. 2013. "Latin American Decolonial Thought, or Making the Subaltern Speak." *Geography Compass* 7, no. 12: 832–42. https://doi.org/10.1111/gec3.12102.
Ayres, Jeffrey, and Michael Bosia. 2011. "Beyond Global Summitry: Food Sovereignty as Localized Resistance to Globalization." *Globalizations* 8, no. 1: 47–63.
Bacon, Christopher. 2010. "Who Decides What Is Fair in Fair Trade? The Agri-environmental Governance of Standards, Access, and Price." *Journal of Peasant Studies* 37, no. 1: 111–47. https://doi.org/10.1080/03066150903498796.
Bacon, Christopher. 2013. "Quality Revolutions, Solidarity Networks, and Sustainability Innovations: Following Fair Trade Coffee from Nicaragua to California." *Ecology* 20, no. 1: 70–179.
Bacon, Christopher. 2015. "Food Sovereignty, Food Security and Fair Trade: The Case of an Influential Nicaraguan Smallholder Cooperative." *Third World Quarterly* 36, no. 3: 469–88. https://doi.org/10.1080/01436597.2015.1002991.
Bacon, Christopher, William A. Sundstrom, María Eugenia Flores Gómez, V. Ernesto Méndez, Rica Santos, Barbara Goldoftas, and Ian Dougherty. 2014. "Explaining the 'Hungry Farmer Paradox': Smallholders and Fair Trade Cooperatives Navigate Seasonality and Change in Nicaragua's Corn and Coffee Markets." *Global Environmental Change* 25, no. 1: 133–49. https://doi.org/10.1016/j.gloenvcha.2014.02.005.
Baronnet, Bruno, Mariana Mora, and Richard Stahler-Sholk, eds. 2011. *Luchas "muy otras": Zapatismo y autonomía en las comunidades indígenas de Chiapas.* México, D.F.: CIESAS, Centro de Investigaciones y Estudios Superiores en Antropología Social: Universidad Autónoma Metropolitana UAM-Xochimilco/Universidad Autónoma de Chiapas.
Baviera, Mara, and Walden F. Bello. 2009. "Food Wars." *Monthly Review* (blog), July 1. https://monthlyreview.org/2009/07/01/food-wars/.

Bennett, Elizabeth A. 2016. "Governance, Legitimacy, and Stakeholder Balance: Lessons from Fairtrade International." *Social Enterprise Journal* 12, no. 3: 322–46. https://doi.org/10.1108/SEJ-08-2016-0038.

Bernstein, Henry. 2014. "Food Sovereignty via the 'Peasant Way': A Sceptical View." *Journal of Peasant Studies* 41, no. 6: 1031–63. https://doi.org/10.1080/03066150.2013.852082.

Beuchelt, Tina, and Detlef Virchow. 2012. "Food Sovereignty or the Human Right to Adequate Food: Which Concept Serves Better as International Development Policy for Global Hunger and Poverty Reduction?" *Agriculture and Human Values* 29, no. 2: 259–73. https://doi.org/10.1007/s10460-012-9355-0.

Block, Daniel R., Noel Chávez, Erika Allen, and Dinah Ramirez. 2012. "Food Sovereignty, Urban Food Access, and Food Activism: Contemplating the Connections through Examples from Chicago." *Agriculture and Human Values* 29, no. 2: 203–15. https://doi.org/10.1007/s10460-011-9336-8.

Bobrow-Strain, Aaron. 2004. "(Dis)Accords: The Politics of Market-Assisted Land Reforms in Chiapas, Mexico." *World Development* 32, no. 6: 887–903.

Bobrow-Strain, Aaron. 2005. "Articulations of Rule: Landowners, Revolution, and Territory in Chiapas, Mexico 1920–1962." *Journal of Historical Geography* 31, no. 4: 744–62.

Bobrow-Strain, Aaron. 2007. *Intimate Enemies: Landowners, Power, and Violence in Chiapas*. Durham, N.C.: Duke University Press.

Borowiak, Craig, Maliha Safri, Stephen Healy, and Marianna Pavlovskaya. 2018. "Navigating the Fault Lines: Race and Class in Philadelphia's Solidarity Economy." *Antipode* 50, no. 3: 577–603. https://doi.org/10.1111/anti.12368.

Boyer, Jefferson. 2010. "Food Security, Food Sovereignty, and Local Challenges for Transnational Agrarian Movements: The Honduras Case." *Journal of Peasant Studies* 37, no. 2: 319–51.

Brandt, Marisa. 2014. "Zapatista Corn: A Case Study in Biocultural Innovation." *Social Studies of Science* 44, no. 6: 874–900.

Brandt, Willy. *North-South, a Programme for Survival: Report of the Independent Commission on International Development Issues*. Cambridge, Mass.: MIT Press, 1980.

Brown, Lester. 2011. "The New Geopolitics of Food." *Foreign Policy*, no. 186, 54–63.

Brown, Peter. 2013. "Mother Seeds in Resistance of Highland Chiapas in Defense of Native Corn." In *Seeds of Resistance, Seeds of Hope: Place and Agency in the Conservation of Biodiversity*, edited by Virginia D. Nazarea, Robert E. Rhoades, and Jenna Andrews-Swann, 151–76. Tucson: University of Arizona Press.

Brown, Sandy, and Christy Getz. 2008. "Privatizing Farm Worker Justice: Regulating Labor through Voluntary Certification and Labeling." *Geoforum* 39, no. 3: 1184–96. https://doi.org/10.1016/j.geoforum.2007.01.002.

Bruce, Analena. 2016. "The Legacy of Agrarian Reform in Latin America:

Foundations of the Fair Trade Cooperative System." *Geography Compass* 10, no. 12: 485–98. https://doi.org/10.1111/gec3.12298.

Burnett, Kim, and Sophia Murphy. 2014. "What Place for International Trade in Food Sovereignty?" *Journal of Peasant Studies* 41, no. 6: 1065–84. https://doi.org/10.1080/03066150.2013.876995.

Buttle, Martin. 2008. "Diverse Economies and the Negotiations and Practices of Ethical Finance: The Case of Charity Bank." *Environment and Planning A* 40, no. 9: 2097–113. https://doi.org/10.1068/a39317.

Cameron, Jenny. 2015. "Enterprise Innovation and Economic Diversity in Community Supported Agriculture." In *Making Other Worlds Possible: Performing Diverse Economies*, edited by Gerda Roelvink, Kevin St. Martin, and J. K. Gibson-Graham, 52–71. Minneapolis: University of Minnesota Press.

Cameron, Jenny, Katherine Gibson, and Ann Hill. 2014. "Cultivating Hybrid Collectives: Research Methods for Enacting Community Food Economies in Australia and the Philippines." *Local Environment* 19, no. 1: 118–32. https://doi.org/10.1080/13549839.2013.855892.

Cameron, Jenny, and Sarah Wright. 2014. "Researching Diverse Food Initiatives: From Backyard and Community Gardens to International Markets." *Local Environment* 19, no. 1: 1–9. https://doi.org/10.1080/13549839.2013.835096.

Castro-Gómez, Santiago. 2007. "The Missing Chapter of Empire." *Cultural Studies* 21, no. 2–3: 428–48. https://doi.org/10.1080/09502380601162639.

Castro-Gómez, Santiago, and Eduardo Mendieta. 1998. *Teorías Sin Disciplina: Latinoamericanismo, Poscolonialidad y Globalización En Debate*. Mexico, D.F.: Miguel Ángel Porrúa México.

Cedillo, Adela. 2012. "Armed Struggle without Revolution, the Organizing Process of the National Liberation Forces (FLN) and the Genesis of Neo-Zapatism (1969–1983)." In *Challenging Authoritarianism in Mexico: Revolutionary Struggles and the Dirty War, 1964–1982*, edited by Fernando Calderón and Adela Cedillo, 148–66. New York: Routledge.

Center for International Development at Harvard University. 2014. "The Chiapas Project." Growth Lab. https://growthlab.cid.harvard.edu/chiapas-project.

Chatterton, Paul, and Nik Heynen. 2011. "Resistance(s) and Collective Social Action." In *A Companion to Social Geography*, edited by Vincent J. Del Casino Jr., Mary E. Thomas, Paul Cloke, and Ruth Panelli, 508–25. Oxford: Wiley-Blackwell. https://doi.org/10.1002/9781444395211.

CLAC. 2004. "Private Plantations and FLO's Future." Unpublished document discussed at the Fairtrade International Meeting of Members and FLO Board.

Clapp, Jennifer. 2014. "Food Security and Food Sovereignty: Getting Past the Binary." *Dialogues in Human Geography* 4, no. 2: 206–11. https://doi.org/10.1177/2043820614537159.

Collier, George Allen, and Elizabeth Lowery Quaratiello. 2005. *Basta! Land and the Zapatista Rebellion in Chiapas*. 3rd ed. Oakland, Calif.: Food First Books.

Collier, Paul. 2008. "The Politics of Hunger: How Illusion and Greed Fan the Food Crisis." *Foreign Affairs*, November/December. https://www.foreignaffairs.com/articles/2008-11-01/politics-hunger.

Comaroff, John L., and Jean Comaroff. 2009. *Ethnicity, Inc.* Chicago: University of Chicago Press.

Congreso Nacional Indígena. n.d. "¿Qué es el CNI?" *Congreso Nacional Indígena* (blog). https://www.congresonacionalindigena.org/que-es-el-cni/.

Consejo Nacional de Población. 2011. *Índice Absoluto de Marginación 2000–2010*. Mexico, D.F.: Consejo Nacional de Población. http://www.conapo.gob.mx/es/CONAPO/Indice_Absoluto_de_Marginacion_2000_2010.

Cook, Maria Lorena, Kevin J. Middlebrook, and Juan Molinar Horcasitas. 1994. *The Politics of Economic Restructuring: State-Society Relations and Regime Change in Mexico*. San Diego, Calif.: Center for US–Mexican Studies, University of California.

Cresswell, Tim. 1996. *In Place/out of Place: Geography, Ideology, and Transgression*. Minneapolis: University of Minnesota Press.

Cumes, Aura. 2014. "La 'India' como 'sirvienta': Servidumbre doméstica, colonialismo y patriarcado en Guatemala." PhD diss., CIESAS, Mexico City.

Daigle, Michelle. 2017. "Tracing the Terrain of Indigenous Food Sovereignties." *Journal of Peasant Studies* 46, no. 2: 297–316. https://doi.org/10.1080/03066150.2017.1324423.

Dalvai, Rudi. 2012. "Metamorphosis of the Fair Trade Movement." *Fair World Project* (blog), Fall. http://fairworldproject.org/voices-of-fair-trade/metamorphosis-of-the-fair-trade-movement/.

Dean, Jodi. 2015. "The Party and Communist Solidarity." *Rethinking Marxism* 27, no. 3: 332–42. https://doi.org/10.1080/08935696.2015.1042701.

Delfín-Fuentes, Yliana, Claudia Brunel-Manse, Eduardo Bello-Baltazar, and Remy Vandame. 2011. "Contribution of Producer Organizations to the Sustainability of Their Territories, Guaya'b (Guatemala) y Maya Vinic (Chiapas)." *Ra Ximhai* 7, no. 2: 313–30.

Dennis, Aaron. 2013. "Connected by Coffee." http://connectedbycoffee.com/.

Desmarais, Annette Aurélie, and Hannah Wittman. 2014. "Farmers, Foodies and First Nations: Getting to Food Sovereignty in Canada." *Journal of Peasant Studies* 41, no. 6: 1153–73. https://doi.org/10.1080/03066150.2013.876623.

Desmarais, Annette Aurélie, Hannah Wittman, and Nettie Wiebe. 2011. "Sovereignty Now!" *Alternatives Journal* 37, no. 2: 19–21.

Diprose, Gradon. 2016. "Negotiating Interdependence and Anxiety in Community Economies." *Environment and Planning A* 48, no. 7: 1411–27. https://doi.org/10.1177/0308518X16638659.

Dixon, Jane. 2011. "Diverse Food Economies, Multivariant Capitalism, and the Community Dynamic Shaping Contemporary Food Systems." *Community Development Journal* 46, Suppl. 1: i20–35. https://doi.org/10.1093/cdj/bsq046.

Dolan, Catherine S. 2008. "In the Mists of Development: Fairtrade in Kenyan Tea Fields." *Globalizations* 5, no. 2: 305–18.

Dolan, Catherine S. 2010. "Virtual Moralities: The Mainstreaming of Fairtrade in Kenyan Tea Fields." *Geoforum* 41, no. 1: 33–43. https://doi.org/10.1016/j.geoforum.2009.01.002.

Dombroski, Kelly. 2016. "Hybrid Activist Collectives: Reframing Mothers' Environmental and Caring Labour." *International Journal of Sociology and Social Policy* 36, no. 9/10: 629–46.

Dombroski, Kelly, Katharine Mckinnon, and Stephen Healy. 2016. "Beyond the Birth Wars: Diverse Assemblages of Care." *New Zealand Geographer* 72, no. 3: 230–39. https://doi.org/10.1111/nzg.12142.

Dussel, Enrique D. 1976. *History and the Theology of Liberation: A Latin American Perspective*. Ossining, N.Y.: Orbis Books.

Dussel, Enrique D. 1995. *The Invention of the Americas: Eclipse of "The Other" and the Myth of Modernity*. New York: Continuum.

Dussel, Enrique D., and Eduardo Mendieta. 1996. *The Underside of Modernity: Apel, Ricoeur, Rorty, Taylor, and the Philosophy of Liberation*. Atlantic Highlands, N.J.: Humanities Press.

Earley, Matt. 2012. "Fair Trade Is Dead." *Just Coffee Cooperative* (blog), January 13. http://www.justcoffee.coop/blog/%5Buser%5D/2012/01/13/fair_trade_is_dead.

Earley, Matt. 2013. "10 Days, 5 Farmer Co-Ops, 4 Countries, 2 Coffee Roasters, 1 Jeep." *Just Coffee Cooperative* (blog), December 20. http://justcoffee.coop/10-days-5-farmer-co-ops-4-countries-2-coffee-roasters-1-jeep/.

Eber, Christine England, and Christine Kovic. 2003. *Women in Chiapas: Making History in Times of Struggle and Hope*. New York: Routledge.

Edelman, Marc. 2014. "The Next Stage of the Food Sovereignty Debate." *Dialogues in Human Geography* 4, no. 2: 182–84. https://doi.org/10.1177/2043820614537153.

Ejército Zapatista de Liberación Nacional. 1993. "The First Declaration of the Lacandon Jungle." Palabra Zapatista. http://palabra.ezln.org.mx/comunicados/1994/1993.htm.

Ejército Zapatista de Liberación Nacional. 1996. "The Fourth Declaration of the Lacandon Jungle." Palabra Zapatista. http://palabra.ezln.org.mx/comunicados/1996/1996_01_01_a.htm.

Ejército Zapatista de Liberación Nacional. 2012. "¿Escucharon? Comunicado Del Comité Clandestino Revolucionario Indígena-Comandancia General Del Ejército Zapatista De Liberación Nacional." Enlace Zapatista. December 21. http://enlacezapatista.ezln.org.mx/2012/12/21/comunicado-del-comite-clandestino-revolucionario-indigena-comandancia-general-del-ejercito-zapatista-de-liberacion-nacional-del-21-de-diciembre-del-2012/.

Elizabeth, De. 2017. "Erica Garner Has Passed Away Following a Heart Attack." *Teen Vogue*, December 27. https://www.teenvogue.com/story/erica-garner-reportedly-declared-brain-dead.

England, Kim V. L. 1994. "Getting Personal: Reflexivity, Positionality, and Feminist Research." *Professional Geographer* 46, no. 1: 80–89.

Escobar, Arturo. 1995. *Encountering Development: The Making and Unmaking of the Third World*. Princeton, N.J.: Princeton University Press.
Escobar, Arturo. 2001. "Culture Sits in Places: Reflections on Globalism and Subaltern Strategies of Localization." *Political Geography* 20, no. 2: 139–74.
Escobar, Arturo. 2007. "Worlds and Knowledges Otherwise." *Cultural Studies* 21, no. 2–3: 179–210.
Escobar, Arturo. 2008. *Territories of Difference: Place, Movements, Life, Redes*. Durham, N.C.: Duke University Press.
Escobar, Arturo. 2018. *Designs for the Pluriverse: Radical Interdependence, Autonomy, and the Making of Worlds*. Durham, N.C.: Duke University Press.
Essex, Jamey. 2012. "Idle Hands Are the Devil's Tools: The Geopolitics and Geoeconomics of Hunger." *Annals of the Association of American Geographers* 102, no. 1: 191–207. https://doi.org/10.1080/00045608.2011.595966.
Essex, Jamey. 2013. *Development, Security, and Aid: Geopolitics and Geoeconomics at the US Agency for International Development*. Vol. 16. Athens: University of Georgia Press.
Fair Trade Advocacy Office. n.d. "The Fair Trade Movement." http://www.fairtrade-advocacy.org/about-fair-trade/the-fair-trade-movement.
Fair Trade USA. 2012. "Fair Trade for All." http://www.fairtradeusa.org/fair_trade_for_all.
Fair Trade USA. 2013. "Trade as One Launches Unique Approach to Buying Fair Trade Products." February 22. http://fairtradeusa.org/press-room/press-release/trade-one-launches-unique-approach-buying-fair-trade-products.
Fair Trade USA. 2016. "Fighting Poverty." 2016. http://fairtradeusa.org/what-is-fair-trade/impact/fighting-poverty.
Fair Trade USA. 2017. "2016 Almanac." https://www.fairtradecertified.org/news/2016-fair-trade-usa-almanac.
Fairbairn, Madeleine. 2010. "Framing Resistance: International Food Regimes and the Roots of Food Sovereignty." In *Food Sovereignty: Reconnecting Food, Nature and Community*, edited by Hannah Wittman, Annette Aurélie Desmarais, and Nettie Wiebe, 15–32. Halifax, N.S.: Fernwood.
Fairbairn, Madeleine. 2012. "Framing Transformation: The Counterhegemonic Potential of Food Sovereignty in the US Context." *Agriculture and Human Values* 29, no. 2: 217–30. https://doi.org/10.1007/s10460-011-9334-x.
Fairtrade International. 2011. *Fairtrade Standard for Small Producer Organizations*. Bonn, Germany: Fairtrade Labelling Organizations International.
Fairtrade International. 2015. *Fairtrade Standard Setting Public System Report*. Bonn, Germany: Fairtrade International. https://www.fairtrade.net/fileadmin/user_upload/content/2009/standards/documents/2016-01-15-FI-PublicSystemReport.pdf.

Fairtrade International. 2016a. *Growing Better Futures, Fairtrade International Annual Report 2015–2016*. Bonn, Germany: Fairtrade International. https://annualreport15–16.fairtrade.net/en/growing-better-futures/.

Fairtrade International. 2016b. *Changing Trade, Changing Lives: A Five-Year Strategy*. Bonn, Germany: Fairtrade International. http://www.fairtrade.net/new/latest-news/single-view/article/changing-trade-changing-lives-a-five-year-strategy.html.

Fairtrade International. 2017. "Fairtrade: Setting Our Sights on the Future." *Fairtrade* (blog), September 21. https://medium.com/@fairtrade/fairtrade-setting-our-sights-on-the-future-f5c5422dfdda.

Fairtrade International. 2018. *Monitoring the Scope and Benefits of Fairtrade*. Monitoring Report. Bonn, Germany: Fairtrade International. https://www.fairtrade.net/fileadmin/user_upload/content/Fairtrade MonitoringReport_9thEdition_lores.pdf.

Fairtrade Labelling Organizations. 2008. "Frequently Asked Questions." http://www.fairtrade.net.

Fairtrade Labelling Organizations. 2013. *Unlocking the Power*. Annual report. Bonn, Germany: Fairtrade International.

Faria, Caroline, and Sharlene Mollett. 2016. "Critical Feminist Reflexivity and the Politics of Whiteness in the 'Field.'" *Gender, Place, and Culture* 23, no. 1: 79–93. https://doi.org/10.1080/0966369X.2014.958065.

Featherstone, David. 2003. "Spatialities of Transnational Resistance to Globalization: The Maps of Grievance of the Inter-continental Caravan." *Transactions of the Institute of British Geographers* 28, no. 4: 404–21. https://doi.org/10.1111/j.0020-2754.2003.00101.x.

Featherstone, David. 2007. "The Spatial Politics of the Past Unbound: Transnational Networks and the Making of Political Identities." *Global Networks* 7, no. 4: 430–52. https://doi.org/10.1111/j.1471-0374.2007.00178.x.

Featherstone, David. 2008. *Resistance, Space and Political Identities: The Making of Counter-global Networks*. Chichester, U.K.: Wiley-Blackwell.

Featherstone, David. 2012. *Solidarity: Hidden Histories and Geographies of Internationalism*. London: Zed Books.

Ferguson, James. 1994. *The Anti-politics Machine: "Development," Depoliticization, and Bureaucratic Power in Lesotho*. Minneapolis: University of Minnesota Press.

Ferguson, James. 2010. "The Uses of Neoliberalism." *Antipode* 41: 166–84. https://doi.org/10.1111/j.1467-8330.2009.00721.x.

Ferguson, James. 2015. *Give a Man a Fish: Reflections on the New Politics of Distribution*. Durham, N.C.: Duke University Press.

Fernandez, Margarita, V. Ernesto Mendez, and Christopher Bacon. 2013. "Seasonal Hunger in Coffee Communities: Integrated Analysis of Livelihoods, Agroecology, and Food Sovereignty with Smallholders of Mexico and Nicaragua." In *Food Sovereignty: A Critical Dialogue*, 1–37. New Haven, Conn.: Yale University Press.

Fisher, Josh. 2013. "Fair or Balanced? The Other Side of Fair Trade in a Nicaraguan Sewing Cooperative." *Anthropological Quarterly* 86, no. 2: 527–57.

Fisher, Josh. 2018. "In Search of Dignified Work: Gender and the Work Ethic in the Crucible of Fair Trade Production." *American Ethnologist* 45, no. 1: 74–86. https://doi.org/10.1111/amet.12600.
FLO-CERT. 2011. "Fair Trade Glossary." Fairtrade International. https://www.flocert.net/glossary/.
FLO-CERT. 2013. *Fee System Small Producer Organization: Explanatory Document*. Bonn, Germany: Fairtrade Labelling Organizations International.
Fluri, Jennifer L. 2017. "Crisis and Consumption: 'Saving' the Poor and the Seductions of Capitalism." *Humanities* 6, no. 2: Article 36. https://doi.org/10.3390/h6020036.
Fobelets, Vincent, Andrea Rusman, and Adrian de Groot Ruiz. 2017. *Assessing Coffee Farmer Household Income*. Bonn, Germany: Fairtrade International.
Foley, Paul, and Charles Mather. 2016. "Making Space for Community Use Rights: Insights From 'Community Economies' in Newfoundland and Labrador." *Society and Natural Resources* 29, no. 8: 965–80. https://doi.org/10.1080/08941920.2015.1089611.
Freidberg, Susanne. 2003. "Cleaning Up down South: Supermarkets, Ethical Trade and African Horticulture." *Social and Cultural Geography* 4, no. 1: 27–43.
Fridell, Gavin. 2007a. "Fair-Trade Coffee and Commodity Fetishism: The Limits of Market-Driven Social Justice." *Historical Materialism* 15, no. 4: 79–104.
Fridell, Gavin. 2007b. *Fair Trade Coffee: The Prospects and Pitfalls of Market-Driven Social Justice*. Toronto, Ont.: University of Toronto Press.
García, Alejandro Cerda. 2011. *Imaginando Zapatismo: Multiculturalidad y autonomía indígena en Chiapas desde un municipio autónomo*. Mexico, D.F.: Universidad Autónoma Metropolitana, Unidad Xochimilco, División de Ciencias Sociales y Humanidades.
Gerber, Philipp. 2005. "'Preguntando caminamos'—Café orgánico Zapatista: los tsotsiles de la cooperativa mut vitz en su caminar autónomo." *Anuario de Estudios Indígenas* 10: 247–300.
Getz, Christy, and Aimee Shreck. 2006. "What Organic and Fair Trade Labels Do Not Tell Us: Towards a Place-Based Understanding of Certification." *International Journal of Consumer Studies* 30, no. 5: 490–501.
Gibson-Graham, J. K. 1993. "Waiting for the Revolution, or How to Smash Capitalism While Working at Home in Your Spare Time." *Rethinking Marxism* 6, no. 2: 10–24.
Gibson-Graham, J. K. 2002. "Beyond Global vs. Local: Economic Politics Outside the Binary Frame." In *Geographies of Power: Placing Scale*, edited by Andrew Herod and Melissa W. Wright, 25–60. Malden, Mass.: John Wiley.
Gibson-Graham, J. K. 2003. "The Impatience of Familiarity: A Commentary on Michael Watts' 'Development and Governmentality.'" *Singapore Journal of Tropical Geography* 24, no. 1: 35–37.
Gibson-Graham, J. K. (1996) 2006a. *The End of Capitalism (as We Knew It):*

A Feminist Critique of Political Economy. Minneapolis: University of Minnesota Press.

Gibson-Graham, J. K. 2006b. *A Postcapitalist Politics.* Minneapolis: University of Minnesota Press.

Gibson-Graham, J. K. 2007. "A Diverse Economy: Rethinking Economy and Economic Representation." http://www.communityeconomies.org/.

Gibson-Graham, J. K. 2008. "Diverse Economies: Performative Practices for 'Other Worlds.'" *Progress in Human Geography* 32, no. 5: 613–32.

Gibson-Graham, J. K., Jenny Cameron, Kelly Dombroski, Stephen Healy, and Ethan Miller. 2017. "Cultivating Community Economies." *The Next System Project* (blog), February 27. http://thenextsystem.org/cultivating-community-economies/.

Gibson-Graham, J. K., Jenny Cameron, and Stephen Healy. 2013. *Take Back the Economy: An Ethical Guide for Transforming Our Communities.* Minneapolis: University of Minnesota Press.

Gibson-Graham, J. K., and Gerda Roelvink. 2009. "Social Innovation for Community Economies." In *Social Innovation and Territorial Development,* edited by Serena Vicari Haddock, Diana MacCallum, Frank Moulaert, and Jean Hillier, 25–39. Farnham, U.K.: Ashgate.

Gibson-Graham, J. K., and Gerda Roelvink. 2011. "The Nitty Gritty of Creating Alternative Economies." *Social Alternatives* 30, no. 1: 29–33.

Giovanni, Michela. 2014. "Indigenous Peoples and Self-Determined Development: The Case of Community Enterprises in Chiapas." PhD diss., University of Trento. http://eprints-phd.biblio.unitn.it/1228/1/Thesis_Giovannini_7Apr2014.pdf.

Giunta, Isabella. 2014. "Food Sovereignty in Ecuador: Peasant Struggles and the Challenge of Institutionalization." *Journal of Peasant Studies* 41, no. 6: 1201–24. https://doi.org/10.1080/03066150.2014.938057.

Glassman, Jim. 2003. "Rethinking Overdetermination, Structural Power, and Social Change: A Critique of Gibson-Graham, Resnick, and Wolff." *Antipode* 35, no. 4: 678–98. https://doi.org/10.1046/j.1467-8330.2003.00345.x.

Gliessman, Stephen R. 2007. *Agroecology: The Ecology of Sustainable Food Systems.* Boca Raton, Fla.: CRC Press.

Gobierno del Estado de Chiapas. 2013. "Plan Estatal De Desarrollo: Chiapas 2013–2018." Tuxtla Gutiérrez, Mexico: Secretaría de Planeación, Gestión Pública y Programa de Gobierno.

Gómez-Barris, Macarena. 2017. *The Extractive Zone: Social Ecologies and Decolonial Perspectives.* Durham, N.C.: Duke University Press.

Goodman, M., and Agatha Herman. 2015. "Connections in Fair Trade Food Networks." In *Handbook of Research on Fair Trade,* edited by Laura T. Raynolds and Elizabeth Bennett, 139–56. Cheltenham, U.K.: Edward Elgar.

Gould, Nicholas J. 2003. "Fair Trade and the Consumer Interest: A Personal Account." *International Journal of Consumer Studies* 27, no. 4: 341–45.

Gritzas, Giorgos, and Karolos Iosif Kavoulakos. 2016. "Diverse Economies and Alternative Spaces: An Overview of Approaches and Prac-

tices." *European Urban and Regional Studies* 23, no. 4. https://doi.org/10.1177/0969776415573778.
Grosfoguel, Ramón. 2008. "Transmodernity, Border Thinking, and Global Coloniality: Decolonizing Political Economy and Postcolonial Studies." *Eurozine*, July 4. http://www.eurozine.com/articles/2008-07-04-grosfoguel-en.html.
Grosfoguel, Ramón. 2011. "Decolonizing Post-colonial Studies and Paradigms of Political Economy: Transmodernity, Decolonial Thinking, and Global Coloniality." *Transmodernity* 1, no. 1: 1–36.
Guthman, Julie. 2007. "The Polanyian Way? Voluntary Food Labels as Neoliberal Governance." *Antipode* 39, no. 3: 456–78. https://doi.org/10.1111/j.1467-8330.2007.00535.x.
Hale, Charles R. 2005. "Neoliberal Multiculturalism." *PoLAR: Political and Legal Anthropology Review* 28, no. 1: 10–19.
Handy, Jim. 2007. "Food Sovereignty: Theory, Praxis and Power." Paper presented at the International Workshop on Food Sovereignty, University of Saskatchewan, Saskatoon.
Haraway, Donna. 1988. "Situated Knowledges: The Science Question in Feminism and the Privilege of Partial Perspective." *Feminist Studies* 14, no. 3: 575–99.
Haraway, Donna. 1991. *Simians, Cyborgs, and Women: The Reinvention of Nature*. New York: Routledge.
Harriss, John. 2002. *Depoliticizing Development: The World Bank and Social Capital*. Cambridge: Anthem Press.
Hart, Gillian. 2001. "Development Critiques in the 1990s: Culs de Sac and Promising Paths." *Progress in Human Geography* 25, no. 4: 649–58.
Harvey, David. 2001. *Spaces of Capital: Towards a Critical Geography*. New York: Routledge.
Harvey, David. 2007. *A Brief History of Neoliberalism*. Oxford: Oxford University Press.
Harvey, Neil. 1993. *Mexico: Dilemmas of Transition*. London: Institute of Latin American Studies, University of London/British Academic Press.
Harvey, Neil. 1998. *The Chiapas Rebellion: The Struggle for Land and Democracy*. Durham, N.C.: Duke University Press.
Healy, Stephen. 2009. "Alternative Economies." In *International Encyclopedia of Human Geography: A 12-Volume Set*, edited by Nigel Thrift and Rob Kitchin, 1st ed., 338–44. Amsterdam: Elsevier Science.
Healy, Stephen. 2014. "The Biopolitics of Community Economies in the Era of the Anthropocene." *Journal of Political Ecology* 21, no. 1: 210–21.
Hernández Castillo, Rosalva Aída. 1994. "Identidades Colectivas En Los Márgenes de La Nación: Etnicidad y Cambio Religioso Entre Los Mames de Chiapas." *Nueva Antropología* 13, no. 45: 83–105.
Hernández Castillo, Rosalva Aída. 1998. "Construyendo La Utopía. Esperanzas y Desafíos de Las Mujeres Chiapanecas de Frente Al Siglo XXI." In *La otra palabra: Mujeres y violencia en Chiapas, antes y después de Acteal*, 125. Mexico: CIESAS/Colmex/CIAM.
Hernández Castillo, Rosalva Aída. 2016. *Multiple Injustices: Indigenous*

Women, Law, and Political Struggle in Latin America. Tucson: University of Arizona Press.

Hill, Ann. 2011. "A Helping Hand and Many Green Thumbs: Local Government, Citizens and the Growth of a Community-Based Food Economy." *Local Environment* 16, no. 6: 539–53.

Hobsbawm, E. J. 1994. *The Age of Extremes: A History of the World, 1914–1991*. New York: Pantheon Books.

Holt-Giménez, Eric. 2009. "From Food Crisis to Food Sovereignty." *Monthly Review: An Independent Socialist Magazine* 61, no. 3: 142–56.

Holt-Giménez, Eric, and Annie Shattuck. 2011. "Food Crises, Food Regimes and Food Movements: Rumblings of Reform or Tides of Transformation?" *Journal of Peasant Studies* 38, no. 1: 109–44. https://doi.org/10.1080/03066150.2010.538578.

hooks, bell. 1992. *Black Looks: Race and Representation*. Boston: South End Press.

hooks, bell. 2000. *Feminism Is for Everybody: Passionate Politics*. Cambridge, Mass.: South End Press.

Hosking, Emma Noëlle, and Marcela Palomino-Schalscha. 2016. "Of Gardens, Hopes, and Spirits: Unravelling (Extra)Ordinary Community Economic Arrangements as Sites of Transformation in Cape Town, South Africa." *Antipode* 48, no. 5: 1249–69. https://doi.org/10.1111/anti.12259.

Hospes, Otto. 2014. "Food Sovereignty: The Debate, the Deadlock, and a Suggested Detour." *Agriculture and Human Values* 31, no. 1: 119–30. https://doi.org/10.1007/s10460-013-9449-3.

Howard, Philip H., and Daniel Jaffee. 2013. "Tensions between Firm Size and Sustainability Goals: Fair Trade Coffee in the United States." *Sustainability* 5, no. 1: 72–89.

Hudson, Ian, and Mark Hudson. 2003. "Removing the Veil? Commodity Fetishism, Fair Trade, and the Environment." *Organization Environment* 16, no. 4: 413–30.

Hudson, Mark, and Ian Hudson. 2004. "Justice, Sustainability, and the Fair Trade Movement: A Case Study of Coffee Production in Chiapas." *Social Justice: A Journal of Crime, Conflict, and World Order* 31, no. 3: 130–46.

Hyndman, Jennifer. 2004. "Mind the Gap: Bridging Feminist and Political Geography through Geopolitics." *Reconceptualizing the State* 23, no. 3: 307–22.

Instituto Nacional de Estadística y Geografía. 2015. *México en Cifras*. Mexico, D.F.: Instituto Nacional de Estadística y Geografía. https://www.inegi.org.mx/

Jaffee, Daniel. 2012. "Weak Coffee: Certification and Co-optation in the Fair Trade Movement." *Social Problems* 59, no. 1: 94–116. https://doi.org/10.1525/sp.2012.59.1.94.

Jaffee, Daniel. 2014. *Brewing Justice: Fair Trade Coffee, Sustainability, and Survival*. Updated ed. Berkeley: University of California Press.

Jaffee, Daniel, and Philip H. Howard. 2010. "Corporate Cooptation of Organic and Fair Trade Standards." *Agriculture and Human Values* 27, no. 4: 387–99. https://doi.org/10.1007/s10460-009-9231-8.

Jaffee, Daniel, and Philip H. Howard. 2016. "Who's the Fairest of Them All? The Fractured Landscape of U.S. Fair Trade Certification." *Agriculture and Human Values* 33, no. 4: 813–26. https://doi.org/10.1007/s10460-015-9663-2.

Jarosz, Lucy. 2014. "Comparing Food Security and Food Sovereignty Discourses." *Dialogues in Human Geography* 4, no. 2: 168–81. https://doi.org/10.1177/2043820614537161.

Kautsky, Karl. (1899) 1988. *The Agrarian Question*. London: Zwan.

Kay, Cristóbal. 2008. "Focus: Reflections on Latin American Rural Studies in the Neoliberal Globalization Period: A New Rurality?" *Development and Change* 39, no. 6: 915–43.

Keck, Margaret E., and Kathryn Sikkink. 1998. *Activists beyond Borders: Advocacy Networks in International Politics*. Ithaca, N.Y.: Cornell University Press.

Kelly, Philip. 2005. "Scale, Power and the Limits to Possibilities." *Singapore Journal of Tropical Geography* 26, no. 1: 39–43. https://doi.org/10.1111/j.0129-7619.2005.00202.x.

Klossner, John. 2013. "Cartoons." http://www.jklossner.com/.

Knapp, Steve. 2009. "Fair Trade at the Centre of Development." In *Fair Trade, Corporate Accountability and Beyond: Experiments in Globalizing Justice*, 1st ed., edited by Kate Macdonald and Shelley Marshall, 37–55. Burlington, Vt.: Ashgate.

Kobayashi, Audrey, and Linda Peake. 1994. "Unnatural Discourse: 'Race' and Gender in Geography." *Gender, Place, and Culture* 1, no. 2: 225–43.

Koopman, Sara. 2008. "El imperialismo adentro: Pueden las herramientas del amo derribar el emperio?" *ACME* 7, no. 2: 283–334.

Krueger, Robert, Christian Schulz, and David C. Gibbs. 2018. "Institutionalizing Alternative Economic Spaces? An Interpretivist Perspective on Diverse Economies." *Progress in Human Geography* 42, no. 4. https://doi.org/10.1177/0309132517694530.

Kurtz, Hilda E. 2015. "Scaling Food Sovereignty: Biopolitics and the Struggle for Local Control of Farm Food in Rural Maine." *Annals of the Association of American Geographers* 105, no. 4: 859–73. https://doi.org/10.1080/00045608.2015.1022127.

Laurie, Nina D. 2005. "Putting the Messiness Back In: Towards a Geography of Development as Creativity." *Singapore Journal of Tropical Geography* 26, no. 1: 32–35. https://doi.org/10.1111/j.0129-7619.2005.00032.x.

Lawson, Victoria. 2005. "Hopeful Geographies: Imagining Ethical Alternatives." *Singapore Journal of Tropical Geography* 26, no. 1: 36–38. https://doi.org/10.1111/j.0129-7619.2005.00201.x.

Lawson, Victoria. 2007. "Geographies of Care and Responsibility." *Annals of the Association of American Geographers* 97, no. 1: 1–11. https://doi.org/10.1111/j.1467-8306.2007.00520.x.

Lekakis, Eleftheria J. 2012. "Will the Fair Trade Revolution Be Marketised? Commodification, Decommodification and the Political Intensity of Consumer Politics." *Culture and Organization* 18, no. 5: 345–58. https://doi.org/10.1080/14759551.2012.728392.

Lepofsky, Jonathan David. 2007. "'In Each Other We Trust': Reimagining Community, Economics and the Region in Central North Carolina." PhD diss., University of North Carolina at Chapel Hill.

Lewis, Stephen. 1997. "Mestizaje." In *Encyclopedia of Mexico: History, Society, and Culture*, edited by Michael S. Werner, 838–42. London: Routledge.

Lewis, Stephen E. 2005. *The Ambivalent Revolution: Forging State and Nation in Chiapas, 1910–1945*. Albuquerque: University of New Mexico Press.

Li, Tania Murray. 2007. *The Will to Improve: Governmentality, Development, and the Practice of Politics*. Durham, N.C.: Duke University Press.

Li, Tania Murray. 2014. *Land's End: Capitalist Relations on an Indigenous Frontier*. Durham, N.C.: Duke University Press.

Little, Ruth, Damian Maye, and Brian Ilbery. 2010. "Collective Purchase: Moving Local and Organic Foods beyond the Niche Market." *Environment and Planning A* 42, no. 8: 1797–1813. https://doi.org/10.1068/a4262.

Lorde, Audre. 2003. "The Master's Tools Will Never Dismantle the Master's House." *Feminist Postcolonial Theory: A Reader* 25: 27.

Low, William, and Eileen Davenport. 2005. "Has the Medium (Roast) Become the Message? The Ethics of Marketing Fair Trade in the Mainstream." *International Marketing Review* 22, no. 5: 494–511.

Low, William, and Eileen Davenport. 2007. "To Boldly Go . . . : Exploring Ethical Spaces to Re-politicise Ethical Consumption and Fair Trade." *Journal of Consumer Behaviour* 6, no. 5: 336–48.

Lugones, María. 2007. "Heterosexualism and the Colonial/Modern Gender System." *Hypatia* 22, no. 1: 186–209.

Lugones, María. 2010. "Toward a Decolonial Feminism." *Hypatia* 25, no. 4: 742–59. https://doi.org/10.1111/j.1527-2001.2010.01137.x.

Lugones, María. 2013. "The Coloniality of Gender." In *Globalization and the Decolonial Option*, reprint ed., edited by Walter D. Mignolo and Arturo Escobar, 369–90. London: Routledge.

Lugones, María, and Elizabeth V. Spelman. 1983. "Have We Got a Theory for You! Feminist Theory, Cultural Imperialism and the Demand for 'the Woman's Voice.'" *Women's Studies International Forum* 6: 573–81.

Lustig, Nora Claudia. 2000. *Mexico: The Remaking of an Economy*. Washington, D.C.: Brookings Institution Press.

Lyon, Sarah. 2006. "Evaluating Fair Trade Consumption: Politics, Defetishization and Producer Participation." *International Journal of Consumer Studies* 30, no. 5: 452–64.

Lyon, Sarah. 2007. "Maya Coffee Farmers and Fair Trade: Assessing the Benefits and Limitations of Alternative Markets." *Culture and Agriculture* 29, no. 2: 100–112.

Lyon, Sarah. 2011. *Coffee and Community: Maya Farmers and Fair-Trade Markets*. Boulder, Colo.: University Press of Colorado.

Lyon, Sarah. 2015a. "The Hidden Labor of Fair Trade." *Labor* 12, no. 1–2: 159–76. https://doi.org/10.1215/15476715-2837652.

Lyon, Sarah. 2015b. "Fair Trade and Indigenous Communities in Latin

America." In *Handbook of Research on Fair Trade*, edited by Laura T. Raynolds and Elizabeth Bennett, 422–40. Northampton, Mass.: Edward Elgar.

Manokha, Ivan. 2004. "Modern Slavery and Fair Trade Products: Buy One and Set Someone Free." In *The Political Economy of New Slavery*, edited by Christien van den Anker, 217–34. New York: Palgrave Macmillan.

Mansvelt, Juliana, and Lawrence D. Berg. 2016. "Writing Qualitative Geographies, Constructing Meaningful Geographical Knowledges." In *Qualitative Research Methods in Human Geography*, 4th ed., edited by Iain Hay, 394–421. Oxford: Oxford University Press.

Marcus, Sharon. 2005. "Queer Theory for Everyone: A Review Essay." *Signs: Journal of Women in Culture and Society* 31, no. 1: 191–218. https://doi.org/10.1086/432743.

Marston, Andrea. 2013. "Justice for All? Material and Semiotic Impacts of Fair Trade Craft Certification." *Geoforum* 44: 162–69. https://doi.org/10.1016/j.geoforum.2012.09.013.

Martínez-Echazábal, Lourdes. 1998. "Mestizaje and the Discourse of National/Cultural Identity in Latin America, 1845–1959." *Latin American Perspectives* 25, no. 3: 21–42.

Martínez-Torres, Maria Elena. 2001. "Civil Society, the Internet, and the Zapatistas." *Peace Review* 13, no. 3: 347–55. https://doi.org/10.1080/13668800120079045.

Martínez-Torres, Maria Elena. 2006. *Organic Coffee: Sustainable Development by Mayan Farmers*. Athens: Ohio University Center for International Studies.

Martínez-Torres, Maria Elena, and Peter M. Rosset. 2010. "La Vía Campesina: The Birth and Evolution of a Transnational Social Movement." *Journal of Peasant Studies* 37, no. 1: 149–75. https://doi.org/10.1080/03066150903498804.

Massey, Doreen B. 1994. *Space, Place, and Gender*. Minneapolis: University of Minnesota Press.

Massicotte, Marie-Josée, Claudia Beaudoin, Thomas Bernier-Villeneuve, and Jessica Brousseau. 2012. "Beyond Borders: The Struggle for Food Sovereignty in the Americas." *Kasarinlan: Philippine Journal of Third World Studies* 26, no. 1–2: 49–67.

Mattiace, Shannan Lorraine. 1998. *Peasant and Indian: Political Identity and Indian Autonomy in Chiapas, Mexico, 1970–1996*. Austin: University of Texas at Austin.

Mattiace, Shannan Lorraine. 2003. *To See with Two Eyes: Peasant Activism and Indian Autonomy in Chiapas, Mexico*. Albuquerque: University of New Mexico Press.

McCarthy, James. 2009. "Social Movements." In *The Dictionary of Human Geography*, 5th ed., edited by Derek Gregory, Ron Johnston, and Geraldine Pratt, 695. Chichester, U.K.: Wiley-Blackwell.

McLees, Leslie. 2012. "Understanding the Urban, the Role of Open Space Agriculture in Dar Es Salaam, Tanzania." PhD diss., University of Oregon, Eugene.

McMichael, Philip. 2006. "Peasant Prospects in the Neoliberal Age." *New Political Economy* 11, no. 3: 407–418.
McMichael, Philip. 2009. "A Food Regime Genealogy." *Journal of Peasant Studies* 36, no. 1: 139–69. https://doi.org/10.1080/03066150902820354.
McMichael, Philip. 2014. "Historicizing Food Sovereignty." *Journal of Peasant Studies* 41, no. 6: 933–57. https://doi.org/10.1080/03066150.2013.876999.
Meek, David, and Rebecca Tarlau. 2016. "Critical Food Systems Education (CFSE): Educating for Food Sovereignty." *Agroecology and Sustainable Food Systems* 40, no. 3: 237–60. https://doi.org/10.1080/21683565.2015.1130764.
Mencher, Joan P. 2013. "Food Sovereignty: How It Turns the Growing Corporate Global Food System Upside Down." In *Food Sovereignty: A Critical Dialogue*. New Haven, Conn.: Yale University Press.
Méndez, V. Ernesto, Christopher Bacon, Meryl Olson, Katlyn S. Morris, and Annie Shattuck. 2010. "Agrobiodiversity and Shade Coffee Smallholder Livelihoods: A Review and Synthesis of Ten Years of Research in Central America." *Professional Geographer* 62, no. 3: 357–76. https://doi.org/10.1080/00330124.2010.483638.
Mendoza, Breny. 2015. "Coloniality of Gender and Power." In *The Oxford Handbook of Feminist Theory*, 100. Oxford: Oxford University Press.
Micheletti, M. 2003. *Political Virtue and Shopping: Individuals, Consumerism, and Collective Action*. New York: Springer.
Mignolo, Walter. 2000. *Local Histories/Global Designs: Coloniality, Subaltern Knowledges, and Border Thinking*. Princeton Studies in Culture/Power/History. Princeton, N.J.: Princeton University Press.
Mignolo, Walter. 2002. "The Geopolitics of Knowledge and the Colonial Difference." *South Atlantic Quarterly* 101, no. 1: 57–96.
Mignolo, Walter. 2009a. "Cosmopolitanism and the De-colonial Option." *Studies in Philosophy and Education* 29, no. 2: 111–27. https://doi.org/10.1007/s11217-009-9163-1.
Mignolo, Walter. 2009b. "Epistemic Disobedience, Independent Thought and Decolonial Freedom." *Theory, Culture, and Society* 26, no. 7–8: 159–81. https://doi.org/10.1177/0263276409349275.
Mignolo, Walter, and Catherine E. Walsh. 2018. *On Decoloniality: Concepts, Analytics, Praxis*. Durham, N.C.: Duke University Press.
Miller, Ethan. 2015. "Anticapitalism or Postcapitalism? Both!" *Rethinking Marxism* 27, no. 3: 364–67. https://doi.org/10.1080/08935696.2015.1042705.
Miller, Ethan, Christian Anderson, Marianna Pavlovskya, and Yahya Madra. 2017. "Gazing at Power in Alternative Economies Research." Paper presented at the annual meeting of the American Association of Geographers, Boston. http://meridian.aag.org/callforpapers/program/SessionDetail.cfm?SessionID=28507.
Moksnes, Heidi. 2004. "Factionalism and Counterinsurgency in Chiapas: Contextualizing the Acteal Massacre." *European Review of Latin American and Caribbean Studies*, no. 76: 109–17.

Moksnes, Heidi. 2012. *Maya Exodus: Indigenous Struggle for Citizenship in Chiapas*. Norman: University of Oklahoma Press.
Mora, Mariana. 2008. "Decolonizing Politics: Zapatista Indigenous Autonomy in an Era of Neoliberal Governance and Low Intensity Warfare." PhD diss., University of Texas at Austin.
Mora, Mariana. 2017. *Kuxlejal Politics: Indigenous Autonomy, Race, and Decolonizing Research in Zapatista Communities*. Austin: University of Texas Press.
Moraga, Cherríe. 2015. Preface to *This Bridge Called My Back: Writings by Radical Women of Color*, 4th ed., edited by Gloria Anzaldúa, xiii–xxi. Albany: State University of New York Press.
Morrow, Oona, and Kelly Dombroski. 2015. "Enacting a Postcapitalist Politics through the Sites and Practices of Life's Work." In *Precarious Worlds: Contested Geographies of Social Reproduction*, edited by Katharine Meehan and Kendra Strauss, 82–98. Athens: University of Georgia Press.
Mosse, David. 2005. *Cultivating Development: An Ethnography of Aid Policy and Practice*. London: Pluto.
Murphy, Alexander B. 2013. "Advancing Geographical Understanding: Why Engaging Grand Regional Narratives Matters." *Dialogues in Human Geography* 3, no. 2: 131–49.
Mutersbaugh, Tad. 2002. "The Number Is the Beast: A Political Economy of Organic-Coffee Certification and Producer Unionism." *Environment and Planning A* 34, no. 7: 1165–84. https://doi.org/10.1068/a3435.
Mutersbaugh, Tad. 2004. "Serve and Certify: Paradoxes of Service Work in Organic-Coffee Certification." *Environment and Planning D* 22, no. 4: 533–52. https://doi.org/10.1068/d396.
Mutersbaugh, Tad. 2005a. "Certifying Rural Spaces: Quality-Certified Products and Rural Governance." *Journal of Rural Studies* 21, no. 4: 381–88.
Mutersbaugh, Tad. 2005b. "Just-in-Space: Certified Rural Products, Labor of Quality, and Regulatory Spaces." *Journal of Rural Studies* 21, no. 4: 389–402.
Mutersbaugh, Tad. 2016. "Environmental Certification and Eco-Labeling." In *International Encyclopedia of Geography: People, the Earth, Environment, and Technology*. Hoboken, N.J.: John Wiley. https://doi.org/10.1002/9781118786352.wbieg0943.
Mutersbaugh, Tad, and Sarah Lyon. 2010. "Transparency and Democracy in Certified Ethical Commodity Networks." *Geoforum* 41, no. 1: 27–32. https://doi.org/10.1016/j.geoforum.2009.11.013.
Nancy, Jean-Luc. 1991. "Of Being-in-Common." In *Community at Loose Ends*, edited by the Miami Theory Collective, 1–12. Minneapolis: University of Minnesota Press.
Nash, June. 2001. *Mayan Visions: The Quest for Autonomy in an Age of Globalization*. New York: Routledge.
Naylor, Lindsay. 2012a. "Food Sovereignty and the Politics of Indigenous Resistance in Chiapas, Mexico." In *Food Politics 1: Food, Race, and National Identity in Mexico*. San Francisco: Latin American Studies Association.

Naylor, Lindsay. 2012b. "Hired Gardens and the Question of Transgression: Lawns, Food Gardens and the Business of 'Alternative' Food Practice." *Cultural Geographies* 19, no. 4: 483–504. https://doi.org/10.1177/1474474012451543.

Naylor, Lindsay. 2014. "'Some Are More Fair than Others': Fair Trade Certification, Development, and North–South Subjects." *Agriculture and Human Values* 31, no. 2: 273–84.

Naylor, Lindsay. 2017a. "Reframing Autonomy in Political Geography: A Feminist Geopolitics of Autonomous Resistance." *Political Geography* 58 (May): 24–35. https://doi.org/10.1016/j.polgeo.2017.01.001.

Naylor, Lindsay. 2017b. "A Place for GMOs in Food Sovereignty?" *Geographical Review* 107, no. 4: 572–77. https://doi.org/10.1111/gere.12258.

Naylor, Lindsay. 2017c. "Auditing the Subjects of Fair Trade: Coffee, Development, and Surveillance in Highland Chiapas." *Environment and Planning D* 35, no. 5: 816–35. https://doi.org/10.1177/0263775817694031.

Naylor, Lindsay. 2018. "Fair Trade Coffee Exchanges and Community Economies." *Environment and Planning A* 50, no. 5: 1027–46. https://doi.org/10.1177/0308518X18768287.

Naylor, Lindsay, Michelle Daigle, Sofia Zaragocin, Margaret Marietta Ramírez, and Mary Gilmartin. 2018. "Interventions: Bringing the Decolonial to Political Geography." *Political Geography* 66: 199–209. https://doi.org/10.1016/j.polgeo.2017.11.002.

Nelson, Lise. 2003. "Decentering the Movement: Collective Action, Place, and the 'Sedimentation' of Radical Political Discourses." *Environment and Planning D* 21, no. 5: 559–82.

Newdick, Vivian. 2012. "'To Know How to Speak': Technologies of Indigenous Women's Activism against Sexual Violence in Chiapas, Mexico." PhD diss., University of Texas at Austin.

Nicholls, Alex. 2010. "Fair Trade: Towards an Economics of Virtue." *Journal of Business Ethics* 92, no. 2: 241–55. https://doi.org/10.1007/s10551-010-0581-3.

Nicholls, Alex, and Charlotte Opal. 2005. *Fair Trade: Market-Driven Ethical Consumption*. London: Sage.

North, Peter. 2015. "The Business of the Anthropocene? Substantivist and Diverse Economies Perspectives on SME Engagement in Local Low Carbon Transitions." *Progress in Human Geography* 40, no. 4: 437–54. https://doi.org/10.1177/0309132515585049.

Oberhauser, Ann M. 2005. "Scaling Gender and Diverse Economies: Perspectives from Appalachia and South Africa." *Antipode* 37, no. 5: 863–74. https://doi.org/10.1111/j.0066-4812.2005.00536.x.

Obringer, Kelsey, and Lindsay Naylor. 2018. "Toward a Theory of Food Politics." Paper presented at the annual conference of the American Political Science Association, San Francisco.

OECD. 2016. "Net ODA (Indicator)." https://doi.org/10.1787/33346549-en.

Ortner, Sherry B. 1995. "Resistance and the Problem of Ethnographic Refusal." *Comparative Studies in Society and History* 37, no. 1: 173–93.

Patel, Raj. 2009. "Food Sovereignty." *Journal of Peasant Studies* 36, no. 3: 663–706.
Pérez Ruiz, Maya Lorena. 2004. *Tejiendo historias: Tierra, género y poder en Chiapas*. Serie Antropología (Mexico City, Mexico), Colección científica (Instituto Nacional de Antropología e Historia (Mexico)). Mexico, D.F.: Conaculta-INAH.
Pile, Steve. 1997. "Introduction: Opposition, Political Identities and Spaces of Resistance." In *Geographies of Resistance*, edited by Steve Pile and Michael Keith, 1–32. London: Routledge.
Pile, Steve, and Michael Keith. 1997. *Geographies of Resistance*. London: Routledge.
Pimbert, Michel P. 2009. *Towards Food Sovereignty*. The Gatekeeper Series 141. London: IIED.
Pimbert, Michel P., John Thompson, William T. Vorley, T. Fox, N. Kanji, and C. Tacoli. 2001. *Global Restructuring, Agri-Food Systems, and Livelihoods*. London: International Institute for Environment and Development.
Ploeg, J. D., van der. 2008. *The New Peasantries: Struggles for Autonomy and Sustainability in an Era of Empire and Globalization*. London: Earthscan.
Ploeg, J. D., van der. 2010. "The Peasantries of the Twenty-First Century: The Commoditisation Debate Revisited." *Journal of Peasant Studies* 37, no. 1: 1–30. https://doi.org/10.1080/03066150903498721.
Ploeg, J. D. van der. 2014. "Peasant-Driven Agricultural Growth and Food Sovereignty." *Journal of Peasant Studies* 41, no. 6: 999–1030. https://doi.org/10.1080/03066150.2013.876997.
Polanyi, Karl. 1957. *The Great Transformation: The Political and Economic Origins of Our Time*. Boston: Beacon Press.
Polynczuk-Alenius, Kinga, and Mervi Pantti. 2017. "Branded Solidarity in Fair Trade Communication on Facebook." *Globalizations* 14, no. 1: 66–80. https://doi.org/10.1080/14747731.2016.1175099.
Popke, Jeff. 2006. "Geography and Ethics: Everyday Mediations through Care and Consumption." *Progress in Human Geography* 30, no. 4: 504–12.
Pratt, Geraldine. 2000. "Research Performances." *Environment and Planning D* 18, no. 5: 639–51.
Probyn, Elspeth. 2016. *Eating the Ocean*. Durham, N.C.: Duke University Press.
Quijano, Aníbal. 1997. "Colonialidad del poder, cultura y conocimiento en America Latina." *Annuario Mariateguiano* 9: 113–21.
Quijano, Aníbal. 2008. "Coloniality of Power, Eurocentrism and Social Classification." In *Coloniality at Large: Latin America and the Postcolonial Debate*, edited by Mabel Moraña, Enrique D. Dussel, and Carlos A. Jáuregui, 181–224. Durham, N.C.: Duke University Press.
Raynolds, Laura T. 2000. "Re-embedding Global Agriculture: The International Organic and Fair Trade Movements." *Agriculture and Human Values* 17, no. 3: 297–309.
Raynolds, Laura T. 2002. "Consumer/Producer Links in Fair Trade Coffee Networks." *Sociologia Ruralis* 42, no. 4: 404–24.

Raynolds, Laura T. 2012. "Fair Trade: Social Regulation in Global Food Markets." *Journal of Rural Studies* 28, no. 3: 276–87. https://doi.org/10.1016/j.jrurstud.2012.03.004.

Raynolds, Laura T. 2017. "Fairtrade Labour Certification: The Contested Incorporation of Plantations and Workers." *Third World Quarterly* 38, no. 7: 1473–92. https://doi.org/10.1080/01436597.2016.1272408.

Raynolds, Laura T., and Nicholas Greenfield. 2015. "Fair Trade: Movement and Markets." In *Handbook of Research on Fair Trade*, edited by Laura T. Raynolds and Elizabeth Bennett, 24–41. Northampton, Mass.: Edward Elgar.

Raynolds, Laura T., Douglas L. Murray, and John Wilkinson. 2007. *Fair Trade: The Challenges of Transforming Globalization*. London: Routledge.

Raynolds, Laura T., Douglas Murray, and Peter Leigh Taylor. 2004. "Fair Trade Coffee: Building Producer Capacity via Global Networks." *Journal of International Development* 16, no. 8: 1109–21.

Renard, Marie-Christine. 2003. "Fair Trade: Quality, Market and Conventions." *Journal of Rural Studies* 19, no. 1: 87–96.

Renard, Marie-Christine. 2005. "Quality Certification, Regulation and Power in Fair Trade." *Journal of Rural Studies* 21, no. 4: 419–31.

Renard, Marie-Christine. 2010. "The Mexican Coffee Crisis." *Latin American Perspectives* 37, no. 2: 21–33. https://doi.org/10.1177/0094582X09356956.

Renard, Marie-Christine. 2015. "Fair Trade for Small Farmer Cooperatives in Latin America." In *Handbook of Research on Fair Trade*, edited by Laura T. Raynolds and Elizabeth Bennett, 475–90. Northampton, Mass.: Edward Elgar.

Renard, Marie-Christine, and Allison Loconto. 2013. "Competing Logics in the Further Standardization of Fair Trade: ISEAL and the Símbolo de Pequeños Productores." *International Journal of Sociology of Agriculture and Food* 20, no. 1: 51–68.

Reyes Ramos, María Eugenia. 1992. *El reparto de tierras y la política agraria en Chiapas, 1914–1988*. Mexico City: Universidad Nacional Autonoma de Mexico y Centro de Investigaciones Humanisticas de Mesoamerica y del Estado de Chiapas.

Reynolds, Kristin, and Nevin Cohen. 2016. *Beyond the Kale: Urban Agriculture and Social Justice Activism in New York City*. Reprint ed. Athens: University of Georgia Press.

Rice, R. A. 2001. "Noble Goals and Challenging Terrain: Organic and Fair Trade Coffee Movements in the Global Marketplace." *Journal of Agricultural and Environmental Ethics* 14, no. 1: 39–66.

Rist, Gilbert. 2008. *The History of Development: From Western Origins to Global Faith*. London: Zed Books.

Roelvink, Gerda. 2016. *Building Dignified Worlds: Geographies of Collective Action*. Minneapolis: University of Minnesota Press.

Roelvink, Gerda, Kevin St. Martin, and J. K. Gibson-Graham. 2015. *Making Other Worlds Possible: Performing Diverse Economies*. Minneapolis: University of Minnesota Press.

Rose, Gillian. 1997. "Situating Knowledges: Positionality, Reflexivities and Other Tactics." *Progress in Human Geography* 21, no. 3: 305–20.

Rose, Mitch. 2002. "The Seductions of Resistance: Power, Politics, and a Performative Style of Systems." *Environment and Planning D* 20, no. 4: 383–400.

Rosset, Peter. 2009. "Fixing Our Global Food System: Food Sovereignty and Redistributive Land Reform." *Monthly Review: An Independent Socialist Magazine* 61, no. 3: 114–28.

Rosset, Peter. 2011. "Food Sovereignty and Alternative Paradigms to Confront Land Grabbing and the Food and Climate Crises." *Development* 54, no. 1: 21–30.

Rosset, Peter, Raj Patel, Michael Courville, and Land Research Action Network. 2006. *Promised Land: Competing Visions of Agrarian Reform*. Oakland, Calif.: Food First Books.

Routledge, Paul. 2002. "Travelling East as Walter Kurtz: Identity, Performance, and Collaboration in Goa, India." *Environment and Planning D* 20, no. 4: 477–98.

Routledge, Paul. 2009. "Transnational Resistance: Global Justice Networks and Spaces of Convergence." *Geography Compass* 3, no. 5: 1881–1901. https://doi.org/10.1111/j.1749-8198.2009.00261.x.

Rus, Jan. 1994. "The 'comunidad revolucionaria institucional': The Subversion of Native Government in Highland Chiapas, 1936–1968." In *Everyday Forms of State Formation: Revolution and the Negotiation of Rule in Modern Mexico*, edited by G. M. Joseph and Daniel Nugent, 265–300. Durham, N.C.: Duke University Press.

Rus, Jan. 2004. "Rereading Tzotzil Ethnography: Recent Scholarship from Chiapas, Mexico." In *Pluralizing Ethnography: Comparison and Representation in Maya Cultures, Histories and Identities*, edited by John Watanabe and Edward Fischer, 199–230. Santa Fe, N.M.: School of American Research.

Rus, Jan, Rosalva Aída Hernández Castillo, and Shannan L. Mattiace. 2003. *Mayan Lives, Mayan Utopias: The Indigenous Peoples of Chiapas and the Zapatista Rebellion*. Lanham, Md.: Rowman and Littlefield.

Sadoulet, Elisabeth, Alain de Janvry, and Benjamin Davis. 2001. "Cash Transfer Programs with Income Multipliers: PROCAMPO in Mexico." *World Development* 29, no. 6: 1043–56.

Saiz, Juan Manuel Ramirez. 1990. "Urban Struggles and Their Political Consequences." In *Popular Movements and Political Change in Mexico*, edited by Joe Foweraker and Ann L. Craig, 234–46. Boulder, Colo.: Lynne Rienner.

Samers, Michael. 2005. "The Myopia of 'Diverse Economies,' or a Critique of the 'Informal Economy.'" *Antipode* 37, no. 5: 875–86. https://doi.org/10.1111/j.0066-4812.2005.00537.x.

Sarcauga, Michael. 2004. "History of Fair Trade." World Fair Trade Organization. January. https://wfto.com/about-us/history-wfto/history-fair-trade.

Schanbacher, William D. 2010. *The Politics of Food: The Global Conflict between Food Security and Food Sovereignty.* Santa Barbara, Calif.: Praeger Security International.

Schiwy, Freya. 2007. "Decolonization and the Question of Subjectivity." *Cultural Studies* 21, no. 2–3: 271–94. https://doi.org/10.1080/09502380601162555.

Scholz, Sally J. 2008. *Political Solidarity.* University Park: Pennsylvania State University Press.

Scott, James C. 1985. *Weapons of the Weak: Everyday Forms of Peasant Resistance.* New Haven, Conn.: Yale University Press.

Sedgwick, Eve Kosofsky. 1993. *Tendencies.* Durham, N.C.: Duke University Press.

Sedgwick, Eve Kosofsky. 2003. *Touching Feeling: Affect, Pedagogy, Performativity.* Durham, N.C.: Duke University Press.

Sharp, Joanne P., Paul Routledge, Chris Philo, and Ronan Paddison. 2000. *Entanglements of Power: Geographies of Domination/Resistance.* London: Routledge.

Shear, Boone. 2010. "The Green Economy: Grounds for a New Revolutionary Imaginary?" *Rethinking Marxism* 22, no. 2: 203–9.

SIPAZ. 2012. "ACTUALIDAD: México—Brecha Entre Gobierno y Sociedad Rumbo a Las Elecciones." *Informe SIPAZ,* March.

Smith, Adrian. 2004. "Regions, Spaces of Economic Practice and Diverse Economies in the 'New Europe.'" *European Urban and Regional Studies* 11, no. 1: 9–25.

Smith, Adrian. 2007. "Articulating Neoliberalism: Diverse Economies and Everyday Life in 'Postsocialist' Cities." In *Contesting Neoliberalism: Urban Frontiers,* edited by Helga Leitner, Jamie Peck, and Eric Sheppard, 204–22. New York: Guilford Press.

Smith, Neil. 1984. *Uneven Development: Nature, Capital, and the Production of Space.* New York: Blackwell.

Snyder, Richard. 2001. *Politics after Neoliberalism: Reregulation in Mexico.* Cambridge: Cambridge University Press.

Snyder, Robert, and Kevin St. Martin. 2015. "A Fishery for the Future: The Midcoast Fishermen's Association and the Work of Economic Being-in-Common." In *Making Other Worlds Possible: Performing Diverse Economies,* edited by Gerda Roelvink, Kevin St. Martin, and J. K. Gibson-Graham, 26–52. Minneapolis: University of Minnesota Press.

Solomon, Joel A., Sebastian Brett, Cynthia G. Brown, Anne Manuel, and Human Rights Watch/Americas. 1997. *Implausible Deniability: State Responsibility for Rural Violence in Mexico.* New York: Human Rights Watch.

Sparke, Matthew. 2000. "Graphing the Geo in Geo-political: Critical Geopolitics and the Re-visioning of Responsibility." *Political Geography* 19, no. 3: 373–80.

Speed, Shannon. 2005. "Dangerous Discourses." *PoLAR: Political and Legal Anthropology Review* 28, no. 1: 29–51. https://doi.org/10.1525/pol.2005.28.1.29.

Speed, Shannon. 2006. "Indigenous Women and Gendered Resistance in the Wake of Acteal." In *Engaged Observer: Anthropology, Advocacy, and Activism*, edited by Victoria Sanford and Asale Angel-Ajani, 170–88. New Brunswick, N.J.: Rutgers University Press.

Speed, Shannon. 2008. *Rights in Rebellion: Indigenous Struggle and Human Rights in Chiapas*. Stanford, Calif.: Stanford University Press.

Speed, Shannon, and Alvaro Reyes. 2002. "'In Our Own Defense': Rights and Resistance in Chiapas." *PoLAR: Political and Legal Anthropology Review* 25, no. 1: 69–89. https://doi.org/10.1525/pol.2002.25.1.69.

Speed, Shannon, and Alvaro Reyes. 2005. "Rights, Resistance, and Radical Alternatives: The Red de Defensores Comunitarios and Zapatismo in Chiapas." *Humboldt Journal of Social Relations* 29, no. 1: 47–82.

Spinney, Justin. 2010. "Performing Resistance? Re-reading Practices of Urban Cycling on London's South Bank." *Environment and Planning A* 42, no. 12: 2914–37.

Spivak, Gayatri Chakravorty. 1988. "Can the Subaltern Speak?" In *Marxism and the Interpretation of Culture*, edited by Lawrence Grossberg and Cary Nelson, 271–316. Champaign: University of Illinois Press.

Spivak, Gayatri Chakravorty. 1999. *A Critique of Postcolonial Reason*. Cambridge, Mass.: Harvard University Press.

Spivak, Gayatri Chakravorty. 2012. *An Aesthetic Education in the Era of Globalization*. Cambridge, Mass.: Harvard University Press.

Springer, Simon. 2012. "Neoliberalising Violence: Of the Exceptional and the Exemplary in Coalescing Moments." *Area* 44, no. 2: 136–43.

St. Martin, Kevin. 2007. "The Difference That Class Makes: Neoliberalization and Non-capitalism in the Fishing Industry of New England." *Antipode* 39, no. 3: 527–49. https://doi.org/10.1111/j.1467-8330.2007.00538.x.

St. Martin, Kevin, Gerda Roelvink, and J. K. Gibson-Graham. 2015. "Introduction: An Economic Politics for Our Times." In *Making Other Worlds Possible: Performing Diverse Economies*, edited by Gerda Roelvink, Kevin St. Martin, and J. K. Gibson-Graham, 1–25. Minneapolis: University of Minnesota Press.

Stahler-Sholk, Richard. 1998. "Massacre in Chiapas." *Latin American Perspectives* 25, no. 4: 63–75.

Stahler-Sholk, Richard. 2005. "Time of the Snails: Autonomy and Resistance in Chiapas." *NACLA Report on the Americas* 38, no. 5: 34–38.

Stahler-Sholk, Richard. 2007. "Resisting Neoliberal Homogenization: The Zapatista Autonomy Movement." *Latin American Perspectives* 34, no. 2: 48–63.

Stahler-Sholk, Richard. 2010. "The Zapatista Social Movement: Innovation and Sustainability." *Alternatives: Global, Local, Political* 35, no. 3: 269–90.

Stahler-Sholk, Richard. 2015. "Resistencia, identidad, y autonomía: La transformación de espacios en las comunidades Zapatistas." *Pueblos y Fronteras* 10, no. 19: 199–227.

Stahler-Sholk, Richard. 2017. "Constructing Autonomy." In *The New Global*

Politics: Global Social Movements in the Twenty-First Century, edited by Harry E. Vanden, Peter N. Funke, and Gary Prevost, 13–28. Abingdon, U.K.: Taylor and Francis.

Stephen, Lynn. 1997. "Redefined Nationalism in Building a Movement for Indigenous Autonomy in Southern Mexico." Journal of Latin American Anthropology 3, no. 1: 72–101.

Stephen, Lynn. 2002. Zapata Lives! Histories and Cultural Politics in Southern Mexico. Berkeley: University of California Press.

Stephen, Lynn. 2013. We Are the Face of Oaxaca: Testimony and Social Movements. Durham, N.C.: Duke University Press.

Suh, Doowon. 2011. "Institutionalizing Social Movements: The Dual Strategy of the Korean Women's Movement." Sociological Quarterly 52, no. 3: 442–71. https://doi.org/10.1111/j.1533-8525.2011.01214.x.

Sundberg, Juanita. 2007. "Reconfiguring North–South Solidarity: Critical Reflections on Experiences of Transnational Resistance." Antipode 39, no. 1: 144–66.

Tavanti, Marco. 2003. Las Abejas: Pacifist Resistance and Syncretic Identities in a Globalizing Chiapas. New York: Routledge.

Trang, Tran Thi Thu. 2012. "Food Security versus Food Sovereignty: Choice of Concept, Policies, and Classes in Vietnam's Post-reform Economy." Kasarinlan: Philippine Journal of Third World Studies 26, no. 1–2: 68–88.

Trauger, Amy. 2014. "Toward a Political Geography of Food Sovereignty: Transforming Territory, Exchange and Power in the Liberal Sovereign State." Journal of Peasant Studies 41, no. 6: 1131–52. https://doi.org/10.1080/03066150.2014.937339.

Trauger, Amy, ed. 2015. Food Sovereignty in International Context: Discourse, Politics and Practice of Place. London: Routledge.

Trauger, Amy. 2017. We Want Land to Live: Making Political Space for Food Sovereignty. Athens: University of Georgia Press.

Treter, Chris. 2013. "Every End Is a New Beginning: Thoughts from Chris Treter on Day 1." Fair Trade Chronicles (blog), January 2. http://fairtradechronicles.com/2013/01/02/every-end-is-a-new-beginning-thoughts-from-chris-treter-on-day-1/.

Tuck, Eve, and K. Wayne Yang. 2012. "Decolonization Is Not a Metaphor." Decolonization: Indigeneity, Education, and Society 1, no. 1: 1–40.

Tuhiwai-Smith, Linda. 1999. Decolonizing Methodologies: Research and Indigenous Peoples. London: Zed Books.

Tyner, James A., and Rachel Will. 2015. "Nature and Post-conflict Violence: Water Management under the Communist Party of Kampuchea, 1975–1979." Transactions of the Institute of British Geographers 40, no. 3: 362–74. https://doi.org/10.1111/tran.12080.

Vallega, Alejandro Arturo. 2014. Latin American Philosophy from Identity to Radical Exteriority. Bloomington: Indiana University Press.

Varul, Matthias Zick. 2008. "Consuming the Campesino." Cultural Studies 22, no. 5: 654–79. https://doi.org/10.1080/09502380802245910.

Wallerstein, Immanuel. 1974. The Modern World-System: Capitalist Agricul-

ture and the Origins of the European World-Economy in the Sixteenth Century. New York: Academic Press.
Walsh, Catherine. 2007. "Shifting the Geopolitics of Critical Knowledge." *Cultural Studies* 21, no. 2–3: 224–39.
Warren, Jeff, and Caroline Wollard. 2016. *Solidarity Economy*. Ink on paper. http://carolinewoolard.com/project/redrawing-economy/.
Watts, Michael. 2002. "Chronicle of a Death Foretold: Some Thoughts on Peasants and the Agrarian Question." *Oesterreichische Zeitschrift Fuer Geschichtswissenschaften* 4: 22–51.
Watts, Michael. 2003. "Development and Governmentality." *Singapore Journal of Tropical Geography* 24, no. 1: 6–34.
Wiggins, Steve, and Stephanie Levy. 2008. *Rising Food Prices: A Global Crisis*. London: Overseas Development Institute.
Wilson, Bradley. 2010. "Indebted to Fair Trade? Coffee and Crisis in Nicaragua." *Geoforum* 41, no. 1: 84–92. https://doi.org/10.1016/j.geoforum.2009.06.008.
Wilson, Bradley. 2013. "Delivering the Goods: Fair Trade, Solidarity, and the Moral Economy of the Coffee Contract in Nicaragua." *Human Organization* 72, no. 3: 177–87.
Wilson, Bradley. 2016. "Food Sovereignty, Agrarian Politics and Certification Enclosures in Nicaragua." Paper presented at the annual meeting of the American Association of Geographers, San Francisco.
Wilson, Bradley, and Joe Curnow. 2013. "Solidarity: Student Activism, Affective Labor, and the Fair Trade Campaign in the United States." *Antipode* 45, no. 3: 565–83. https://doi.org/10.1111/j.1467-8330.2012.01051.x.
Wilson, Bradley, and Tad Mutersbaugh. 2015. "Fair Trade Certification, Performance and Practice." In *Handbook of Research on Fair Trade*, edited by Laura T. Raynolds and Elizabeth Bennett, 281–96. Northampton, Mass.: Edward Elgar.
Wimborne Minster. 2006. "A Fair Trade Town." Wimborne Minster Town Council. http://www.wimborne.gov.uk/the-town/wimborne-minster-a-fair-trade-town/.
Wittman, Hannah. 2009. "Reworking the Metabolic Rift: La Vía Campesina, Agrarian Citizenship, and Food Sovereignty." *Journal of Peasant Studies* 36, no. 4: 805–26.
Wittman, Hannah, Annette Aurélie Desmarais, and Nettie Wiebe. 2010. *Food Sovereignty: Reconnecting Food, Nature, and Community*. Halifax, N.S.: Fernwood.
Wittman, Hannah, Annette Aurélie Desmarais, and Nettie Wiebe, eds. 2011. *Food Sovereignty in Canada: Creating Just and Sustainable Food Systems*. Halifax, N.S.: Fernwood.
Wolford, Wendy. 2010. *This Land Is Ours Now: Social Mobilization and the Meanings of Land in Brazil*. Durham, N.C.: Duke University Press.
Womack, John. 2011. *Zapata and the Mexican Revolution*. New York: Knopf Doubleday.
Wynter, Sylvia. 2003. "Unsettling the Coloniality of Being/Power/Truth/

Freedom: Towards the Human, after Man, Its Overrepresentation—An Argument." *New Centennial Review* 3, no. 3: 257–337.
Young, I. M. 2013. "The Ideal of Community and the Politics of Difference." In *Feminism/Postmodernism*, edited by Linda Nicholson, 300–323. New York: Routledge.
Zaragocin, Sofia. 2017. "Feminismo decolonial y buen vivir." In *Feminismo y buen vivir: Utopías decoloniales*, edited by Soledad Varea and Sofia Zaragocin, 17–25. Cuenca, Ecuador: PYDLOS Ediciones/Universidad de Cuenca.http://dspace.ucuenca.edu.ec/jspui/bitstream/123456789/27831/1/feminismo%20y%20buen%20vivir%20pdf%20PARA%20IMPRESION%20%281%29.pdf.
Zaragocin, Sofia. 2018. "Geopolitica del utero, hacia una geografia feminista decolonial." In *Cuerpos, territorios y feminismos*, edited by D. Cruz and M. Bayon, 195–204. Quito: AbyaYala y Estudios Ecologistas del Tercer Mundo.
Zaragocin, Sofia, Melissa Moreano Venegas, and Soledad Álvarez Velasco. 2018. "Presentación del dossier: Hacia una reapropiación de la geografía crítica en América Latina." *Íconos—Revista de Ciencias Sociales*, no. 61 (May), 11–32. https://doi.org/10.17141/iconos.61.2018.3020.
Zibechi, Raúl. 2016. "La Candidatura Presidencial Del Zapatismo." *Viento Sur*, November 7. http://vientosur.info/spip.php?article11883.

Index

abarrote, 121
Abejas, Las, 7, 51, 53, 75, 76, 79; coffee production, 11, 12; formation, 10; indigenous rights, 75; pacifism, 7, 10, 81, 83; religion, 132, 224n7. *See also* social movements
accumulation by dispossession, 23, 102, 126
Acteal, 79
Acteal Massacre, 80–85, 118, 157, 163, 225n20; international involvement, 81, 157–58; Máscara Roja, 80. *See also* paramilitaries
ageographical, 211
agricultural production, 49, 51, 52, 58, 59, 61, 91–92; chemical use, 58, 59; perspectives on, 91–92, 184–85; practices, 196–201, 230n14. See also *cafetal*; *milpa*; subsistence
agroecology, 59, 182–84
alternatives, 27–28, 112
apolitical, 110, 117, 119, 121, 127
autonomy, 2, 6, 7, 16–17, 36–37, 190–91; agriculture and, 1, 123, 206, 226n3; borders and, 76; rebel, 56, 64, 76–79, 85, 122, 209, 221n4

being in common, 133, 140, 144–45, 150–51, 157–58, 204–6
binaries, 3, 41, 45, 50, 52, 61, 91, 100–102, 118, 135, 141
bodies, 121, 123–24, 227n8

cafetal, 80, 89, 95, 118, 136, 196, 197, 230n13

campesinos/as, 51; in resistance, 6–11, 75, 221n4
capitalism, 14, 20–21, 26–32, 33–35; capitalist relations, 2, 24
capitalocentrism, 26, 28, 32, 42, 52, 61–62, 93, 100–101, 118–19, 126–27
cargo, 95, 137
Chenalhó, 10, 63, 80
Chiapas State, 33, 62–77; research in, 13–14, 222n8
CLAC. *See* Latin American and Caribbean Network of Fair Trade Small Producers and Workers
climate change, 198
coffee, 23, 24, 25, 66, 69–77, 78, 112; adoption of, 33, 69–71; corporatist state, 69–71; coyotes and, 11–12, 70, 158, 161, 209; crisis, 73, 140–41; depulping, 89; farming practices, 7, 53, 183; labor, 66, 136; organizing, 69, 71, 73, 141; plantation certification, 106; price, 9, 10, 11, 16, 21, 84; producer cooperatives, 161–66. *See also* INMECAFE
colonial difference, 39–40, 120, 126, 151
colonial–imperial, 23, 25, 34, 37–38, 110–11, 208–9
coloniality of power, 39, 41
community economies, 29–31, 92, 100, 138, 147, 151, 152, 170, 190, 191, 202–6
Comunidades Eclesiales de Base (CEBs), 69, 224n10
conflict, 118, 176; autonomous communities in, 79–85, 159;

257

counterinsurgency, 78; low-intensity war, 77, 78, 80, 118, 177; third-party fair trade certifiers, 43–44, 152, 153
conquest, 4–5, 34, 38, 61
consumer imaginaries, 119, 147–49
consumers, 111, 113, 119–25, 227n2
consumption, 31, 113, 119, 136; market goods and consumer durables, 124–25. *See also* ethical consumption
Cooperative Coffees, 135, 156, 158
corn, 49, 91–92, 95, 124, 183, 185, 196–201. See also *milpa*; seeds

debt crisis, 71–72
decolonial, 15, 120
decoloniality, 15
decolonial theory, 29, 37–43
decolonizing, 17, 24, 37–43, 56, 57, 66, 91–96, 100, 126, 206
development, 7, 18, 23–25, 26, 33–37, 42, 57–59, 60–62, 63, 66, 68, 74, 91–96, 168, 223n1, 225n1; coffee as, 11, 66–77; discourses, 2, 23, 33–34, 46, 57, 58, 93, 111, 223n1, 227n10; fair trade as, 12, 61, 91; fair trade standard, 18, 85–91; state discourses, 57, 60, 63, 64, 68, 74; state programs, 59, 64, 65, 68, 71, 74, 91–92, 96–98
development aid, 26, 102, 110. *See also* economic aid
dignified livelihoods, 2, 18, 24, 36, 43, 45, 47, 51, 56, 94, 104, 122–23, 143, 168, 175, 177, 190, 204
dignity, 4
displacement, 7, 80, 84, 133, 163, 176. *See also* Acteal Massacre
diverse economies, 13, 14, 24, 26–32, 46, 93, 134, 169, 189, 193, 194, 195, 202, 211, 223n2; Community Economies Collective, 28; critiques, 30–31; J. K. Gibson-Graham, 27–29; reframing, 29–30, 100, 147, 179, 191

economic aid, 35, 102, 110, 225n1, 226n5
economic development. *See* development
economic diversity, 14, 27–32, 40, 41–42, 120, 123, 206. *See also* diverse economies
economic exchange, 28–29, 122–23, 144–45, 150, 157, 167, 210–12
economic identities, 30, 32, 36, 42, 101, 118–19, 121, 122–25, 144, 168, 177, 178, 212. *See also* consumers; producers
economies, 93–95. *See also* diverse economies
education, 55, 85, 122, 162–63
Ejército Zapatista de Liberación Nacional (EZLN). *See* Zapatistas
ejidos, 53, 65, 72, 95, 181, 202, 224n8. *See also* land; privatization; PROCEDE
electricity, 125
elote. *See* corn
embodiment, 6, 9, 10, 15, 17, 39, 95, 113, 123–25, 151, 194, 206
encubrimiento, 4–5, 96
epistemology, 15, 24, 37, 42, 50, 56, 99, 120, 151
ethical consumption, 134, 169–70; buy and let live, 134. *See also* consumption
ethical encounter, 29, 30, 101, 144
ethic of care, 101, 133–34, 168

Fair Trade Advocacy Office (FTAO), 115, 146
fair trade audit, 87, 90, 103–4
fair trade certification, 2, 11, 24, 26, 27, 33, 35–37, 43–44, 209, 224n8, 226n6; as alternative, 18–19, 27, 29, 31, 32, 35;

buy and let live, 134, 147–52; *comercio justo*, 85; commodity chain, 135–36, 159, 227n1; development "fix," 36, 42, 43, 44, 86–91, 103–4, 109, 136, 210; fairness, 11, 16, 26, 85, 86, 128–30, 206–7; fair rebels and, 11–13, 18, 109; income, 108–9, 143, 150, 162, 209; price, 2, 3, 8, 11, 12, 16, 52, 88, 89, 108–9, 138, 150, 156, 163, 227n3, 228n11; producer subjects, 36, 85–91, 101–2, 105, 109–10, 111, 113, 117, 119, 126; rational economic actors, 18, 101, 103, 104, 211; "working" for producers, 12, 26, 32, 35, 36, 45, 46, 52, 128, 223n4
fair trade discourses, 35, 44, 86, 91, 92, 100, 101, 110, 114, 141–42; movement and a market, 111–18; producer–consumer linkages, 119–25, 140–44, 149–50, 162; trade not aid, 102–11
fair trade in movement, 43, 45, 112, 134, 166–71, 184, 212
Fairtrade International, 26, 44, 83, 87–88, 104, 105, 106, 107, 108–9, 110–11, 115, 119, 127, 139, 226n6
fair trade market, 12, 32, 43, 45, 52, 105, 111–18
Fair Trade Month, 128–30
fair trade movement, 12, 32, 43, 44–45, 52, 86, 111–18. *See also* trade
fair trade premium, 35, 89, 90, 127
fair trade standards, 86–91, 104–5, 109, 136, 138, 149
Fair Trade USA, 26, 44, 106, 111, 112, 115, 127, 128, 139, 143, 167, 226nn5–6, 227n4
feminist thinking, 15, 28, 39, 40, 41, 99, 120
First Declaration of the Lacandón Jungle, 5
five-hundred-year struggle, 1, 4–6, 42, 50, 52, 57, 58. *See also* war of five hundred years
FLO. *See* Fairtrade International
FLO-CERT, 88–89, 139
food sovereignty, 178, 184–93, 229nn6–7, 229n11; critiques, 187, 194; definition, 185–87, 191; practices, 188, 193–206, 229n9

gender, 23, 38, 39, 40, 66, 121, 221n1, 222n7, 222n12, 226n2
geography and geographers, 27, 29, 34, 35, 39, 42, 47, 48, 50, 121, 215
geopolitics of knowledge, 17, 29, 36, 40–41, 48, 51, 57, 60, 64, 72, 90, 93, 99, 109, 126–27, 151, 191, 211
governance: fair trade coffee cooperatives, 137, 164–65; fair trade third-party certifiers, 105–7, 184; producer representation, 105–8, 116; by the state, 61; by the Zapatistas, 137, 225n15

Higher Grounds Trading Company, 78, 131, 153–61, 171, 225n18, 229n3
honey, 84, 96, 197
hope, 16, 30, 31, 42, 83, 132–33, 171, 188, 211
hunger, 47, 92, 93, 187, 195

indigeneity, 48, 49, 50, 51, 65, 68, 213
indigenous peoples of Chiapas, 62, 64, 221n3, 222n5, 224n5. *See also* Mayan peoples
indigenous rights, 17, 18
"Indio," 4, 67. *See also* race; racism
INMECAFE, 11, 37, 70, 73, 149, 223n5
interdependence, 29, 113
International Coffee Agreement (ICA), 11, 70, 73, 149

Just Coffee Cooperative, 44–45, 135, 153–61, 170–71, 228nn5–6, 229n3

knowledge exchange, 2, 177, 183, 198, 210
knowledge production, 14, 17, 24, 27, 29, 33, 36, 37–43, 47–48, 52, 56–57, 59–60, 72, 77, 81, 85, 90–91, 96, 99, 110, 125–26, 145, 157, 183, 191, 210
knowledges, 3, 7, 14, 17, 37, 41, 42, 49, 76, 120, 212

labor, 2, 4, 27, 28, 32, 39, 45, 55, 58, 65, 67, 73, 110, 121–22, 123, 136, 165, 166, 228n1. *See also* social reproduction
Lacandón Jungle, 63, 222n6
land, 8, 59, 180–82, 199; access, 8, 57, 70, 184; conflict, 10, 66, 70, 79, 80, 224n9, 225n11, 228n1; control, 8; displacement, 67; privatization, 8, 72, 74, 180–81; redistribution, 8, 53, 74, 181; reform, 8, 67, 68, 74, 224n8; resources, 8, 199; women's claims, 10. See also *ejidos*; PROCEDE
Latin American and Caribbean Network of Fair Trade Small Producers and Workers (CLAC), 108, 226n4
"lean months." *See* hunger
livable worlds, 12, 14, 17, 19, 24, 28, 32, 43, 47, 60, 96, 125, 157, 159, 178, 189, 191, 206
local, 13, 29, 30, 36, 42, 43, 46, 47, 57
low-intensity warfare. *See* conflict

maize. *See* corn
market, 26, 32, 61, 109, 111, 112, 113, 143
Max Havelaar, 26, 106, 107

MAYACERT, 139
Mayan peoples, 56, 64
Maya Vinic, 12, 52, 79–85, 96, 121–22, 131–33, 153, 161–64, 175–76, 183, 206, 210, 228n7; *abarrote*, 121; bodega, 121, 138, 209; formation, 83–85, 176; leadership, 137, 161, 228n9
mestizaje, 67
methodology, 14–17, 100, 222nn9–10
Mexican Revolution, 8, 67
militarization, 58, 77, 78, 80, 81, 118
milpa, 49, 59, 76, 78, 81, 91–92, 136, 177, 182, 193, 196. *See also* corn; seeds

NAFTA, 5, 53, 58, 72, 73, 74, 223n2, 224n3; Article 27, 8, 72, 74
National Indigenous Congress, 6, 221n5, 225n14
neoliberalism, 3, 7, 11, 14, 27, 32, 36–37, 43, 50, 59–61, 66, 71–77, 92–93, 99, 100, 102–3, 105, 114, 183, 203, 212
networks, 13, 18, 25, 31, 43, 57, 121, 183, 198, 202, 207, 212, 222n11; fair trade based, 11, 116, 133, 135–40, 152–61, 190–91, 210; international, 2, 7, 85; solidarity, 7, 12, 18, 49, 51, 81, 84, 88, 133, 140–47

ontology, 24, 37, 40, 56, 99, 120, 151, 194
Oportunidades, 59, 60, 65–66, 224n6
Oventik, 21

paramilitaries, 77, 80, 81, 94, 118, 225n16; Máscara Roja, 80. *See also* Acteal Massacre; conflict; militarization
paranoid theory, 100
partidistas, 80, 122, 158

parties: Mexican political, 67, 80
patron–client relations, 59, 65, 66–69, 73, 94
peace, 12, 75, 81, 94, 167
peasants, 7–8, 51, 57–59, 61, 67, 91, 93, 109, 125, 178, 183, 186, 193. See also *campesinos/as*
place, 13, 18, 29, 33, 38, 41, 42, 45, 46, 47, 48, 49, 56, 57, 60, 65, 84, 90, 95, 109, 114, 117, 121, 122, 192, 195, 204, 211
pluriversal, 40, 42, 96, 168, 210, 212
Polanyian countermovement, 112–13
poverty, 26, 33, 35, 36, 43, 60, 62, 63, 88, 104, 108, 109, 136, 155, 177, 211, 224n3
power, 13, 15, 17, 30–31, 32, 38, 47–49, 50–51, 64, 76, 86, 88, 105, 110, 116–17, 135, 138–39, 149, 157, 160, 186, 202, 208–9, 223n3
pozol, 124. See also corn
privatization, 8. See also *ejidos*; land
PROCAMPO, 59, 65, 224n3
PROCEDE, 8, 53–54, 59, 65, 74, 225n12, 229n2
producers, 119–25, 161–62
Progresa, 59. See also Oportunidades
Prospera, 59, 60, 65, 230n12. See also Oportunidades

race, 4, 6, 17, 23, 38, 39, 41, 60, 66–67, 85, 110, 113, 117, 119, 166; whiteness, 14–15, 24, 42, 68, 93, 119, 146, 166
racism, 37, 68, 80, 171–73, 225n17
rebellion, 5–6
resistance, 7, 16, 17, 24, 41, 42, 46, 47–51, 54, 57, 59, 64, 76, 99, 123, 150; agriculture as tool of, 1, 10, 49, 50, 79, 92, 95, 179, 180, 204; autonomous, 48, 204; *campesinos/as*, 6–11, 221n4; to capitalism, 116, 226n7; collective protest, 8–9, 10, 55–56; embodied, 9, 10, 78, 80; fair trade as tool of, 3, 36–37, 43, 45, 79, 143, 150, 158, 204; state interference and, 58, 59, 77, 177; *stzi'kel vocol*, 47–51, 151, 177

San Andrés Accords, 58, 75–76, 77, 158
San Cristóbal de las Casas, 81, 131, 221n5; Maya Vinic coffee shop, 131–32; Zapatista uprising, 5–6
schools. See education
seeds, 49, 95, 198, 230n15
self-determination, 17, 65, 66. See also resistance
situated knowledge, 15, 19
Sixth Declaration of the Lacandón Jungle, 7
sixth sun, 4, 55–56
social movements, 2, 6, 9, 37, 45, 47, 48, 50, 64, 113–15, 134; Ejército Zapatista de Liberación Nacional (EZLN), 5–7, 9, 48, 56, 77, 221n4; Fuerzas de Liberación Nacional (FLN), 9; Sociedad Civil Las Abejas, 7, 10, 79–85; La Vía Campesina, 185, 229n4
social reproduction, 105, 123, 127, 138. See also labor
Sociedad Civil Las Abejas. See Abejas, Las
socios, 7, 16, 26, 83, 89–90, 98, 121–22, 161
solidarity, 7, 12, 25, 45, 46, 49, 52, 57, 77, 78, 81, 119, 132–33, 135, 140–49, 155, 169, 171–74, 176, 221n4; "helper" forms, 88, 119, 138–39, 146–47, 167
struggle, 6, 10–11, 25, 43, 46–50, 54, 56–57, 66, 76, 93, 95, 122–23, 159, 177, 190, 195, 198, 210

subsistence, 2, 39, 49, 59, 60, 69, 91–93, 95, 124, 196–201, 207
sustainable development, 86, 87, 88, 92, 110–11, 116

third-party certifiers, 26, 85–87, 113, 148–49. *See also* fair trade certification; Fairtrade International; fair trade standards; Fair Trade USA
tortillas, 124, 227n9
trade, 25, 35, 45, 103, 111; making trade fairer, 111, 113. *See also* fair trade movement

violence. *See* conflict

waged work. *See* labor
war of five hundred years, 1, 4, 58, 75, 94, 182. *See also* five-hundred-year struggle
women, 9, 16, 60, 65, 78, 123, 136, 166

Zapata, Emiliano, 8, 9
Zapatistas, 48, 51, 53, 55, 56, 75, 77, 125, 158, 171–74, 207, 221nn3–4, 223n6, 225n13, 226n7; coffee cooperatives, 78–79, 153; coffee production, 11, 12, 172–74; formation, 9–10; indigenous rights, 75–76; MAREZ, 76, 137; support bases, 123, 177, 192–93, 198, 199–201, 202, 221n3; uprising, 5–6, 8, 12, 14, 48, 75, 209; uprising impact of, 57–60, 79–85, 181, 228n1

Lindsay Naylor is assistant professor of geography at the University of Delaware.

www.ingramcontent.com/pod-product-compliance
Lightning Source LLC
Jackson TN
JSHW070314120426
100741JS00008B/64